"We need an approach to social justice in higher education more rooted in care; many people have written about this kind of social justice. *Teaching, Learning, and Caring in Higher Education* transitions us to something more: an approach to care more rooted in social justice—not the hollow, fluffy kind of care we often find in higher education, but the intentional, transformative kind. This book has helped me, and can help you, to make that transition."

Paul Gorski, co-author with Seema Pothini of *Case Studies for Diversity and Social Justice Education*

TEACHING, LEARNING, AND CARING IN HIGHER EDUCATION

This practical resource illustrates how to establish and nurture relationships with intention, paving the way for meaningful student, instructor, and content engagement.

Torres expertly peels back the layers of disengagement prevalent in today's college classroom and demonstrates how in-person and online courses can form ecologies that empower students and teachers rather than exhaust them. Informed by a rich blend of pedagogical research, case studies, and social interdependence learning theory, this book features plentiful activities, suggestions, and templates for cultivating and connecting care throughout learning environments. A worthwhile read for any faculty member regardless of level or discipline, this book is especially relevant for those who are new to teaching, concerned with student engagement, or interested in redesigning their courses.

JT Torres is Director of the Harte Center for Teaching and Learning at Washington & Lee University, USA. He is an award-winning educator and scholar who has published several articles and books about how we learn to perform particular identities as part of cultural practices and social networks.

TEACHING, LEARNING, AND CARING IN HIGHER EDUCATION

How to Cultivate an Interdependent Classroom

JT Torres

Routledge
Taylor & Francis Group

NEW YORK AND LONDON

Designed cover image: Getty Images

First published 2026
by Routledge
605 Third Avenue, New York, NY 10158

and by Routledge
4 Park Square, Milton Park, Abingdon, Oxon, OX14 4RN

Routledge is an imprint of the Taylor & Francis Group, an informa business

© 2026 JT Torres

The right of JT Torres to be identified as author of this work has been asserted in accordance with sections 77 and 78 of the Copyright, Designs and Patents Act 1988.

All rights reserved. No part of this book may be reprinted or reproduced or utilised in any form or by any electronic, mechanical, or other means, now known or hereafter invented, including photocopying and recording, or in any information storage or retrieval system, without permission in writing from the publishers.

Trademark notice: Product or corporate names may be trademarks or registered trademarks, and are used only for identification and explanation without intent to infringe.

ISBN: 978-1-032-96871-1 (hbk)
ISBN: 978-1-032-96870-4 (pbk)
ISBN: 978-1-003-59100-9 (ebk)

DOI: 10.4324/9781003591009

Typeset in Times New Roman
by Apex CoVantage, LLC

CONTENTS

Acknowledgments   *viii*

     Introduction: Who Cares?   1

1   An Interdependent Perspective of Care   12

2   Higher Education as an Ecology in Need of Care   30

3   Care Between Teachers and Content   52

4   Care Between Teachers and Students   70

5   Care Between Students   87

6   Care Between Students and Content   105

7   Care Between Teachers   124

     Conclusion: We Care!   142

Index   *150*

ACKNOWLEDGMENTS

This book feels less like a single-authored project and more like the voices, ideas, scholarship, insight, and care I gathered on my journey. I have so many people to acknowledge and thank for caring for me in ways that nurtured my curiosity and commitment to helping create a more just world. Many of these individuals populate the pages of this book, and so I hope I have done them honor in representing our conversations, collaborations, and email exchanges. Below are a few statements of thanks for shaping my understanding of social interdependence as pedagogical practice.

Beauty Bragg taught me how to approach creativity with a critical framework. She was the first person to teach me about this art: it cannot be separated from its cultural contexts, meaning art must always question and be questioned. Ever since being Beauty Bragg's student, I have pursued critical questions, connecting with amazing humans Jotwan Daniels, Trymaine Gaither, Lance Eaton, and Deborah Kronenberg.

Liz Qualman and Leticia Burbano de Lara taught me how to teach. They modeled care-in-action as an instructional method, mentorship, and way of life. Thanks to them, I know how to pursue relationships that model similar practices. Those include Lisa Johnson Shull, Poonam Arora, Khalilah Brown-Dean, Don Sawyer III, Leslie Cunningham, Rachel Sanchez, Emma McMain, and Chris Hakala.

These individuals, and many more, helped define my interdependent authorial identity. More directly, individuals helped more directly with the formation of this book, including Sheri Rysdam, Poonam Arora, and Jeff Saerys-Foy for collaborating with me on similar projects; Kate McConnell, Eddie Watson, and Lynn Pasquarella (and the entire American Association of Colleges and Universities family) for supporting the development of the framework that informs this book; and Alex Andrews, Kyanna Nusom, and the Routledge team for making this book a reality.

INTRODUCTION

Who Cares?

Chapter Contents
Learning Care   2
Defining Care   3
Teaching Care   7
Alone Together in Higher Education   9
References   10

As an educational developer, I frequently consult with educators across the country working in various learning environments, from higher education to community organizations. Recently, a college professor at a research institution requested help with class engagement. He lamented that students today seem so overwhelmed. Social media demands their constant attention. They feel powerless to change unjust systems or address the climate crisis. And now artificial intelligence (AI) threatens the long-held promise that justifies the high cost of college: a professional career.

He said to me, "I always felt like I was paid to do research, but I was fulfilled by teaching. Teaching, however, is no longer fulfilling. No one seems to care."

Certainly, this professor is not alone in his observation. College students today experience a host of mental health challenges, from increased depression (Liu et al., 2022) to widespread loneliness (Haikalis et al., 2022), all of which impacts their academic performance. COVID-19 disrupted educational trajectories and eroded important opportunities for many people to develop social identities, meaning that traditionally aged college students have weaker relational ties and fewer social experiences from which to draw as they enter adulthood (Salimi et al., 2023). COVID-19, however, did not introduce these challenges. For that matter, neither did social media—the other culprit—introduce these challenges. In 2000, three years before MySpace debuted and seven years before the introduction of the iPhone, Robert Putnam published *Bowling Alone: The Collapse and Revival of American Community*. In it, Putnam argues that social capital has dramatically declined due to the increased emphasis on individualism, isolation, and separation. Disconnection from one another has been increasing in virtually all demographics for many years.

Many educators, from college faculty to pre-school teachers, have also not felt cared about for decades. The possible contributing factors have long been studied. Researchers rang the alarm about teacher burnout in the 1980s (Cunningham, 1983). Despite the alarm, legislation in the 1990s required institutions to quantify and justify faculty workload, influencing a new obsession around "productivity" that ushered in a culture of overwork and delegitimized professorship as a professional field (Townsend & Rosser, 2007). The rising cost of colleges and universities in particular has been accompanied by an increasingly consumerist mindset among their stakeholders, introducing new pressures to an already stressed ecosystem. If students are expected to take on massive debt, they want some assurance they can pay it back. Unfortunately, grades, majors, and campus experiences are then rendered as high-stakes investments rather than enriching social experiences. Many other tensions, such as the neoliberalization of education, increased political tensions around systemic racism, sexism, and ableism, and the colonial legacy of academia, as well as the persistent culture wars attacking science and scholarship, from denying climate change to crucifying diversity, equity, and inclusion (DEI), have all made care difficult.

I'm already out of breath, and this is just the first page.

It is hard not to empathize with the college professor who believes that "no one seems to care."

But I believe care is not only possible, it is necessary. For that matter, teaching and learning—at least the teaching and learning principles endorsed by most scholars—directly depend on a foundation of care.

Learning Care

Because of my own unstable identity as a white Latino, I have experienced variations of care depending on the environment I inhabited at the time. In an overcrowded Hispanic-serving high school in Orlando, Florida, I certainly felt like no one cared whether I obtained a degree or ended up dropping out. The school resembled a maximum security prison, with barbed-wire fences enclosing the perimeter and a uniformed police officer stationed at the only entrance.

My skin complexion also meant that I was not treated as harshly as my classmates, sending a message that I could bend some rules just because I was recognized differently. As the whitest kid in my friend group, I was always elected to "do the talking" whenever we got in trouble. We knew that, regardless of my communication skills, my presented whiteness offered us the best chance at grace.

Even the care directed at my professional work changed with the social contexts. I began my career in academia as an adjunct faculty who loved leading pedagogy workshops supporting other adjuncts. Most of the time, these workshops were entirely voluntary, from the presenters to the participants. I could not even get funding approval for coffee or snacks. Then, in 2020, disrupting forces demanded calls for faculty support. Quarantine suddenly dissolved classroom boundaries separating "in-person students" from "online students." The murder of George Floyd amplified the need to teach for racial justice. Meanwhile, the demographic cliff among white, middle-class high school graduates highlights the need for more inclusive recruitment strategies. Institutions scrambled to put together centers for teaching and learning. I was plucked from the trenches and placed in such a role, and for the next five years the most frequent request I received was to help increase "engagement" and "care" in their students.

Rarely, though, have educators approached care using a shared vocabulary or framework, something this book aims to address. While many have expressed the desire to increase the sense of care—in one way or another—in their courses, many others have cautioned that today's students might receive too much care. In the *New York Times* best-selling *The Coddling of the American Mind: How Good Intentions and Bad Ideas Are Setting Up a Generation for Failure*, psychologists Greg Lukianoff and Jonathan Haidt (2019) critique the "safetyism" of many educational settings. They argue that recent movements toward overprotection, safe spaces, trigger warnings, and censorship have contributed to a generation of "fragile" students who avoid challenges, give up easily, and succumb to past traumas. Coddling humans to the point of fragility, Lukianoff and Haidt write, is "based on a fundamental misunderstanding of human nature and of the dynamics of trauma and recovery. It is vital that people who have survived violence become habituated to ordinary cues and reminders woven into the fabric of daily life" (p. 29). While this might sound harsh, empirical evidence does suggest that avoidance of potentially troubling experiences can exacerbate the severity and duration of Post Traumatic Stress Disorder (PTSD) symptoms (Badour et al., 2012). Debates around definitions of care should be carefully approached.

Defining Care

Let us first clarify that care is *not* coddling. This is not a book that will tell you to drop your expectations of what students can do and what you can accomplish as an educator. I will not suggest that you make your courses less rigorous or turn every class meeting into therapy or counseling sessions. In fact, care, as I will use the term, and resilience share a positive relationship. Patients who survived a life-threatening cardiac event are more likely to change dangerous behaviors (e.g., quit smoking) if they have strong social connections (Pinquart & Duberstein, 2010). Social connectedness and feeling cared about can dramatically increase cancer survival rates (Boen et al., 2018). On the converse, social isolation has been shown to be just as deadly as drug or alcohol use (Ozbay et al., 2007). These findings strongly suggest that we are happier, healthier, and more capable when we work together to sustain social interdependence. I draw inspiration from Robin Wall Kimmerer's (2013) definition of "ecology" as a "shared home," in which the well-being and survivability of all the home's inhabitants depend on one another (p. 85). Interdependent classrooms can be thought of as social ecologies.

Robert Barr and John Tagg (1995) declared an important paradigm shift in education when they argued for learner-centeredness. In contrast to an instructional paradigm that centers all responsibility and value on faculty, such as measuring and evaluating teaching as the only metric of educational success, a learning paradigm centers responsibility and value on students. According to Barr and Tagg (1995), "the chief agent in the process is the learner. Thus, students must be active discoverers and constructors of their own knowledge. In the Learning Paradigm, knowledge consists of frameworks or wholes that are created or constructed by the learner" (p. 22). Of course, teachers should not be held solely responsible for institutional success. Of course, empirical evidence strongly supports active learning. And, of course, students should share the responsibility of educational success. But perhaps an ecological framing helps more than an individualized one. Rather than choosing a teacher-centered or student-centered approach, why not center them both?

Wright et al. (2018) made this case. Writing in the same magazine—*Change: The Magazine of Higher Learning*—as Barr and Tagg, Wright et al. (2018) call for

> an expanded vision of ways to develop, design, and deliver learning to allow for a more democratic or reciprocal relationship between instructor, learner, and material. It also includes an increasingly disrupted sense of what higher education institutions do or could look like.
>
> *(p. 39)*

Wright et al. (2018) call this new paradigm a de-centered approach.

> Rather than a "sage on the stage" (Instruction-centered) or even a "guide on the side" (Learner-centered), de-centered pedagogical approaches encourage . . . instructor and student to reconceptualize social presence and positions in real or virtual spaces—or even, in the case of Virtual Reality or Alternative Reality, to de-center "reality" itself.
>
> *(p. 39)*

In this book, I take the opportunity offered by de-centering paradigms as a chance to re-center relationships and the connective spaces that make possible individual identities that always exist in relation to one another, like teacher and student.

Chapter 1 explores care as a relational concept with a genealogy that includes ethics, philosophy, psychology, sociology, political science, and critical theory.

The goal is to provide readers with a framework for how terms like *care, ecology*, and *interdependence* are used in this book to inform teaching and learning, especially since such terms are hotly contested.

As a historic term, care has taken on vastly different meanings, shaped by cultural worldviews, social hierarchies, and relationships to the land. Many North American Indigenous communities practice care as a reciprocal, relational ethic grounded in kinship with people, land, and the natural world. Care was holistic—sustaining ecosystems, community well-being, and future generations through mutual respect and responsibility. As Leslie Marmon Silko (2013) realized as a child wandering the hills and mesas around Laguna, "the land all around me is teeming with creatures related to human beings and to me" (p. 42). By recognizing self and world as interconnected, care becomes a requirement for collective survival.

Colonial settlers redefined care through a framework of domination and religious paternalism, where controlling land and "civilizing" Native peoples was framed as benevolence. Land was no longer a relative to care for but a resource to own and exploit, feeding a logic that deepened under Manifest Destiny and capitalism, where care was equated with productivity, ownership, and economic gain. Communal care gave way to individualism, and unpaid or marginalized care labor (especially by women and people of color) became invisible or devalued.

In the industrial and neoliberal eras, care became increasingly commodified—sold as a service while still largely expected from families and communities without support. Emotional labor and caregiving roles were underpaid, despite being essential. Fraser (2016) argues that capitalism has created a "crisis of care," exploiting the very social bonds and human capacities it depends on while failing to support or replenish them. Today's care crisis is linked to both social and ecological degradation—systems that extract without renewing lead to burnout, inequality, and environmental collapse.

As a gendered term, care has been framed as feminine, meaning that, due to the patriarchal structures of Western society, care has not been valued as highly as masculine traits like competition or individualism. It also means that women have been historically expected to provide care to a society in disrepair, often due to the aforementioned masculine traits that enjoy privileged status. Of course, I do not suggest that men are destroying society while women repair it. Rather, particular ideologies—namely, care—tend to operate as performances of social identities, which then have very real effects on the individuals who present the associated identities. For instance, Purvanova and Muros's (2010) meta-analysis of workplace burnout finds that women are more likely to feel emotionally exhausted whereas men are more likely to depersonalize. When social expectations gender care as feminine, women do not always get the same affordances to withdraw or check out as men. In fact, when situations become stressful, women might be expected to provide even more care.

Fortunately, the work of care theorists such as Nel Noddings and Joan Tronto and psychologists like Carol Gilligan has called attention to the importance of care while also critiquing its gendered expectations. They questioned the individualist and universalist ethics (all based on male experiences) accepted in their fields and positioned feminine voices as critical to science and society, emphasizing the ways in which relationships both constitute and are constituted by the world we build. These theories connect with instructional concepts in educational research, such as Sarah Rose Cavanagh's (2016) presentation of "emotional contagion," which demonstrates the celerity with which emotional experiences like care can spread throughout social groups. Through relational practices that model for students what it means to be a caring human, we can demonstrate different ways of relating to one another. Through interdependent experiences in which students learn with and through one another, we move from the individualist paradigm that favors self-specific benefits (e.g., grades) into a relational paradigm that favors self-shared benefits (e.g., a classroom that empowers everyone).

María Puig de la Bellacasa (2017) brilliantly extends care into interdependent frameworks, expanding our focus to notice all of the complex relationships and factors that constitute care. Bellacasa shows how interdependence helps to position care as inherently fluid, emerging as a socially situated action. In such situations, all forms of interdependence should be considered, not just between humans but also between things, more-than-human life, technology, ideologies, etc. Expanded notions of relational ecologies are critical for a future that includes the rapid development of AI. In a compelling TED Talk about the rise of market-driven AI technologies that might be creating a dystopia, Zeynep Tufecki (2017) claims, "[T]he algorithms don't care if they are selling you a product or influencing your politics." Critically, Lynn Pasquarella (2022) adds to the concern: "[T]echnology develops faster than our ability to reflect on [or care about] it" (p. 32).

For this reason, French philosopher Bruno Latour (2011) quixotically encourages us to "love our monsters," such as environmentalists committing to care for Sport Utility Vehicles (SUVs). Our cultural appetite for private transportation and suburban lifestyles that require roads and highways made possible the emergence of gas-guzzling SUVs. Even if we made the individual choice of using public transportation or riding a bicycle, the SUVs exist. Someone, somewhere, is driving one at this very moment! SUVs (and AI, social media, plastic, guns, etc.) are already organisms within our social ecologies, meaning that we are already in relation to them. To deny them care, according to Latour, could mean additional damage to our social and environmental ecologies. As an entertaining example, Latour offers a reading of Mary Shelley's *Frankenstein* in which he claims that Dr. Frankenstein's "crime was not that he invented a creature through some combination of hubris and high technology, but rather that he abandoned the creature to itself"

(p. 19). Whether or not we condone the emergence of such technologies, they exist in our ecologies and require our care.

Like Bellacasa and Kimmerer, I extend theories of care into understandings of interdependence. Such an extension helps consider care beyond dyadic relationships (e.g., mother and child, and student and teacher) and into complex networks of social connectedness that make possible many different kinds of relationships (e.g., mother—and all of their friendships, family connections, and professional mentors—and child—and all of their social networks). Where I take the theoretical thread into new territory is by emphasizing a particular aspect of interdependence—social interdependence learning theory (SILT). While SILT has its roots in Vygotsky's theory that culture mediates learning through social interaction, empirical evidence supporting SILT's significance emerged in landmark studies conducted by David and Roger Johnson, which I'll cover in Chapter 1.

Teaching Care

Here, the theoretical becomes pedagogical. We all need care.

But: we live in a world that can feel very careless.
But: we can cultivate interdependence within our classrooms.
So: We can feel care *and* we can enjoy teaching and learning because interdependence is how we do those things well.

One of the most effective things educators can do is show students that they matter. Cate Denial (2024) shows how intentionally equitable hospitality (IEH) can do just that. "The instructor of a class is the host of a gathering," Denial (2024) writes, "and [as hosts, instructors] must think critically about the welcome their course offers to students all semester long" (p. 82). As an example, Denial populates her Learning Management System (LMS) with time management and self-care resources and activities, directly incorporating care into the classroom environment. Research consistently demonstrates that when students feel seen, valued, and cared for, their academic engagement and long-term success significantly improve. A large-scale Gallup-Purdue Index study of over 30,000 college graduates identified six key college experiences—dubbed the "Big Six"—that are most strongly associated with success after graduation. Chief among them: "I had a professor who cared about me as a person" (Seymour & Lopez, 2015). This single indicator outperformed many traditional academic measures, highlighting that personal connection can be as impactful as pedagogy.

Another study in undergraduate biology courses found that something as simple as the instructor learning and using students' names significantly enhanced students' perceptions of being cared for, which in turn supported their motivation and academic engagement (Cooper et al., 2017). These findings suggest that demonstrating care doesn't require grand gestures; instead, small, consistent acts of acknowledgment and empathy—like learning a student's name—can deeply influence how they experience learning and see themselves within it.

We are always already in relation to others in one ecology or another (Latremouille et al., 2020). When I describe creating or cultivating an ecology of care, this does not mean we will be doing so from scratch. Rather, we will be operating within the ecologies that have been historically and culturally reinforced (Lee, 2017). Current systems and structures are not always receptive to pedagogical practices resulting in care, and so it is important to understand where we might find possibilities for care. Chapter 2 provides a brief survey of the higher education ecology within which many of us operate. Even for readers who do not live and work in higher education, features of the higher education ecology ripple across other learning environments that might make the chapter relevant.

Chapters 3–7 share a Care Kit for cultivating interdependent classrooms through care. While this book can certainly be read in any order based on the reader's needs and learning contexts, the presented order follows the methodology I formed based on my scholarship and experience with wonderful caring mentors, like Leticia Burbano de Lara, a critical teacher educator, who taught me that "learning follows community." Instead of structuring courses around content, Leti structures courses around developing relationships; therefore, the chapters progress through layers of relationships (both human and nonhuman) that shape our identities as educators. Other mentors, like the deeply reflective facilitator Trymaine Gaither, taught me that if we can tap into shared interests—affinities—we can increase both political power and our own well-being; therefore, the methodology begins with the affinities that likely connect many educators—the content they teach. Building from our care for content, the book then examines ways to share the care teachers have cultivated with their content with their students. Next, the book expands care across and between students, reducing the pressure on teachers to be the "care center" so that the labor of care becomes relational and communal. Learning is inherently community based, and so once community takes root, the book directs the relationships cultivated throughout the classroom toward content. At the end, care between teachers and academic support staff demonstrates the importance of true "self-care" and provides insights into strategies for making sure that teachers are cared about and valued. The conclusion will reflect on the impact interdependent care can have on everything from learning outcomes to social well-being and help transform education for a new and difficult world.

Social interaction is messy and stochastic. Meaning emerges through real-time relationships and dynamics that we cannot always predict or replicate. I cannot count the times a lesson plan worked wonders with one class, only to fall apart during the very next section. As we develop our Care Kit, keep in mind that I am sharing the approaches that worked for me in particular situations. Yes, these approaches are based in evidence and supported by the science of learning, but how they might be used depends on the ecology in which the learning takes place. Anything from institutional culture to the extended communities from which students and teachers come will shape the possibilities. While all the Care Kit entries are appropriate for in-person or online settings, for instance, each entry will change depending on the modality. Interdependent care unfolds through dynamic relationships. No set of strategies will work for all students in all situations. Context will determine what kinds of relationships are possible and how an ecology of care can be cultivated.

With these considerations in mind, each Care Kit provides two approaches to meet needs that change with space and time. *Remedies* offer gifts for quick steps into interdependence. These include strategies and suggestions for single presentations or immediate interventions in a learning environment. They do not require a lot of planning or preparation, making them easy to adopt, adapt, or become something else. *Roots* offer gifts for structural transformation, helping teachers design assignments, sequences, or entire courses founded upon interdependent care. While roots require time, labor, and commitment to take hold, their rewards tend to be more sustainable, as the cultivated models become transferable to new contexts.

Remedies and *Roots* are not necessarily mutually exclusive choices. We know that systemic transformation is required to ensure care for all people, but that does not mean we can afford to wait around for a revolution to help those who are in front of us in the present moment. Yes, we need to keep addressing systems and structures and cultivate networks of action and activism. But we cannot wait for Godot when a human student in our classroom today asks for care. At the same time, any remedy to address an emerging concern, possibly in response to a single individual, can take root, setting precedent for organizational or institutional change. Remembering that we all exist in interconnected ecologies, individual impact can include collective ripples. Implementing a remedy from any of the Care Kits for a single class or course can become a routine throughout a semester, a curricular element across courses, or a programmatic change. The Care Kit shared in this book provides situational possibilities in ways that avoid either/or decision-making. While the division of Remedy and Root helps readers cultivate interdependent care based on the appropriate context of their classrooms, the two sections should not be read as firmly divided. Remedies can take root, and roots need responsive remedies to flourish.

Alone Together in Higher Education

For many teachers, disengaged students can be a heartbreaking challenge. We are trained to help students close the gap between what they know and do not know, but that does not mean we can instantly open someone's mind. And when students turn their nose up at the ideas that bring us joy, we can take it personally. Before anyone questions their teaching skills, know that the majority of teachers identify apathy and technology distraction as the biggest classroom challenges today (Will, 2024). We are all asking the same question: how do we motivate and inspire students?

No single classroom can contain these challenges. Today's students are more disengaged than previous generations. Young people in America face a dangerous epidemic of loneliness, depression, and anxiety. Teachers worry about soaring absenteeism. Sociologists worry about the dramatic decline in friendships, romantic relationships, and sexual activity. Psychologists worry about increased isolation, suicide rates, and participation in radical ideologies such as white nationalism. This is not just a social epidemic. Books like *The Anxious Generation* by Jonathan Haidt describe how the conditions contributing to disengagement are "rewiring" minds. In fact, recent studies indicate that growing up with rapidly available information—via Google, for instance—changes how our brains function when faced with a difficult question. In an often-cited study, Sparrow et al. (2011) found that people who grew up using the Internet actually use their memories differently than those with less Internet exposure. Specifically, Internet users are more likely to remember *how to access* information rather than remember the information, a stark contrast from how most educators define and assess learning. The longer we allow current systems to operate out of alignment with who students are becoming, the more likely that higher education will disconnect students—and itself—from social relevance.

Care is the heart of desire, interest, and action. It is what gives us meaning and what connects us through empathy and shared interest. To teach care, we need to understand it for what it is: a relational bond. Care emerges through interdependent relationships. In other words, care inspires action for/with others who matter a great deal to us. Not only can care bring back the joy and engagement of teaching and learning, but it might also provide a strategy for healing a disconnected world. This book is my invitation to other caring teachers: an offering of vocabulary, research, and practices that help us build classrooms rooted in relationships, shared responsibility, and collective well-being. By centering care—not as coddling or overprotection, but as mutual investment and interdependence—I aim to restore some of the joy, purpose, and meaning that drew many of us to teaching in the first place. This is a book for those of us who still care, and maybe especially for those who are struggling to remember how.

References

Badour, C. L., Blonigen, D. M., Boden, M. T., Feldner, M. T., & Bonn-Miller, M. O. (2012). A longitudinal test of the bi-directional relations between avoidance coping and PTSD severity during and after PTSD treatment. *Behaviour Research and Therapy, 50*(10), 610–616.

Barr, R. B., & Tagg, J. (1995). From teaching to learning—a new paradigm for undergraduate education. *Change: The Magazine of Higher Learning, 27*(6), 12–26.

Boen, C. E., Barrow, D. A., Bensen, J. T., Farnan, L., Gerstel, A., Hendrix, L. H., & Yang, Y. C. (2018). Social relationships, inflammation, and cancer survival. *Cancer Epidemiology, Biomarkers & Prevention, 27*(5), 541–549.

Cavanagh, S. R. (2016). *The spark of learning: Energizing the college classroom with the science of emotion.* West Virginia University Press.

Cooper, K. M., Haney, B., Krieg, A., & Brownell, S. E. (2017). What's in a name? The importance of students perceiving that an instructor knows their names in a high-enrollment biology classroom. *CBE—Life Sciences Education, 16*(1), ar8.

Cunningham, W. G. (1983). Teacher burnout—solutions for the 1980s: A review of the literature. *The Urban Review, 15*(1), 37–51.

de la Bellacasa, M. P. (2017). *Matters of care: Speculative ethics in more than human worlds* (Vol. 41). University of Minnesota Press.

Denial, C. J. (2024). *A pedagogy of kindness.* University of Oklahoma Press.

Fraser, N. (2016). Capitalism's crisis of care. *Dissent, 63*(4), 30–37.

Haikalis, M., Doucette, H., Meisel, M. K., Birch, K., & Barnett, N. P. (2022). Changes in college student anxiety and depression from pre-to during-COVID-19: Perceived stress, academic challenges, loneliness, and positive perceptions. *Emerging Adulthood, 10*(2), 534–545.

Kimmerer, R. (2013). *Braiding sweetgrass: Indigenous wisdom, scientific knowledge and the teachings of plants.* Milkweed Editions.

Latour, B. (2011). Love your monsters. *Breakthrough Journal, 2*(11), 21–28.

Latremouille, J., et al. (Eds.). (2020). An ecological pedagogy of joy. In *The SAGE handbook of critical pedagogies* (Vol. 3, pp. 1543–1558). Sage.

Lee, C. (2017). An ecological framework for enacting culturally sustaining pedagogy. In D. Paris, & H. S. Alim (Eds.), *Culturally sustaining pedagogies: Teaching and learning for justice in a changing world.* Teachers College Press.

Liu, X. Q., Guo, Y. X., Zhang, W. J., & Gao, W. J. (2022). Influencing factors, prediction and prevention of depression in college students: a literature review. *World journal of psychiatry, 12*(7), 860.

Lukianoff, G., & Haidt, J. (2019). *The coddling of the American mind: How good intentions and bad ideas are setting up a generation for failure.* Penguin.

Ozbay, F., Johnson, D. C., Dimoulas, E., Morgan III, C. A., Charney, D., & Southwick, S. (2007). Social support and resilience to stress: From neurobiology to clinical practice. *Psychiatry, 4*(5), 35–52.

Pasquarella, L. (2022). *What we value: Public health, social justice, and educating for democracy.* University of Virginia Press.

Pinquart, M., & Duberstein, P. R. (2010). Associations of social networks with cancer mortality: A meta-analysis. *Critical Reviews in Oncology/Hematology, 75*(2), 122–137.

Purvanova, R. K., & Muros, J. P. (2010). Gender differences in burnout: A meta-analysis. *Journal of vocational behavior, 77*(2), 168–185.

Salimi, N., Gere, B., Talley, W., & Irioogbe, B. (2023). College students mental health challenges: Concerns and considerations in the COVID-19 pandemic. *Journal of College Student Psychotherapy, 37*(1), 39–51.

Seymour, S., & Lopez, S. J. (2015, May 6). Big six college experiences linked to life preparedness. *Gallup News.* https://news.gallup.com/poll/182306/big-six-college-experiences-linked-life-preparedness.aspx.

Silko, L. M. (2013). *Yellow woman and a beauty of the spirit.* Simon and Schuster.

Sparrow, B., Liu, J., & Wegner, D. M. (2011). Google effects on memory: Cognitive consequences of having information at our fingertips. *Science, 333*(6043), 776–778.

Townsend, B. K., & Rosser, V. J. (2007). Workload issues and measures of faculty productivity. *Thought & Action, 23*(1), 7–19.

Tufekci, Z. (2017, September). We're building a dystopia just to make people click on ads [Video]. *TED.* https://www.ted.com/talks/zeynep_tufekci_we_re_building_a_dystopia_just_to_make_people_click_on_ads.

Will, M. (2024). Student Apathy Is a Big Classroom Challenge, Teachers Say. Cellphones Aren't Helping. *Education Week.* https://www.edweek.org/teaching-learning/student-apathy-is-a-big-classroom-challenge-teachers-say-cellphones-arent-helping/2024/04

Wright, M. C., Lohe, D. R., & Little, D. (2018). The role of a center for teaching and learning in a de-centered educational world. *Change: The Magazine of Higher Learning, 50*(6), 38–44.

1
AN INTERDEPENDENT PERSPECTIVE OF CARE

Chapter Contents
Care About/For/With   13
A Brief History of Interdependence   17
Interdependent Classrooms   24
Teaching Care and the Honorable Harvest   27
References   28

In *Braiding Sweetgrass*, Robin Wall Kimmerer (2013) reflects on her experience restoring a pond in her backyard. The pond had become overrun by eutrophication, sediment buildup caused by years of algae growth, lily pad overpopulation, and falling leaves and apples. Instead of clear water, thick layers of plants became so dense the pond even ensnared goslings. Kimmerer had imagined a natural pool safe for her daughters to swim and play, but that could not safely happen in the viscous mud and muck. She decided to get to work.

Kimmerer raked the algal strands from the water into a wheelbarrow and removed the slippery mesh from the environment. She discovered, though, that she did not just rake algae but also the lifeforms living with, depending on, and providing for the algae: diving beetles, tadpoles, crawfish, dragonfly larvae, invertebrates, and protozoans. Despite the heartbreak of her discovery—that her desire for a pond that might give life to geese and human children meant the demise of other lifeforms—she continued the restoration. As she realized, morality is definitely not as clear as a maintained pond.

Kimmerer's experience illustrates that we all live in various ecologies, systems of abundant relationships in which life, death, success, failure, and everything else depend on our connections with one another. While an algal pond may not be suitable for goslings and children, it serves as a healthy habitat for many other lifeforms. In order for Kimmerer to care for the pond in ways that benefited her daughters, she had to decide *not* to care for the pond in ways that benefited the beasties depending on the plant and algae growth. In an ecology, one thing is never just one thing.

To better understand the complexities of incorporating care within teaching, this chapter considers care beyond the traditional moral confines that have traditionally framed such discussions. Kimmerer's experience illustrates the definition of care that informs this book: a committed action with and for (human and more-than-human) others who *matter a great deal to us*. The italicized phrase points to the difficult political and moral considerations that make care complex. Because care gets directed toward those who matter a great deal to the carer, care is an inherently political act, something the scholars from whom I draw below have consistently argued. For instance, Joan Tronto's (1993) definition of care as "everything we do to maintain, continue and repair our world" resonates with the idea that we actively choose when, where, and how we center care on the things that matter to us and "our worlds" (p. 103). When we care about something or someone, we are more likely to care for them. How care gets directed depends on relational bonds, forming reciprocal channels that constitute mattering a great deal to one another. Teachers, for example, always share how much they learn from their students. Similarly, Kimmerer reflects on her experience restoring the pond, "Our lives became entwined in ways both material and spiritual. It's been a balanced exchange: I worked on the pond and the pond worked on me, and together we made a good home" (p. 95). What I hope to add is a cognitive dimension, demonstrating how attention, for example, shapes the selectivity with which we direct care.

Care About/For/With

In stark contrast with Kimmerer's reflection, Western culture's fascination with individualism continues to drive a more transactional understanding of care. Extreme examples of such an understanding include billionaire philanthropists, who make extraordinary efforts to demonstrate how much they care about the world's injustices, despite their role in sustaining those very injustices. In *Winner Takes All: The Elite Charade of Changing the World*, Anand Giridharadas (2019) investigates the problematic entanglement of capitalism and charity. Take, for instance, Bill Gates, who has poured enormous resources into his education foundation. While those resources certainly reach many students across the world, the resources direct students to solutions consistent with Gates's ideology. Student benefactors typically receive Microsoft products or enroll in programs that reward skills and knowledge directly relevant for a field in which Bill Gates sits at the top. Treated as a transaction or an investment, care becomes a currency that is explicitly self-serving on a purely individualistic basis. Giridharadas (2019) argues that philanthropy ultimately becomes a tool used by the elite to shape the world in their image, allowing extremely wealthy individuals to act as unelected officials and implement class-based colonialist strategies. Gates's attempt to use philanthropy to shape global agricultural practices has resulted in headlines such as this one in *Scientific American*: "Bill Gates Should Stop Telling Africans What Kind of Agriculture Africans Need" (Belay & Mugambe, 2021). Of course, transactional care extends beyond corporate behavior. Missionaries might withhold aid from impoverished communities until they convert to the desired religion, and states might withhold welfare until arbitrary work requirements are met. These examples expect a return on care-based investments.

Transactional care not only extends power, but it also absolves individuals in power of responsibility, reducing the burden of committed action, by emphasizing intent rather than collective impact. British Petroleum will say they did not intend to destroy the Gulf of Mexico and kill thousands of species. That is not in their mission statement, at least. Their only intention, in fact, is to sell oil. They can distance themselves from the very effects they created, and they can celebrate the amount of money they have donated to ocean cleanup all they want; however, continuing to drill in deepwater sites and even rushing safety inspections tell a different story (McGill & Brown, 2020). On a more personal level, if I truly cared about how my behavior made others feel, I would prioritize how they felt, not how I intended them to feel. Making an offensive joke is careless, even if it is followed up with, "I didn't mean for it to be offensive." When action and impact define care, we all become accountable to the well-being of one another (Butler, 2020).

Nel Noddings remains one of the most influential thinkers around the ethics of care, especially as a relational practice that can transform education. She questioned the traditional notions of care described in the previous paragraphs and offered models for approaching care from a feminist position of relationships and empathy. In her work, Noddings (2013) makes an important distinction between caring-about and caring-for. The former, caring about, draws upon our natural empathy and concern. We might feel for someone who experiences a particular struggle, or we might have a special interest in an issue or injustice. However, as Noddings (2013) suggests, while caring-about can move us to address the issue or injustice, it tends to remain in the abstract. I might care about the planet but never engage in environmental activism, for instance. Caring-about can even be reduced to the more problematic experience of "pity," in which we become spectators who can benignly ignore the connections between ourselves and the "distant others who suffer" (Zembylas, 2013, p. 509).

This is not to say that caring-about is a less preferable version of care. It is difficult, if not impossible, to care about everyone and everything. Similar to the ways in which cognitive load functions when presented with too much information at once, compassion fatigue can be induced when we feel overwhelmed with issues and people who need to be cared about. Compassion fatigue refers to the emotional and physical exhaustion that individuals may experience when they are repeatedly exposed to the suffering of others, often in caregiving or helping roles. It can result from the cumulative stress of the emotional labor dedicated to those who are experiencing trauma, pain, or distress. Over time, this constant exposure can lead to feelings of helplessness, emotional numbness, and a decreased ability over time to emotionally connect. Also known as the "cost of caring" (Roney & Acri, 2018), compassion fatigue is particularly common among healthcare workers, therapists, social workers, educators, and others in caregiving professions. It differs from burnout in that it specifically stems from the emotional toll of caring for others, rather than general work-related stress.

Caring-about aligns with cognitive science's understanding of attention. If our brains (and hearts) absorbed all the information they encountered, our cognitive systems would overload and shut down. Imagine standing in front of an enormous room filled with all of the world's injustices. The room would be more expansive than the Grand Canyon. A sense of awe might even be induced by its vastness. Considering the vastness of injustice all at once would likely be so awe-inducing that we feel completely incapable of doing anything about injustice at all. When we start focusing on one element, issue, or person in that vastness, important details clarify, including details about how we might act to address the injustice related to that specific focal point. Scientists, like Cave and Bichot (1999), describe attention as working like a spotlight, where we selectively focus on specific information while filtering out irrelevant details to prevent cognitive overload. The spotlight metaphor suggests that attention allows us to direct our mental and emotional resources toward particular stimuli, while the rest of the environment remains blurred in the background.

Like attention, caring-about requires us to direct our focus and concern toward issues that may otherwise be lost to us in the vastness of human experience, such as social justice or global problems. Just as attention filters and prioritizes certain stimuli to avoid overload, caring-about helps us focus on the broader concerns we deem important while not getting overwhelmed by the vast number of issues that might demand our empathy. This selective focus helps us manage the vast amount of sensory information our brains encounter at any given moment. Our brains protect us from being overwhelmed by overexcited senses by filtering and prioritizing stimuli into patterns based on factors like novelty, relevance, or personal goals. In the process of prioritization, however, we often miss or ignore other potential information outside of our attention's spotlight. The sharper our spotlight, the more of the vast room of injustice we miss, but that narrower focus makes it more possible to act on what we do see. While climate change itself might be too overwhelming to inspire action, replacing my lawn with wildflowers, inconsequential as it may seem, is more achievable.

Importantly, caring-about and caring-for should not be considered as developmental stages on a linear trajectory. Although Noddings (2010) illustrates that we first experience being "cared for" as children in maternal care and then learn to "care about" others, she also stresses that these forms of caring co-create each other in various contexts. Considering our very limited cognitive resources, as well as the fact that time itself is incredibly finite, we cannot care for everything we care about. Every day, we scan our environments for relevant and novel information. When something, like a particular need tugging on our empathy, catches our attention, we beam our spotlight onto it. Then we become motivated to act, moving into the ethical practice of caring-for. Noddings (2002) clarifies that caring-about

> must be seen as instrumental in establishing the conditions under which caring-for can flourish. Although the preferred form of caring is cared-for, caring-about can help in establishing, maintaining, and enhancing it. Those who care about others in the justice sense must keep in mind that the objective is to ensure that caring actually occurs. Caring-about is empty if it does not culminate in caring relations.
>
> *(p. 24)*

Though Noddings received criticism for emphasizing caring-for over caring-about as ethical practice, the distinction she provides aligns with cognitive science and is an important reminder that we cannot act on every cared-about feeling we have. I hope that my contribution to Noddings' work, by approaching care interdependently, can help address some of these criticisms. As we will see later in this chapter and throughout this book, while I (as an individual) cannot care about everything and everyone, as part of an interdependent community, or ecology, *we* can collectively care about a multitude of things.

Maria Puig de la Bellacasa's (2017) *Matters of Care* suggests a third dimension to Noddings' distinction: *caring-with*. Inspired by Noddings, Bellacasa differentiates "matter of fact" from "matter of concern." Matters of fact refer to things that are presented as objective truths, often in the context of science and technology. These are facts assumed to be neutral, detached from human or nonhuman concerns, and independent of context. They emphasize empirical verification and cling to the belief that things simply exist, without the interference of subjective experience. Rhetorically and epistemologically, "matter fact" can be a phrase that limits inquiry and imagination. Can you remember a time when someone shut down an idea by claiming that "X cannot be true because Y is a matter of fact"? I have often heard that climate change cannot be anthropogenic because "it is a matter of fact that Earth experienced an Ice Age before human industrialization."

By drawing upon standpoint feminism, Bellacasa reminds us that facts are always entangled in relationships, values, and ethical considerations. Instead of seeing knowledge or facts as isolated from subjective experiences, Bellacasa suggests that they should be understood as part of a broader network of human and nonhuman interests, values, and attachments. In contrast to matters of fact, matters of concern are explicitly relational; they invite us to reverse the phrase "matter of fact" and instead ask how facts matter in the world—how they affect others and how they are part of ethical and political considerations. The fact that the earth has undergone ice ages, for instance, is a very convenient fact for polluters that prevents them from needing to be concerned about anthropogenic climate change.

Bellacasa (2017) argues that "knowing and thinking are unconceivable without the multitude of relations that make possible the world we think with" (p. 69). Our thoughts, capacities for care, agency, and our very existence are rooted in relationships. Caring-with calls attention to our inherent ontological relatedness; we are always "with" others, human and more than human, engaging already existing thoughts, ideas, voices, and others. The boundaries between our individual selves and the individual selves of others constantly change and, to use Haraway's (1997) term, diffract, creating both differences and similarities within a collective that, while perpetually unstable, keeps us connected. Bellacasa (2017) tells us that caring-with, or "thinking-with," "creates new patterns out of previous multiplicities, intervening by adding layers of meaning rather than merely deconstructing or conforming to ready-made categories" (p. 72). As an imaginative and speculative opportunity to co-create relational realities, caring-with begins to illuminate pedagogical insights.

Many other scholars, such as Carol Gilligan (1993), have questioned the political boundaries determining who gets to define the knowledge, facts, or identities that matter. Historically, the answer has been particularly wealthy white male technicians trained by Western academies. By questioning political motivations and histories, Judith Butler (2020) challenges us to think about the kinds of action care might make possible, especially in the context of nonviolence. Butler (2020) describes care and nonviolence as political forces that do not mean simply the absence of violence but rather an active force aimed at preserving life. Butler (2020) goes further to argue that nonviolence as a force is not just about restoring the social structures determining who is worthy of care. Nonviolence as a force is a call to transform society around principles of care. These principles, articulated by Joan Tronto (1993), include attentiveness, responsibility, competence, and responsiveness. The insight most relevant to this book is that these principles entail interdependence. As a concept, interdependence has enjoyed interest from several disciplinary fields as more diverse scholars recognize the interconnectedness of life. Before we can ethically and authentically cultivate an interdependent classroom, it is important to consider the genealogy of interdependence as a concept.

A Brief History of Interdependence

A critical concern with educational research is that it favors a history of ideas that originate with empirical evidence. For many, this might seem like common sense. After all, even this book promises to be "evidence-based." Additionally, I often cite David Johnson and Roger Johnson as pillars of SILT. Their work is highly celebrated and regarded as the authority on cooperative and interconnected learning based on the impressive and extensive data they have accumulated over hundreds of publications. That said, given Western industry's entanglement with colonialism, even ideas around learning and knowledge are not innocent. The problem, as we now learned from Bellacasa (2017), lay in the tendency to privilege evidence (matter of fact) over care (matters of concern). One consequence of this privileging is that science often discounts the contributions of Indigenous epistemologies, which tend to be oral performances preserved in social memory as opposed to text citations saved in journal archives.

As I narrate this book's version of the theoretical landscape giving rise to interdependence, I begin with a land acknowledgment of sorts, acknowledging the Western theorizing of many Indigenous belief systems. It took me a long time to become comfortable with the idea that knowledge predates evidence published in an academic journal. I did not begin learning from and with epistemological systems outside of academia until my graduate school research took me to Cuba to work with Arará communities. The Arará people of Cuba are a cultural group descended from West African ethnic groups, particularly from the Ewe, Fon, and other populations of Dahomey, which is today Benin, Togo, and parts of Ghana. The Arará were forcefully brought to Cuba through the transatlantic slave trade, primarily in the 18th and early 19th centuries. Though once enslaved, Arará communities maintained aspects of their African heritage, particularly through religion, music, dance, and other cultural practices, which continue to define Cuban identity around the world.

I spent four years working with a team of artists, ethnographers, and anthropologists in Havana, Perico, and Agramonte, exploring how Arará maintained a sacred identity despite oppressive violence. Much of what we learned pointed to the transformative power of interdependence. Colonial Cuba reinforced the matter of fact that African religion, especially traditions closely related to Voodoo, represented evil forces. The ascription of evil served to justify slavery and the attempted erasure of ethnic identities. In response to state-sanctioned violence, the Arará engaged in syncretic practices, incorporating elements, such as the names of European deities, Catholic saints, or ceremonial traditions, into Arará, in effect both disguising and protecting African heritage in Cuba. Arará religiosity, in other words, survived by interconnecting religious expressions (Crosby & Torres, 2023). Despite the cultural blending and syncretic practices, Arará has maintained a distinct cultural identity through their religious practices and communal activities, separate from other Afro-Cuban religious traditions like Santería (which is more associated with Yoruba influences). While Arará people are a minority within Cuba, their cultural and religious practices have contributed significantly to the broader spectrum of Afro-Cuban identity.

Arará culture is particularly known for its ceremonial music and dance traditions, which are essential components of their religious and social life. Drums are a prominent feature in their ceremonies, and the dances often mimic movements that are intended to honor the spirits or communicate with the divine. While Arará drumming has a distinctive style, many of the rhythms and instruments are shared with other African traditions, such as Santería and Palo Monte. Arará music and dance are sometimes performed publicly during festivals and celebrations in Cuba, keeping the traditions alive across generations. In many ways, artistic performance is a revolutionary practice that reminds each generation of their matter of concern for survival, community, and connection to a shared history.

Over the course of our research, we spent significant time in Matanzas Province, a region known for its committed preservation of Arará traditions through museums, cultural centers, and widely attended ceremonies. Some of the San Lázaro ceremonies I attended each December included around 100 people. Given the importance of community, we wanted to maintain a relationship of researching with one another. Every aspect of the project, from the questions we asked to the forms of expression we described, resulted from a conversation with Arará elders, partners, and practitioners. We did not just interview and observe with a desire for objectivity. Instead, we lived and worked with the community throughout the entire process of organizing a ceremony meant to affirm a collective sacred identity. Since we rented a car in Havana, we could help gather food (or even the animal sacrifices) for the ceremonies or provide transportation for elders who could not walk the distance to the hosting house. These experiences first introduced me to interdependence as not just an idea, but a way of being.

The Arará practice interdependence through a deeply integrated social, spiritual, and ecological framework. Central to their way of life is a strong emphasis on reciprocal relationships between individuals, ancestors, deities, and the natural world. Their ceremonies are essential for maintaining balance and harmony between the living, the spiritual realm, and nature, ensuring protection, guidance, and sustenance. Additionally, Arará culture fosters strong community-based relationships where individuals are embedded in an interconnected web of familial and communal bonds. These relationships are nurtured through mutual aid, shared responsibilities, and collective ceremonies, reflecting the broader values of care, cooperation, and respect for all life. Through these practices, the Arará demonstrate a holistic understanding of interdependence that permeates all aspects of their social and spiritual life. While the extent to which the Arará exchanged ideas with Indigenous peoples in Cuba is not highly documented, much of their conception of interdependence reflects beliefs and practices of the Taíno, who lived in Cuba as well as Puerto Rico, the Dominican Republic, Haiti, Jamaica, and the Bahamas. Religious attributes between African and Indigenous religions highlight the importance of solidarity and connection in the face of empire (Hardt & Negri, 2005).

The Taíno had a rich worldview deeply rooted in concepts of interdependence, particularly with nature and the spiritual world (Neeganagwedgin, 2015). While much of the Taíno culture was disrupted by European colonization, the remnants of their beliefs, oral traditions, and archeological evidence provide insight into their understanding of interdependence. The Taíno believed in spiritual beings called zemí, which were closely tied to natural elements such as mountains, rivers, and forests. Each zemí was thought to govern aspects of the natural world and human life. This belief system reinforced a sense of deep interdependence between the Taíno people and the environment, where maintaining harmonious relationships with these spirits was crucial for survival, prosperity, and well-being. The Taíno saw their connection to the zemí as reciprocal: humans offered respect, rituals, and offerings, while the zemí provided protection, fertility, and balance to their communities. Creation stories and deities also reflect a clear understanding of interdependence between humans and nature. Yúcahu was the god of cassava (their main staple crop) and agriculture, while Atabey was the goddess of fresh water, fertility, and childbirth. These two deities were central to the Taíno worldview, emphasizing the people's reliance on the land, crops, and water for sustenance and survival.

The symbiotic relationship between the Taíno people and their environment was reflected in agricultural practices and rituals, where care for the land was seen as integral to the community's well-being. The Taíno used a sustainable form of agriculture called conuco, a mound-planting method that allowed for multiple crops to grow together, improving soil fertility and maximizing yields (Keegan, 2022). Conuco techniques demonstrated a deep understanding of ecological interdependence, where different plant species supported each other's growth, reflecting an early form of what we now call permaculture. The Taíno organized yucayeques (villages) led by caciques (chiefs) around farms, where collective labor and communal living were fundamental to their society. Their social organization was based on shared resources and cooperative work, particularly in agriculture, fishing, and building. Their communal way of life ensured that everyone contributed to and benefited from the village's resources, reflecting interdependence not only with nature but also within the community. The Taíno also practiced a communal ritual known as cohoba, where they used hallucinogenic substances to communicate with the spirits, especially their zemí ancestors, maintaining spiritual and social balance and reinforcing the idea that the Taíno viewed their existence as interdependent with both the physical and spiritual realms. Other rituals such as the game batay served as both a ceremonial and recreational activity that reminded one another of balance and cooperation within the community. The game emphasized group effort and shared enjoyment, reinforcing social cohesion and interdependence within the tribe.

Beyond Cuba and the Caribbean, many Indigenous cultures view the world as a web of life where all beings—humans, animals, plants, bacteria, and all life—are interconnected. A brief survey of Indigenous peoples and cultures suggests an important theme: the well-being of one part of the system affects the entire system, encouraging respect for the natural world and community. The Lakota phrase Mitákuye Oyás'iŋ, "All My Relations," expresses the spiritual and ethical concept acknowledging that all living things are interrelated and part of a larger whole (Posthumus, 2022). The Andean concept of Ayni, a Quechua word for reciprocity, reflects the idea of mutual dependence and exchange between people and nature. In these communities, survival and harmony rely on shared responsibilities and the continuous giving and receiving between individuals, their communities, and the Earth, Pachamama (Broda, 2015). The Maori of New Zealand have a deep sense of interdependence embodied in whakapapa, which refers to genealogy or layers of connection, not only between people but also between humans and nature. Whakapapa teaches that all life forms are genealogically connected and that respect for the land, whenua, is essential for the health of the community (Mahuika, 2019). South Africa introduced ubuntu to the world. Ubuntu emphasizes the interconnectedness of humanity. The Zulu proverb "Umuntu ngumuntu ngabantu" translates to "I am because we are," underscoring that a person's well-being and identity are deeply intertwined with their relationships with others (Kamwangamalu, 1999, p. 26). The phrase highlights collective well-being and social harmony as central to a balanced life. Aboriginal activist Oodgeroo illustrated the challenge of preserving interdependent dreamtime stories despite dominant colonialist narratives (Jones, 2003). Dreamtime stories integrate the belief that all elements of nature are kin and that human survival depends on living in harmony with the land. Finally, though not Indigenous in the Western sense, Confucianism and Daoism in East Asia have long reflected interdependence. Confucian ideals emphasize the relational nature of human existence, while Daoism teaches that humans must harmonize with the natural flow of the universe, the Dao (Lai, 2007). These examples show that Indigenous and non-Western worldviews have long recognized interdependence as a foundational concept, predating and influencing Western academic discussions.

These histories are important reminders of the shared beliefs that always being in relationship carries important implications. As someone with a dominant identity (whiteness), I also operate within my relationship to colonialism, realizing that a certain amount of privilege accompanies a white Cuban-American. Depending on what others know about me or how they recognize me, I can benefit from positive relationships with (white) people in power. Privilege can also blur the lens of experience, meaning those positive relationships with power can color how I make sense of the world. It can make it easy for me to reside in the comfort of privilege while expressing how much I care about, or pity, something or someone distant. Ethically, then, we cannot engage in decolonial practices simply by announcing the relationality of the world. Rather, through critical practices, we must work to decolonize those relationships that have positioned us with particular dominant identities in social hierarchies.

Given the West's attachment to the rugged individualist orientation of the world, accepting interdependence can be disorienting. Western scholars who studied interdependence often came off as radicals for opposing the Enlightenment-derived matter of fact of individualism. A founding figure in sociology, Emile Durkheim explored the idea of social interdependence in his studies of social cohesion and the division of labor. His work emphasized how individuals and groups rely on each other within a society to maintain social order and stability. Karl Marx's theory of historical materialism involves the idea of interdependence among social classes and economic systems. Marxists examine how the relationships between different classes and modes of production shape society and historical development. In economics, John Maynard Keynes discussed interdependence in the context of global economic systems, particularly through his work on international trade and monetary policies, which highlight how economies are interconnected. Kenneth Boulding, an economist and systems theorist, introduced the concept of interdependence in his work on general systems theory and the dynamics of complex systems, including economic and social systems. In international relations, James Rosenau examined the concept of interdependence in the context of global politics and the complexities of modern international systems. Each of these scholars had to defend against criticism and controversy because of their challenges to Western matters of fact that privileged individualism.

John Thibaut and Harold Kelley established interdependence as a subject of study in social psychology. They defined interdependence theory as a way of explaining how individuals' behaviors and outcomes are influenced by their relationships with others. Interdependence theory posits that six dimensions delineate the variations and commonalities found across interdependent situations: mutual dependence, power, conflict, coordination, future interdependence, and information certainty (Kelley et al., 2003; Kelley & Thibaut, 1978). While it might seem antithetical to interdependence to reduce it to separate parts, these dimensions help provide a vocabulary, even if limited, to explain how situations shape group dynamics.

Mutual dependence refers to the extent to which individuals rely on one another to achieve their goals. In situations of high mutual dependence, individuals recognize that their success is intertwined, fostering collaboration and promoting cooperative behaviors. Conversely, low mutual dependence may lead to more competitive or self-serving behaviors, as individuals may prioritize personal goals over group objectives. Power encompasses the distribution of influence among individuals in an interdependent situation. Those with greater power may have more control over resources or decision-making processes, which can affect the dynamics of interaction. Power imbalances can shape behavior by fostering compliance or resistance, influencing how individuals negotiate and assert their interests. Additionally, perceptions of power can alter cognition, as individuals may adjust their strategies based on their sense of agency or vulnerability within the relationship and may influence behavior based on a desire to reduce conflict. Indeed, power shapes who we are allowed to be in an interdependent situation; individuals may engage in constructive dialogue to resolve issues, or they might resort to avoidance or aggression. How conflict is managed also shapes cognitive processes, as individuals may develop coping mechanisms or adopt different perspectives based on their experiences of conflict. Coordination involves the organization of activities and efforts among interdependent individuals. Effective coordination requires clear communication and shared understanding of roles and tasks. When coordination is high, behaviors are synchronized, leading to efficient outcomes. However, poor coordination can result in confusion and frustration, influencing individuals' perceptions of each other and their overall experience in the interdependent situation. Future interdependence reflects the expectation of ongoing relationships and interactions. When individuals anticipate future interdependence, they may be more inclined to invest in building trust and nurturing relationships. This foresight shapes behavior by promoting long-term thinking and collaboration, whereas a lack of future interdependence might lead individuals to act more opportunistically or selfishly, focusing on immediate gains rather than sustainable partnerships. Information certainty pertains to the degree of clarity and predictability in the information available to individuals, which determines the effectiveness of decision-making and fostered trust, depending on the extent to which individuals feel confident in their understanding of one another's intentions and actions. In contrast, low information certainty can lead to anxiety and mistrust, prompting individuals to behave defensively or competitively as they navigate the uncertainty of the relationship.

Evidence from psychological studies suggests that individuals who recognize interdependence maintain well-being and authenticity even when situations change. Cross et al. (2003), for instance, developed a scale for measuring individuals' relational-interdependent self-construal (RISC), which refers to how individuals define themselves through close personal relationships. Those with a high RISC include their connections with others as essential parts of their self-identity, prioritizing relationships in shaping their behavior and self-concept. Meanwhile, self-consistency is the extent to which people perceive themselves as stable and coherent across different situations or relationships. Individuals with high self-consistency tend to behave similarly across various social contexts, whereas those with low self-consistency show more variation in how they act and define themselves based on their environment. To assess self-consistency, participants described themselves across different close relationships, rating either their traits (Study 1) or emotions (Study 2). Study 3 added a measure of authenticity in relationships. The studies used the RISC Scale to measure how many participants, who consisted of undergraduate students, define themselves through close relationships. Participants also completed well-being measures, such as life satisfaction, self-esteem, depression, and stress. The results revealed that for individuals with a highly relational self-construal, self-consistency was less crucial for well-being. People with high RISC were more likely to adapt their behavior to different social contexts because they understood the role that relationships play in shaping their actions and feelings. For them, being flexible and adjusting to others' needs was more important than consistently displaying the same traits across situations. Additionally, people with a high relational self-construal also reported feeling more authentic in their relationships, even when their behavior varied across different social contexts. In contrast, those with a low relational self-construal placed more value on consistency across relationships and felt better when they could maintain a stable self-concept. They also experienced higher stress and more threats to well-being when experiencing changes in their social contexts. Considering that one of the most important things teachers can do is "teach for transfer," which means helping students apply newly learned content to new situations (Perkins & Salomon, 2012), interdependence promises to be a critical element of any classroom.

As interdependent organisms, we exist through the care of others, such as how humans breathe oxygen due, in part, to their relationships with oxygen-producing plants and trees. In turn, humans help spread tree species by carrying their seeds across geographical distances. This does not mean that care as a committed action is the same as care as a conscious action. Trees certainly do not produce oxygen because they adore humans or other oxygen-dependent beings, and humans do not always intentionally contribute to tree dissemination, especially considering that humans can be very good at consciously cutting down trees. As an instructional approach, care offers a stark reminder that all of our actions impact one another in interconnected ways, regardless of how conscious an actor might be while acting. Care is a constant (conscious and unconscious) form of maintenance to repair, restore, or—when we need to—transform our life worlds to sustain our sense of wholeness. Pedagogically, such a definition of care reveals wonderful opportunities for how we might think about teaching and learning.

Interdependent Classrooms

Care as a committed action is never linear—a singular actor acting upon a thing. Screenwriting guru Robert McKee (2010) states that every story is the relationship between "action/reaction" (p. 178). Every action is itself a reaction as well as the catalyst for any number of other reactions. Within the vibrations of action/reaction, we determine what we can do and who we can become. However, we live in a culture that is strongly obsessed with the idea of individual actions, evidenced by Western countries' strong focus on prisons and a disdain for social safety nets. This obsession impacts instruction, evidenced by the treatment of assessment as an accountability measure. For years, educators have lamented that Edward Thorndike, a pioneer for increased testing, won the battle for America's educational future over John Dewey, a pioneer for student exploration and reflection (Levin, 1991). While interdependence reminds us that failure is never the fault of a single person, it also means that success is more systemic than it is individually determined. This change in thinking might make some people feel like all the work they committed to their achievements was for naught, as if achievement that does not come from individual grit is not valuable achievement. Interdependence disrupts this binary and reminds us that not only does the work we commit help shape our individual achievements, but our efforts also determine the achievement of others, and not just in competitive terms (e.g., "I need my competition to fail so that I can succeed"), but much more frequently in cooperative terms (e.g., "I need others in my community to succeed so that I can succeed"). Similarly, thinking of classrooms as collections of mutually exclusive individuals places potentially unreasonable expectations on a teacher to care for—or, "manage"—several different students in terms of personalities, cultural backgrounds, or neurodiverse behaviors. An interdependent perspective liberates a teacher to cultivate the relationships that connect each member of a classroom, creating a system of care in which everyone contributes to achievement.

For too long, the science of learning has failed to broadly inform most classroom practices (McMurtie, 2022). Considering the harm that has resulted from individualism—polarization, isolation, and loneliness, to name a few—interdependence provides clear evidence for its adoption. This is not my hyperbole, by the way. Johnson & Johnson (2009) literally say, "The application of social interdependence theory to education has become one of the most successful and widespread applications of social and educational psychology to practice" (p. 368). Dan Johnson and Roger Johnson, as I have mentioned earlier, positioned interdependence at the heart of teaching and learning. They argue that the most effective learning occurs in cooperative environments where individuals work together toward common goals. Their take on the theory is built on the idea that knowledge is constructed through interaction and dialogue among learners. SILT "exists when the outcomes of individuals are affected by their own and others' actions" (Johnson & Johnson, 2009, p. 368). In a learning environment, this means that classroom design emphasizes the relational bonds between students, prioritizing collaboration and cooperation as methods upon which success depends. These bonds can be understood in two primary ways, positive and negative interdependence. Positive interdependence occurs when students adopt the perception that they can reach their goals if, and only if, others in the group also reach their goals. In contrast, negative interdependence occurs when students believe that they can reach their goals only if others do not reach their goals, such as the perception that only a certain number of As can be rewarded in a particular course, pitting students in competition for a scarce resource. Finally, no interdependence indicates an environment in which students think their goals are unrelated to others' goals.

Distilling these principles into an actionable pedagogy calls attention to positive interdependence, individual accountability, and promotive interaction. Positive interdependence means that the success of each individual is linked to the success of the group. Individual accountability ensures that each member contributes to the group's work. Promotive interaction involves individuals encouraging and facilitating each other's efforts. In such environments, learners are more likely to challenge each other's ideas, ask questions, and provide feedback, leading to a deeper understanding and more robust knowledge creation. Experts argue that the process of engaging with others in the co-construction of knowledge leads to more critical and reflective scholarship. This collaborative dynamic fosters a more thorough and critical examination of the subject matter. When individuals collaborate, they can combine their strengths and compensate for each other's weaknesses, leading to more comprehensive and well-rounded scholarship. The dialogue and negotiation involved can spark new ideas and approaches that might not emerge in solitary work.

SILT is not just a mindset or belief system about how cooperative or competitive students should be. Empirical evidence consistently suggests that cultivating positive interdependence results in impressive learning gains. In their systematic review of almost 1,000 studies of SILT, Johnson and Johnson (2005) found that students who cooperate rather than compete with other students put forth more effort in the learning task, persist when faced with challenges, engage in critical thinking, and transfer learning to novel situations (pp. 304–306). Before these learning gains can be realized, however, students must commit to interdependence as a theory as well as a practice. Johnson and Johnson (2009) suggest that teachers clarify objectives and the social skills required to achieve the course objectives. They also design groups appropriate for the objectives. Next, they recommend that teachers explain the interdependent processes that align with the class content, crystallizing criteria for success and individual accountability to the group. Then teachers monitor students' learning as well as their engagement in the group. When needed, teachers provide guidance or intervene (like Kimmerer with her pond) to sustain positive interdependence. Finally, teachers include students in the evaluation of their group's success (p. 370).

Reflection remains a critical step for both teachers and students. We cannot care about everything and everyone at the same time. Besides cognitive load exhausting our working memory and narrowing the scope of our attention, enacting boundless care might also result in compassion fatigue (Sinclair et al., 2017). Because of these limitations, we need to also avoid teaching oppression and diversity Olympics, the former signifying a competition among oppressed groups over whose oppression deserves the most attention and the latter signifying a competition among allies and activists over whose work deserves the most attention. An interdependent classroom needs to establish shared trust, especially between people who are engaged in care work in different contexts. I spent much of my life sharply focused on environmental justice, but I did so because I had wonderful mentors engaged in accessibility justice, antiracist justice, sex identity justice, etc. Interdependence allows us to pursue different goals through shared strategies and collective support. Additionally, interdependence entails solidarity—we accomplish our "individual" goals only when we *all* accomplish our "individual" goals. We create a just world when we transform systems in particular contexts, which intersect other systems and create ripples of change beyond the spheres of our individual influence. Alone, we cannot do it all. Connected, our agency is infinite.

When I am invited to facilitate events focused on collaboration and community building, I often begin by asking participants to think about a current project of which they are proud. Then I ask them to create a mental list of everyone who made that project possible. Most people will name formal collaborators, colleagues, mentors, editors, foundations, and other professionals, resembling an acknowledgment section of a publication. We dig deeper. I encourage participants to widen the frame and consider all the ways they replenished themselves. All the ways they maintained care for themselves and their projects. Now people started listing family members and friends, but some say things like, "If my barista did not have my Americano ready for me at 8 am, I would have crashed long ago." Others mentioned the custodial staff who entered the building late at night, invisible to the project leaders, and made sure labs, offices, and classrooms were ready by the break of dawn. Finally, participants pair up and challenge one another to create the longest list of all agents—human and more than human—that make their projects possible. At this stage, entomologists credit and thank the insects they study. Pedestrians credit and thank the construction of crosswalks and traffic lights. Commuters credit and thank the construction of parking lots (even when there aren't enough!). Windows that provide much-needed sunlight, facility services that ensure the A/C keeps running, and furniture designers all receive thanks. Usually, people are surprised by how long their lists can grow. What they realize: despite how lonely our work can often feel, we actually never work alone.

Teaching Care and the Honorable Harvest

We begin and end this chapter with Kimmerer. Her illustration of the Honorable Harvest—that even though we always take from the world for our purposes, we can do so in ways that restore the world—suggests that in a complex ecology, care is not a simple moral/immoral binary. This advice should certainly inspire teachers, who often find themselves giving a great deal of their emotional and intellectual labor and then feeling guilty if they take something as small as a day off. Disentangling "honorable harvests" from "extractive practices" is certainly no easy feat, however. Kimmerer (2013) tells the story of a trapper named Lionel who goes to great lengths to take care of female martens, especially when they have kits. Despite such care, Lionel makes a living by trapping, killing, and skinning martens to sell their pelts and fur. For Kimmerer (2013), the complexity of care, including what may seem like contradictions, begins to make sense when understood through the wisdom of interdependence. She explains:

> The teachings tell us that a harvest is made honorable by what you give in return for what you take. There is no escaping the fact that Lionel's care will result in more martens on his trapline. There is no escaping the fact that they will also be killed. Feeding mama martens is not altruism; it is deep respect for the way the world works, for the connections between us, of life flowing into life. The more he gives, the more he can take, and he goes the extra mile to give more than he takes.
>
> *(p. 194)*

Understanding interdependence within particular ecologies helps guide a notion of care as a committed action. The particular ecology we will explore in the next chapter is that of higher education, which faces increasing challenges to its identity, values, and future. What might an interdependent way of being in the higher education ecology resemble? Let's explore this question in the next chapter.

References

Belay, M., & Mugambe, B. (2021). Bill Gates should stop telling Africans what kind of agriculture Africans need. *Scientific American*. https://www.scientificamerican.com/article/bill-gates-should-stop-telling-africans-what-kind-of-agriculture-africans-need1/.

Broda, J. (2015). Political expansion and the creation of ritual landscapes: A comparative study of Inca and Aztec cosmovision. *Cambridge Archaeological Journal, 25*(1), 219–238.

Butler, J. (2020). *The force of nonviolence: An ethico-political bind*. New York: Verso.

Cave, K. R., & Bichot, N. P. (1999). Visuospatial attention: Beyond a spotlight model. *Psychonomic Bulletin & Review, 6*, 204–223.

Crosby, J. F., & Torres, J. T. (2023). *Situated narratives and sacred dance: Performing the entangled histories of Cuba and West Africa*. University Press of Florida.

Cross, S. E., Gore, J. S., & Morris, M. L. (2003). The relational-interdependent self-construal, self-concept consistency, and well-being. *Journal of Personality and Social Psychology, 85*(5), 933–944. https://doi.org/10.1037/0022-3514.85.5.933.

de la Bellacasa, M. P. (2017). *Matters of care: Speculative ethics in more than human worlds* (Vol. 41). University of Minnesota Press.

Gilligan, C. (1993). *In a different voice: Psychological theory and women's development*. Harvard University Press.

Giridharadas, A. (2019). *Winners take all: The elite charade of changing the world*. Vintage.

Haraway, D. J. (1997). *Modest_Witness@Second_Millennium: FemaleMan©_Meets_OncoMouse™: Feminism and Technoscience*. Routledge.

Hardt, M., & Negri, A. (2005). *Multitude: War and democracy in the age of empire*. Penguin.

Johnson, D. W., & Johnson, R. T. (2005). New developments in social interdependence theory. *Genetic, Social, and General Psychology Monographs, 131*(4), 285–358.

Johnson, D. W., & Johnson, R. T. (2009). An educational psychology success story: Social interdependence theory and cooperative learning. *Educational Researcher, 38*(5), 365–379.

Jones, J. (2003). Oodgeroo and her editor: The production of stradbroke dreamtime. *Journal of Australian Studies, 27*(76), 45–56.

Kamwangamalu, N. M. (1999). Ubuntu in South Africa: A sociolinguistic perspective to a pan-African concept. *Critical Arts, 13*(2), 24–41.

Keegan, W. F. (2022). *Taíno Indian myth and practice: The arrival of the stranger king.* University Press of Florida.

Kelley, H. H., Holmes, J. G., Kerr, N. L., Reis, H. T., Rusbult, C. E., & Van Lange, P. A. M. (2003). *An atlas of interpersonal situations.* Cambridge, UK: Cambridge University Press. http://dx.doi.org/10.1017/CBO9780511499845.

Kelley, H. H., & Thibaut, J. W. (1978). *Interpersonal relations: A theory of interdependence.* New York, NY: Wiley.

Kimmerer, R. (2013). *Braiding sweetgrass: Indigenous wisdom, scientific knowledge and the teachings of plants.* Milkweed Editions.

Lai, K. L. (2007). Understanding change: The interdependent self in its environment. *Journal of Chinese Philosophy, 34*(5), 81–99.

Levin, R. A. (1991). The debate over schooling: Influences of Dewey and Thorndike. *Childhood Education, 68*(2), 71–75.

Mahuika, N. (2019). A brief history of whakapapa: Māori approaches to genealogy. *Genealogy, 3*(2), 32.

McGill, K., & Brown, M. (2020). 10 years after BP spill: Oil drilled deeper; rules relaxed. *Phys Org.* https://phys.org/news/2020-04-years-bp-oil-drilled-deeper.html#google_vignette.

McKee, R. (2010). *Story: Style, structure, substance, and the principles of screenwriting.* Harper Collins.

McMurtie, B. (2022). Why the Science of Teaching is Often Ignored. *Chronicle of Higher Education.* https://www.chronicle.com/article/why-the-science-of-teaching-is-often-ignored

Neeganagwedgin, E. (2015). Rooted in the land: Taíno identity, oral history and stories of reclamation in contemporary contexts. *AlterNative: An International Journal of Indigenous Peoples, 11*(4), 376–388.

Noddings, N. (2002). *Starting at home: Caring and social policy.* University of California Press.

Noddings, N. (2010). *The maternal factor: Two paths to morality.* University of California Press.

Noddings, N. (2013). *Caring: A relational approach to ethics and moral education.* University of California Press.

Perkins, D. N., & Salomon, G. (2012). Knowledge to go: A motivational and dispositional view of transfer. *Educational Psychologist, 47*(3), 248–258.

Posthumus, D. (2022). *All my relatives: Exploring lakota ontology, belief, and ritual.* University of Nebraska Press.

Roney, L. N., & Acri, M. C. (2018). The cost of caring: An exploration of compassion fatigue, compassion satisfaction, and job satisfaction in pediatric nurses. *Journal of Pediatric Nursing, 40*, 74–80.

Sinclair, S., Raffin-Bouchal, S., Venturato, L., Mijovic-Kondejewski, J., & Smith-MacDonald, L. (2017). Compassion fatigue: A meta-narrative review of the healthcare literature. *International Journal of Nursing Studies, 69*, 9–24.

Tronto, J. (1993). *Moral Boundaries: A political argument for an ethic of care.* Routledge.

Zembylas, M. (2013). The "crisis of pity" and the radicalization of solidarity: Toward critical pedagogies of compassion. *Educational Studies, 49*(6), 504–521.

2
HIGHER EDUCATION AS AN ECOLOGY IN NEED OF CARE

Chapter Contents
From the Monastery to the Marketplace: Higher Education's
History of Care   31
   Medieval Care for Religious Doctrine   31
   Enlightenment Care for Reason   32
   Post-War Care for National Security   33
   Postmodern Care for Democratic Rights   33
   Neoliberal Care for Market Value   34
The Current Culture War Over Care   38
   Navigating an Ecology of Stress   39
   Stress as Structure: An Example   42
Cracks in the System   43
Imagining an Era of Caring With Higher Education   45
References   48

Once during a faculty senate meeting at my previous institution, the Provost led a discussion about the frequent calls for curricular innovation. The Provost challenged faculty to evaluate whether their courses served the needs of a 21st-century education, one driven by increasing diversity of students and multiplicity of modalities, including working with AI. Tensions came to a head when faculty expressed that although they also desire opportunities to revise their existing courses and programs, they do not have the capacity to engage in the labor required to do so.

"Between hybrid teaching, federal government hostility towards higher education, and new social dynamics of students who spent the majority of their high school education on Zoom," one faculty member shared, "I haven't had the chance to catch my breath."

"It's not just students who had their lives disrupted," another faculty member chimed in. "We are exhausted, too."

The Provost responded: "I hear you. But the fact remains: if we stand still, we die."

Yes, the Provost comes dangerously close to echoing Zuckerberg ("move fast and break things"); however, to some degree the Provost was, and still is, right. The tectonic shifts unsettling much of the higher education landscape have demanded that educators innovate the idea of a college experience so that it includes increasingly diverse learners, rapidly advancing AI, and dramatically changing political contexts and responds to rising costs that require students to either take out significant loans or work their way through college.

Many might believe that higher education in the Western world is made of immovable structures. Even I fall into despair when watching good ideas die by committee every semester. However, as others have noted, higher education in the West has undergone profound transformations from its medieval origins to the present. Over the centuries, universities have shifted from monastic and church-controlled institutions to secular, state-funded centers of research and finally to today's neoliberal, corporate-driven models. Each era re-centered care in terms of what knowledge was valued and who was worthy of pursuing it. These shifts, reviewed below, reflect interlocking ecologies, not only natural ones like the land colleges and universities occupy but also political, social, and cultural priorities that direct how, and to what, care gets directed. I also provide an historical review to remind us that change is not only possible, but it has always already been in effect.

From the Monastery to the Marketplace: Higher Education's History of Care

Medieval Care for Religious Doctrine

Prominent medieval universities, such as Bologna and Oxford, were founded during a time of increasing heresy and skepticism around the Papacy's spiritual authority. The Church's sanctions that made universities possible came with a specific agenda: to stamp out heresy and train scholars to uphold Church doctrine. Thomas Aquinas, for instance, dedicated much of his career to reconcile Aristotle's philosophy with accepted theology. Meanwhile, scholars like Peter Abelard, who made no such attempt at theological reconciliation, suffered public humiliation and, in some cases, threats to their lives.

Peter Abelard's most famous work, *Sic et Non* (*Yes and No*), compiled contradictory statements from Church authorities. Abelard published the text as a challenge to scholars to resolve theological contradictions through critical reasoning rather than unquestioned acceptance. Suggesting that scholars should think critically and ask questions did not fare well as a learning objective. During the Council of Soissons in 1121, Abelard was forced to burn his own book as punishment. Abelard continued to teach and write until 1140, when the Church silenced him once and for all, condemning his works and ordering him to a life of exile (Brower & Guilfoy, 2004).

Driven by environmental conditions, such as the Little Ice Age, as well as religious challenges to the Catholic Church, historian Philipp Blom (2019) details the educational revolution toward humanism and science in the late 16th century. "The ability to read the Bible and enter into a direct conversation with God" via interpretation became an educational mission that extended schooling to new populations, fostering a more democratic approach to literacy that challenged centralized Papal authority on exegesis (Blom, 2019, p. 109). Gradually, universities in Europe transitioned from purely ecclesiastical institutions to ones under the patronage of nation-states or private scholars. By the 18th and 19th centuries, the Enlightenment ethos—emphasizing reason, empirical science, and intellectual freedom—took hold in academia.

Enlightenment Care for Reason

In this period, knowledge that proved itself through reason or scientific experiment gained prestige alongside (or even above) theological knowledge. Astronomers and physicists from Galileo to Newton advanced knowledge based on observation and mathematics, at times clashing with church doctrine (as in the famous case of Galileo's trial for advocating a heliocentric solar system). While theology remained in the curriculum, European universities increasingly valued discoveries in natural science and the humanities that expanded human understanding of the world. The modern research university model, epitomized by the University of Berlin in the early 19th century, declared the creation of new knowledge a central mission. Academic freedom became an ideal as care for truth was prioritized by scholars and students.

Industrialization of the Western world directly shaped education operations. The industrial model that arranged students into production lines (e.g., disciplines organized by year of study) has been criticized by the likes of Cathy Davidson in *The New Education: How to revolutionize the university to prepare students for a world in flux* and Arthur Levine and Scott Van Pelt in *The Great Upheaval: Higher education's past, present, and uncertain future*. Davidson (2017), for instance, details the history of the current education system, conceived in the 19th century in order to "train farmers to be factory workers and shopkeepers to be managers, supervisors, regulators, bureaucrats, and policymakers" for the new industries replacing agriculture and local community-based business (p. 23). By design, education was molded in the image of the factory: "with nailed-down desks, standardized curriculum, and division of knowledge into discrete subjects to be studied for a specific amount of time each day," regulated by a bell that signaled the next stop on the educational assembly line (p. 24). The system, problematic as it may seem, fit the particular needs of the 19th century, needs that have since been upended by a globalized consumer economy.

Industrialization and its economic contributions to a swelling middle class who mostly provided universities with students shifted epistemic care from religious affirmation to national interests. Knowledge was seen as valuable for strengthening the nation's economy, culture, and power. For example, scientific research might be funded to improve industry or weaponry, and social research to inform governance. Care became redirected within a new alignment of academic priorities: from serving God to serving the state.

Post-War Care for National Security

After World War II, higher education in the Western world, especially the United States, entered a phase of massive expansion and public investment. In the United States, the GI Bill opened college to millions of veterans, and policymakers embraced universities as engines of economic growth and technological supremacy. The Cold War competition between the United States and the Soviet Union further heightened national interest in higher education. The U.S. government poured unprecedented funding into research universities to spur advances in physics, engineering, chemistry, and later computer science, all seen as crucial in the ideological and military rivalry with the Soviet bloc. Forming a military-industrial-academic complex, the decade following World War II saw the U.S. Department of Defense become the single largest patron of scientific research on American campuses (Giroux, 2015). Entire fields of study were cultivated with defense grants, such as nuclear physics and aerospace engineering. Universities like Massachusetts Institute of Technology (MIT) and Stanford grew into research powerhouses thanks to defense contracts. Ethical questions about knowledge production emerged as scholars grappled with the implications of working on weapons or military technology (Hartung, 2024). Nevertheless, the prevailing paradigm in mid-20th-century American higher education cared for knowledge that could yield defensive, often military or economic, benefits to the nation.

Meanwhile, student populations swelled and diversified. Students demanded a role in determining the role of higher education in caring for human and civil rights. In direct opposition to the authority of the nation-state, students especially opposed acts of war, including the one in Vietnam.

Postmodern Care for Democratic Rights

In the 1960s, student protests erupted across Europe and the United States, challenging university authorities and national policies. Inspired by demonstrations in Paris in May 1968 and the Free Speech Movement at the University of California, Berkeley, in 1964, students demanded a say in how universities were run and what they taught. Students protested rigid curricula, authoritarian governance structures, racial segregation, and universities' collaboration with military endeavors. As students succeeded in redirecting care from military interests to social justice, new fields of study emerged. For example, both ethnic studies and women's studies programs were established at several American universities after student demonstrations called for curricula that addressed the history and concerns of marginalized groups.

Crucially, the wave of 1960s campus activism democratized notions of knowledge worthy of care. Rather than accepting government- or administration-set agendas, students and sympathetic faculty insisted that universities serve broader social needs and critical exploration. Issues of social justice, equality, and peace became part of the academic conversation. However, economic crises, such as the global oil crisis in the 1970s, complicated currents of social justice-oriented care, leading to a significant backlash that defines our era today. The backlash, known as neoliberalism, refers to a philosophy that applies market-oriented principles across society, caring only about privatization, competition, and profit. In fact, before 1960, less than half of first-year college students stated that money was "important" to their success. By 2012, more than 90% of college students claimed money was "important or essential" to their success (Twenge et al., 2012).

In higher education, neoliberalism translated into reduced government funding, increased tuition and student fees, and a greater reliance on private sector money, ultimately repositioning higher education as an industry rather than a public trust (Giroux, 2015). Many scholars, journalists, and thinkers continue to address the question: How did neoliberalism so effectively transform higher education?

Neoliberal Care for Market Value

The progressive activism of the preceding era had attracted increasing criticism from conservative media and politicians. In the United States particularly, outlets like *Fox News* have routinely portrayed higher education as a bastion of liberal indoctrination out of touch with populist values. I have caught myself falling into the trap of spending my energy clarifying the correct understanding of critical race theory or DEI in public spheres, as if offering an academic seminar to an audience who certainly did not ask for one. Meanwhile, the audience I addressed cared less about theoretical frameworks in general and more about rising food costs, vanishing job prospects, and fear of losing position in social status. As a scholar who researches socially situated identity, I became easily positioned as the out-of-touch academic. The manufactured disconnect between academia and the lived experiences of many Westerners has contributed to the erosion of public trust and provided justification for certain policymakers to slash university budgets.

Since the 1980s, many state legislatures, mostly conservative, have reduced funding for public colleges. Famously, as California Governor, Ronald Reagan cut state university funding and remarked that taxpayers shouldn't subsidize "intellectual curiosity" (Berrett, 2015). That set a pattern. Public investment in higher education, once justified as building informed citizens and national prosperity, gave way to skepticism about universities' value. Over time, right-wing critics succeeded in decimating state funding for higher education, driving tuition costs up and shifting the burden to students and families. What started in Reagan's California became a nationwide policy shift: by the end of his presidency, students at public universities were covering nearly half the cost of their education out-of-pocket, a dramatic change from the mid-20th-century model of low tuition and high public subsidy (Brownlee & Graham, 2003).

Justifying these cuts, *Fox News* hosts and guests frequently cast universities as elitist, wasteful, or hostile to conservative values. For example, popular commentator Tucker Carlson (a previous Fox personality) argued that college education "diminishes" students and advised that "everyone should opt out" unless they have a very specific career goal (Lemon, 2021). Such rhetoric, amplified to millions of viewers, bolsters a narrative that higher education is not a public good but rather a suspect enterprise. In a climate of polarization, Republican voters have grown increasingly suspicious of universities (Kreighbaum, 2019; Ubell, 2022). Surveys by the Pew Research Center in recent years show a stark partisan divide: as of 2019, 59% of Republicans believed that colleges had a negative effect on the country, while only 33% saw their impact as positive (Parker, 2019). By contrast, strong majorities of Democrats still viewed colleges positively, even though less than half of all Americans have "confidence" in higher education (Brenan, 2023). Exhausted and lacking the resources, universities have not been very successful in making stating a public defense. Lynn Pasquarella's (2022) *What We Value: Public Health, Social Justice, and Educating for Democracy* investigates the difficulty higher education has faced in communicating to the public its value as a public good. Pasquarella asks a difficult question that currently lacks a clear answer: What does higher education care about, and why should the public care about higher education?

For conservatives, the answer is an obsession with efficiency and productivity. Despite the fact that learning is a slow, lifelong process (Eyler, 2018), misconceptions that higher education wastes time and effort continue today. Pressures grew for faculty to prove they deserved their salaries and tenure, resulting in policies requiring more transparency around faculty hours and outputs. Scrutiny came from both government bodies and the public, driven by the manufactured belief that faculty, particularly tenured professors, did not work as hard as they should for the compensation they received (Slaughter & Leslie, 1997; Slaughter & Rhoades, 2004). Such changes contributed to historically high rates of faculty burnout by increasing job insecurity, workload, and micromanagement from emerging university leaders with corporate rather than academic backgrounds (Cunningham, 1983).

By the mid-1990s, more than a third of states in America mandated accountability reporting with a focus on productivity measures of faculty (Gaither, 1995). Universities started to quantify faculty performance in terms of hours worked, research published, and grants secured. This obsession with productivity meant faculty were increasingly judged by metrics that did not always align with the qualitative aspects of teaching and research. As these metrics grew more prominent, faculty experienced more administrative oversight and reporting requirements. As a result, instead of engaging in scholarship or mentoring students, faculty spent their time tracking their hours, committing to more institutional service, and documenting advancements in disciplinary fields in order to warrant the discipline's existence (Cunningham, 1983). Efficiency and productivity also defined intellectual efforts.

Curricula focused on hyper-specialized majors. While deep expertise is necessary in certain fields, it can also create intellectual monocultures where broader perspectives become unimportant or even antagonistic to specialized task completion. The assembly line worker cutting meat into consumable sirloins and filets who thinks about the once-living animal or the human consumer likely becomes more inefficient in their processing. Efficiency, according to Marxist critique, depends on alienating workers from the products of their labor—the slaughterhouse worker likely cannot afford a sirloin or a filet—and from one another, preventing unionization or solidarity (Szadkowski, 2019; Øversveen, 2022). In other words, silos preserve efficiency, even as they limit interdependent thinking. By fragmenting tasks into smaller, repetitive functions, the capitalist system increases production speed and output. Workers specialize in narrow tasks, which streamline processes and reduces the time needed to complete products. Controlling the means of production allows managers to dictate the pace and methods of work, ensuring predictable and efficient outcomes, often at the expense of workers' individual creativity and autonomy. Alienated labor enables capitalism to extract surplus value from workers' labor, since the workers do not control the means of production or the value of their labor. This exploitation drives greater profits for the capitalist, further entrenching the system and its emphasis on efficiency over equity. Since the goal of modern education is to turn students into workers, managing them as individual units with little relational value to one another becomes the pedagogical prerogative. One explicit illustration of this prerogative: the aggressively individualized standardized assessment. I often tell my students, "In the real world, working together is called *collaboration*. In school, it's called *cheating*."

By the 1990s and 2000s, many universities in the United States and Europe narrowed their academic priorities toward economically focused disciplines and programs. STEM fields (science, technology, engineering, and math), business and finance programs, and any research areas with corporate sponsorship or patent potential received growing emphasis. Conversely, humanities and fundamental social sciences, which are less directly tied to economic growth, often saw declining support. For faculty, this has meant that the latitude to pursue truth for its own sake has narrowed. A medieval scholar risked charges of heresy; a modern scholar may risk losing a grant or their job if their research questions powerful economic interests or fails to secure outside funding. The modes of suppression differ—burning at the stake versus budget cuts—but the effect of discouraging certain lines of thought can feel alarmingly familiar. Today's researchers might avoid controversial topics (such as studying the health impacts of a product made by a major donor's company) out of concern for repercussions, just as in the past a philosopher avoided contradicting the Church's teachings. For students, the prevailing belief that education's value lies in earnings after graduation limits their intellectual exploration. Outcomes such as critical and creative thinking only make sense as marketable skills (Vassallo, 2020). If critical thinking leads to asking too many on-the-job questions, then critical thinking as a skillset might have a negative value. Imagine if Chevron hires a newly graduated college student who cares deeply about the environment and wonders why Chevron continues to damage it while also silencing climate science? That student probably will not remain very "employable." On the other hand, if creative thinking helps a company make even more money, then such a skill is especially valued. A campus climate focused on career outcomes and run with corporate efficiency leaves little room for the kind of political engagement and experimentation that once flourished. Student activism itself is sometimes cast as an impediment to the university's brand or a liability in attracting donors, leading administrators to enforce stricter protest policies, all in the desperate pursuit of constantly receding funding lines.

And as public funding for higher education recedes, wealthy private donors and corporations gladly step in to fill the gap, of course with strings attached. The late 20th and early 21st centuries saw an influx of money from billionaire philanthropists, some with strong ideological agendas. In the past few decades, universities have begun to depend more on private sector partnerships. Beyond Bill Gates's philanthropy, which we briefly critiqued in Chapter 1, the Koch family, fossil fuel magnates who long criticized higher education's audacity to teach climate science, invested millions in institutions that promised to minimize environmental concerns (Levinthal, 2015). Rather than these partnerships violating conflicts of interest, they formed an accepted logic.

By 2011, the Koch Foundation was funding programs at 187 different colleges and universities across the United States. Often these gifts come with detailed conditions. At Florida State University, a well-publicized 2008 grant from the Koch Foundation to the economics department included provisions giving a Koch-appointed advisory board a role in approving faculty hires and evaluating their research output for alignment with the foundation's "objectives and purposes" (Palast, 2014). Essentially, Koch representatives sought to ensure the professors hired with their money would promote laissez-faire economic ideas, and they reserved the right to withdraw funding if dissatisfied.

And the Kochs are not alone. Other donors and corporate sponsors have used their wealth to tilt the academic agenda. Pharmaceutical companies fund biomedical research chairs, oil companies endow energy institutes, and tech giants like OpenAI sponsor programs, labs, and scholarships (Kirschenbaum & Raley, 2024). Brendan Cantwell and Ilkka Kauppinen's (2014) *Academic Capitalism in the Age of Globalization* examines how universities, in the context of globalization, have become vulnerable to corporatization. The authors discuss the rise of "academic capitalism," where the pursuit of external funding and partnerships with industry takes precedence over traditional academic values like public scholarship and intellectual freedom. Corporate-groomed individuals often become university leaders, intersecting profit motives from privately held interests with public funding for a social institution. Cantwell and Kauppinen's (2014) book raises the alarm over the current trend of universities blurring "boundaries between state and society and privatizing policy making" (p. 29). When these boundaries become blurred in an educational context, Wendy Brown (2015) argues in *Undoing the Demos: Neoliberalism's Stealth Revolution*, the traditional liberal arts value of educating for citizenship gets replaced with educating for human capital. The "governing rationality" of the neoliberal university, Brown (2015) explains, "formulates everything, everywhere in terms of capital investment and appreciation, including and especially humans themselves" (p. 176). When Florida Senator Rick Scott decried the number of students who majored in the social sciences as a "waste of state money," he directly reflected the neoliberalization of college students, who, in his view, should care about marketplace value over democratic participation (Jaschik, 2011).

Tensions around care, either for marketplace value or for democratic participation, have become a powder keg under the second Trump Administration. Under Trump, the federal government has launched a direct attack against social justice and DEI. Programs, curricula, organizations, and offices that support marginalized identities or teach content related to slavery, identity, or, more broadly, sociology have been eliminated across America. These changes have left higher education in a constant pivot within a grueling culture war.

The Current Culture War Over Care

For many institutions across America, DEI eliminations resulted in the sudden termination of several professional faculty and staff and the loss of scholarships for students with diverse identities (Zeeble, 2024). Community groups, cultural centers, and resources dedicated to minoritized student populations vanished in a matter of days (Gretzinger & Hicks, 2024; Marzia, 2024). Many institutions have been forced to negotiate their care for democratic values of teaching and learning with their care about public opinion and private funding. These negotiations often mean no longer caring-with minoritized and underrepresented populations, theories of knowledge that challenge neoliberal rationality, or purposes of higher education beyond corporate employability.

In general, DEI cares about/for/with students who have been historically excluded from social participation. Almost all American students who hope to go to college take the SAT, a standardized test assessing aptitude. The long-standing evidence of the SAT's historic cultural bias against Black and Latino students, drastically reducing the chances for these students to attend college, is one example of historical exclusion that requires specific interventions (Droege, 2003). On the other hand, the right for women to vote, special education programs, and racial desegregation of schools can all be broadly considered as examples of DEI initiatives. At its heart, DEI is about thoughtfully directing care to populations who have historically been denied care. For example, we know that historically fewer women graduate in STEM fields than men not because they can't succeed in STEM but because they aren't as likely to feel valued as a STEM student (Kim et al., 2018). Many studies find that developing learning experiences with care for particular student identities in mind does not just result in improved academic performance for that particular identity group (Sawyer III et al., 2024). Collectively, DEI strategies, which are rooted in interdependent care, benefit all students (Roldán et al., 2021).

In my experiences working with students labeled as "nontraditional," either because of their age, economic, ethnic, or cultural background, or educational preparation, I have found it impossible to do any teaching before there is a strong sense of belonging (Sawyer III et al., 2024). The same could be said for us teachers: it is difficult to teach well when we do not feel valued by the institution. In a competitive environment, we become trained not only to distrust others but also to exploit any perceived weakness in them, replacing belonging and affirmation of one another with the increased anxiety and stress of being in a constant state of competition (Wilder & Shapiro, 1989). In a collective environment, we practice trust and interdependence so that any one person's perceived weakness is complemented by someone else's strength, or cultural capital, centering the social context on belonging (Yosso, 2005). In contrast to the anxiety-induced competition of individualist orientations, collectivist orientations strongly correlate with positive psychological adjustment to major stressors like COVID-19 (Germani et al., 2020). Unfortunately, the culture war against DEI preserves the high-stress orientation of neoliberal competition and elimination.

Navigating an Ecology of Stress

One of the most prominent features of academic life today is the perceived loss of time. At all levels, those of us in higher education desperately secure any moment we can to work on our publishing, student support, or class preps. Time chasing likely produces burnout (a topic we'll cover in more detail in Chapter 7), a growing phenomenon that affects faculty (Pope-Ruark, 2022) and students (Jagodics & Szabó, 2023). Maggie Berg and Barbara Seeber (2016) remark how higher education's ecology of stress has reconfigured our relationship to time, positioning us as meticulous log keepers of our precious hours, scheduling meetings and classes down to the minute to ensure some level of control over our labor. The increased pressure to "manage" time diverts us from one of the most powerful opportunities education can provide: timelessness, which Berg and Steener (2016) define as moments of "escape from time," opportunities that are vital to "deep thought, creativity, and problem solving" (p. 26).

Very rarely do today's students experience timelessness. In a study of high school students, Caetano et al. (2024) suggest that college admissions pressures have contributed to over-engagement in clubs, organizations, committees, and courses in an attempt to rack up credentials. Once students spend more than an hour each day on activities beyond academic learning, they not only report higher levels of stress, but they also demonstrate zero cognitive or social benefits from the activity (Caetano et al., 2024). These pressures continue in college, as students rack up even more credentials to compete in an ever-shrinking job market.

I remember when my niece, a brilliant young woman who loved discussing social theory, politics, and philosophy despite majoring in industrial engineering, graduated from a leading university. She exhibited the ideal liberal arts student—being well-rounded, critical, and highly skilled. In college, she led sorority events, volunteered throughout the community, joined the dance team, helped take care of our elders in our family who struggled with health challenges, held down a job, and maintained diverse academic interests. I was so excited by her intellectual journey that immediately upon graduation, I encouraged her to continue graduate school. I shared a program at Yale that seemed suited to her interests. She responded by letting me know she had applied for a job at Proctor & Gamble that would fast-track her to a management position overseeing a processing plant.

"That's great," I said. "But graduate school is not a factory (at least not technically). You can continue thinking about complicated problems and pursue research projects. And then later you could always."

"To be honest," she interrupted, her tone becoming impatient. I knew whatever she was about to say would be the final word on the matter. "I don't think my mental health will survive any more time at a university."

In other words, an *actual* factory promised a healthier environment.

Many scholars suggest that much of the Western world exists in perpetual crisis. Crisis has been so normalized that institutions like universities play a discourse of crisis on repeat. On a macro level of analysis, Naomi Klein (2007) described how disaster capitalism and what she termed the "shock doctrine" create conditions for accelerating neoliberalism. Klein shows how throughout history moments of crisis, such as economic recessions or depressions, international wars, or pandemics, tend to result in the rapid deterioration of welfare and other care systems. Depression-era welfare in the form of the New Deal crumbled at the crisis of the Cold War and the fear of communism. Human rights protections did not apply to the United States following the crisis of the September 11 terrorist attacks. Environmental regulation lost its importance when inflation resulted in high energy costs. While the crises themselves may not be orchestrated by proponents of neoliberalism, their transformation into structural discourses is. Klein (2007) quotes economist and primary architect of the U.S. economic system, Milton Friedman, who said: "Only a crisis—actual or perceived—produces real change. [Our basic function is to] develop alternatives to existing policies, to keep them alive and available until the politically impossible becomes politically inevitable" (p. 166).

Scholars Ramírez et al. (2015) studied how the shock doctrine and the discourse of crisis legitimize neoliberal policies at public universities. In three different cases in both Canada and the United States, Ramírez et al. (2015) found that university leaders relied on the same strategy when introducing policies that led to the elimination of faculty positions, departments, or programs; the silencing of student groups and organizations engaged in protest; or the termination of academic staff who questioned such policies. They each explicitly referenced a "crisis" as a level larger than the university (e.g., "global" or "across higher education") as a way to

> justify their attacks on academic freedom and collegial governance by [for example] underscoring the need for austerity in light of a financial crisis. However, the crisis is mostly a mirage, a made-up challenge supported by hortatory technocratic discourse with circular logic that serves and protects managerial interests.
>
> *(p. 172)*

In all three cases of Ramírez et al.'s (2015) study, despite cuts to academic programming and faculty positions, the universities also launched new capital projects in the forms of new buildings and executive positions. Even in an academic setting, in which circular logic can be debated, the cognitive and social tolls of operating within crisis leave a lasting impact. Life in an ecology of stress is not sustainable.

According to Barrett (2019), the brain continuously constructs predictions based on past experiences to minimize uncertainty and conserve energy, which becomes difficult in a crisis mode. In this heightened state, the brain detects threat, often triggering an overproduction of cortisol that keeps the body in a prolonged fight-or-flight response. This state not only exhausts our physical resources but also disrupts the brain's ability to process new information, thereby impeding learning, creativity, and sustained focus. Damasio's (2021) work further illustrates how sustained stress affects our somatic markers, the body-based signals that influence decision-making. Prolonged activation of these signals in crisis mode can desensitize our cognitive responses to stress, making us hypervigilant, overly reactive, and less able to engage in reflective thinking. When we remain in this state, the body's natural rhythms are disrupted, leading to difficulties in engaging with others, working productively, and maintaining overall well-being. Reflecting on Friedman's ominous strategy: it does not matter if the crisis is actual or perceived. It hits us the same.

Beyond the individual effects, higher education as an ecology of stress also emphasizes the hegemonic ideal that the most able-bodied and minded folks, regardless of privilege or starting point, should succeed in society. This ideal cares only for the strongest, reinforcing the "might is right" mentality of Western morality. Hegemony is not just social thought but also the material infrastructures that emerge as a product of dominant social thought (Gramsci, 2000). Consider, for example, how gateway courses—foundational or introductory classes in fields like STEM (Science, Technology, Engineering, and Mathematics), business, and the social sciences—function. They tend to be large classes with more students than a teacher can effectively support whose purpose is to weed out potentially poor-performing students. The logic behind this weeding-out process is rooted in a neoliberal framework, where the emphasis on individual performance, efficiency, and meritocracy often overshadows educational values like inclusivity, relational learning, and student-centered pedagogy. By design, a few students will succeed, usually those with prior experience or knowledge in the class, and the majority will fail.

Stress as Structure: An Example

Gateway courses are used to assess which students have the capability, persistence, and discipline to succeed in the field. In many cases, they are structured to challenge students to the point of failure, functioning as a filter to remove those who are deemed not fit for the major or program. They frequently adopt a "survival of the fittest" mentality, where students are pitted against one another, and only the "strongest" or most prepared make it through to the next level. Years ago, I taught a gateway course for an English department at a liberal arts university. I remember being told by the chair to create a syllabus that seemed so daunting with long readings and multi-page writing assignments that students would drop the course. Somewhat ironically, recently that same English department has launched efforts at attracting students to account for declining English majors.

Rather than helping students discover their strengths and supporting them in overcoming their weaknesses, the spirit of many gateway courses is to separate students into those who are "fit" from those who are not. For instance, grading serves to stratify students, sometimes using rigid curves or harsh grading scales to ensure that only a portion of the class advances. Attrition is often seen as a natural outcome rather than a problem to be addressed. As a result, students who may not have had the same academic preparation or resources (such as first-generation or underrepresented students) are disproportionately impacted. The idea that students who perform well in gateway courses "deserve" to advance, while those who struggle do not, reflects neoliberal meritocratic ideologies. In particular, the essentialist assumption paints a picture of students who have inherent ability worthy of advancement and students who have no essential qualities worthy of academic nourishment and therefore fail because of their own shortcomings, rather than being failed by a system that was not designed to support diverse learners.

The weeding-out process in gateway courses not only operates on a neoliberal framework but also fails to fulfill the broader goals of higher education, which should be to help students find their place in the world and contribute to the common good. Instead of serving as opportunities for exploration, growth, and identity formation, gateway courses often turn into obstacle courses. In direct contrast to this spirit, interdependence understands "fitness" as an adaptable practice of educators and institutions working to create environments that allow a diversity of students to "fit."

In the competitive, individualistic environment of gateway courses, students may feel isolated rather than supported. Rather than fostering interdependence and collaboration, these courses often encourage students to focus on their own success at the expense of others, undermining the development of strong relational ties that could help students build resilience and navigate the challenges of college life. As we know from studies on relational self-construal (Cross et al., 2003), individuals with strong connections to others are better able to maintain their well-being in the face of new and challenging situations. The rising challenges in student mental health and well-being, largely due to a system that refuses relational self-construal through structural dynamics, have, at least, raised questions about neoliberalism.

Cracks in the System

It should be no surprise that neoliberalism has failed to deliver its promise that caring with the market would enable us to live meaningful lives. Younger generations, for instance, continue a recent trend of increasing depression and isolation (Twenge, 2020). While the concern with financial success might not directly cause the decrease in mental health, many believe the obsession with individualist conceptions of success (e.g., personal wealth) might explain the correlation (Hari, 2018; Cavanagh, 2019). As a response, the modern capitalist manipulation of self-care, in which one can supposedly achieve care for a significant price, has dominated marketplace discourse. Care became a commodity for those who could afford it (Barber, 2021). Individual materialism replaced community responsibility, and efficiency of production replaced quality of goods (Martin, 2019). These notions of "care" further stress and harm the self because they depend on repeat customers who associate healing with purchasing. Sharma (2024) illustrates this manufactured cycle of consumption/self-care:

> Companies market skin care products, for example, to prevent the formation of fine lines, supposedly a consequence of a stressful life. Consumers buy the lotions to solve this problem, lather themselves in solitude, and feel at peace for a little while. Once the anxiety, the exhaustion, and the insufficiency creeps in again, as it inevitably does, the routine begins anew. Buy a new eyeshadow, a bullet journal, Botox, a vacation to fill the need for care that never seems to abate. Because buying things does not solve existential dread, we are then flooded with guilt for being unable to adequately tend to our minds and bodies. We just have to self-care harder, and so the consumerism masquerading as a practice that can fix something broken becomes another rote to-do list item.

Despite the infinite attention we can draw to ourselves via social media, loneliness and depression are at all-time highs. Despite the infinite ways we can feed ourselves, most of the available food lacks important nutritional values, resulting in all-time highs of heart disease, obesity, and the existence of food deserts. Despite the economic wealth in America, the majority of its citizens face all-time highs in feeling overworked, exhausted, and burned out. Despite the hyper-individualized approach to learning, with increased specialization/credentialism of knowledge, Americans face all-time highs in disinformation and confusion. Despite the massive availability of consumer choices in capitalist powerhouses like America, the quality of goods and services has declined (Mas, 2023). Meanwhile, the social institutions that had been in prime position to help restore collective care for one another continue to take a reactionary approach, often resulting in the further entrenchment of corporate values in public life (Giroux, 2014; Davidson, 2017). Not only do we need healthy social institutions to respond to the growth of neoliberalism as a prevailing ideology, but we also need colleges and universities that care about values other than those offered by neoliberalism.

If we want to care for a future that includes higher education, it is probably better not to do so under the anxiety and pressure we currently face. We must take up Giroux's (2014) challenge facing educators today: reclaiming "the language of the social, agency, solidarity, democracy, and public life as the basis for rethinking how to name, theorize, and strategize a new kind of education" (p. 47). Now might be our chance to model, promote, and cultivate a system of caring-with one another, as an ecology.

Innovation *is* necessary for higher education to survive. We cannot stand still, but we do not have to move so fast we break things (including ourselves). Considering the snowballing crises that educators have endured, including labor inequities, the pandemic, and AI, asking teachers to once again lead the transformation is like asking the global south to solve climate change. The increased pressure to live faster (and faster, and faster) lifestyles continues to challenge our collective and individual health both in and beyond academia (Berg & Seeber, 2016; Hari, 2018). As an ecology, higher education is indeed under a lot of stress.

In many ways, higher education's ecological stress has clouded any possible vision of what higher education can do to meet the particular needs of the 21st century. In his recent *Inside Higher Education* article, professor Patrick J. Casey (2024) examines the conflicting messages of higher education around workplace preparation. On the one hand, universities have historically claimed that their mission is to prepare students for democratic citizenship through critical and creative praxis, outcomes that include but certainly are not limited to workplace readiness. As part of this mission, universities have provided students with additional support in order to emphasize intellectual development over compliance with workplace norms, such as reducing or eliminating deadlines in order to emphasize creative freedom and revision of ideas. On the other hand, universities have attempted to assert their relevance by insisting that they do make students "job ready," but Casey cites a study of employers who are reluctant to hire new graduates because

> 63 percent [of employers claim] that recent graduates frequently can't handle their workload, 61 percent saying they are frequently late to work, 59 percent saying they often miss deadlines and assignments, 58 percent saying that they get offended too easily, 57 percent saying they lack professionalism, 53 percent saying they struggle with eye contact during interviews and 52 percent saying they have poor communication skills.

The ultimate question Casey raises is not whether universities should lean into job readiness; rather, Casey encourages those of us working in higher education to reflect honestly and courageously about the role higher education should play in society. To once again ask Lynn Pasquarella's (2022) question: What does higher education care about and why should the public care about higher education?

Imagining an Era of Caring With Higher Education

As Joan Tronto (1993) shows in her work, teaching care entails teaching justice. The division of labor and resources necessary to build a caring world should not be shouldered by everyone, especially since many communities have been excluded from the material benefits of capitalist systems. Care is inherently political in that it can reinforce injustice—teachers get blamed for schools closing during a strike, and women are expected to be "caregivers" in an economy that does not value caregiving labor. Care can also, however, disrupt unjust systems by caring for those who have been positioned as not "grievable" (Butler, 2020). Drawing from necropolitics, the idea that those in power make decisions about whose lives are expendable, Butler shows how some lives in particular societies deserve mourning whereas others do not. In the context of terrorism, applying the label "terrorist" to an individual automatically precludes that individual from being mourned, grieved, or cared about. In a much less extreme example, particular students—such as those whose behaviors do not conform to classroom norms—might be positioned as "deserving to fail." Falling squarely into the discussion of interdependence, Butler encourages us to think systemically about care as a political force. Instead of just caring for others on an individual basis, Butler makes a compelling case for care as structural transformation.

Structural transformation entails a critical focus on systems of relationships as opposed to individuals. Only with such a focus can we identify opportunities for transformation. Despite our long-time focus on individuals, such a strategy has proven ineffective. Individual impact plans, individualized education programs, "bad apple" mentality, and victim shaming/blaming all miss the powerful relationships that reproduce the problems individual intervention hoped to solve. Pathologizing and treating individuals represent restorative approaches that, while certainly helping some, allow the system of injustice to persist. adrienne maree brown (2021) and Alicia Garza (2021) define the difference between restoration and transformation: the former retains the current system, albeit with repairs, whereas transformation imagines and cultivates a new system. When it comes to environmental care, transformation depends on redistributing the accumulated capital of the global north, such as through de-industrialization and restoring communities harmed by the previous century. When it comes to social care, transformation depends on those with privilege to both step aside to make room for different forms of leadership and mobilize their privilege in support of new leaders. Based on the power each of us holds in relation to others in society, the actions we take will be different. The labor of care needs to be equitable, not equal. Pedagogically, due to existing inequities faced by students who might be first-generation, international, or of a marginalized identity, this might mean that some students need more care (e.g., attention, support, resources, feedback) than others. And it also might mean that some teachers should carry the labor of care in support of historically marginalized caregivers (e.g., not reserving discussions of diversity only for diverse educators).

Interdependence calls attention to equitable, not equal, relationality. We all exist with varying degrees of power, even as we remain connected to one another. Rampant consumption of everything from oil to t-shirts in the global north has contributed to environmental crises in the global south (Barber, 2021). However, one would not think to blame residents of Flint, Michigan, or Jackson, Mississippi, for purchasing plastic water bottles if they do not have access to clean public water. Individuals are positioned within society due to various systems: economic, social, cultural, etc. Individualist approaches, then, are doomed to fail, or at least be perceived as intractable in the face of systemic problems like climate change (Xiang et al., 2019). Collectively, change becomes likely. The most important thing educators can do today is teach students how to care with others, even if it means caring with and for difficult subjects, such as Bruno Latour's challenge to environmentalists to also care for SUVs.

The coupling of neoliberalism and higher education places colleges and universities in a losing race. Corporate degrees already seek to replace the college-to-job narrative (Intelligent, 2023). Google, Microsoft, Amazon, and many other monoliths no longer require college for high-paying positions. Instead, these corporations provide internal education and training, fast-tracking students to jobs and income. Meanwhile, informal learning environments continue to transform in ways that render higher education unnecessary. The internet, for better and definitely for worse, replaces libraries. YouTube replaces textbooks. And Zoom replaces classrooms. All of these replacements, however, are continued forms of disconnection. We Zoom alone from our rooms rather than work with others in a shared classroom. We watch YouTube and leave anonymous comments rather than talk through ideas in seminars or book clubs. Corporate training prepares students for a particular corporate setting, making transfer to new contexts more difficult. In summary, our culture of neoliberal care has contributed to ecological and social harms largely by alienating us from one another to the point of polarization. Current higher education practices contribute to disconnection by trying to remain relevant in public discourse. And yet, I remain radically hopeful.

Students want to learn, but they need to experience care (Guzzardo et al., 2021). Care can be cultivated through in-class teaching practices that benefit everyone involved (Miller & Mills, 2019). Interdependence defines caring, teaching, and learning as entangled processes that nurture one another. Remove one element, and the ecology changes.

Imagine a higher education ecology with the following roots:

1. Courses that create spaces where students can support one another, building resilience through collective effort. Group projects, peer mentoring, and collaborative problem-solving that help students form strong relational ties that allow them to thrive academically and emotionally.
2. Formative assessments that allow students to learn from failure and improve over time. Feedback promotes a culture where students are encouraged to engage deeply with the material, reflect on their learning, and take intellectual risks.

3. Flexible, student-driven pathways to mastery that democratize opportunities and position teachers as guides along multiple interdependent journeys.
4. Course content that prioritizes intellectual curiosity and exploration by connecting new knowledge to students' interests and passions. Teachers encourage mind-wandering, reflective practices, and the cognitive complexity of unanswerable questions.

Higher education has always been a gateway for young people to become leaders of a new world. This is its chance to do so once more. And considering the environmental, economic, and technological challenges we face, we need higher education to cultivate new solutions and paradigms and to help us imagine a way of life that does not rely on careless destruction of the natural and social worlds that give us life. If we can save higher education, maybe—just maybe—it can help save us.

So where do we begin such a monumental task of transforming higher education by creating interdependent classrooms? In my experience and research, starting with our love for what we teach can be a powerful reminder of our agency and capabilities.

References

Barber, A. (2021). *Consumed: The need for collective change: Colonialism, climate change, and consumerism.* Balance.
Barrett, L. F. (2019). *How emotions are made.* Macmillan.
Berg, M., & Seeber, B. K. (2016). *The slow professor: Challenging the culture of speed in the academy.* University of Toronto Press.
Berrett, D. (2015). The day the purpose of college changed. *The Chronicle of Higher Education.* https://www.chronicle.com/article/the-day-the-purpose-of-college-changed/?sra=true
Blom, P. (2019). *Nature's mutiny: How the Little Ice Age of the long seventeenth century transformed the West and shaped the present.* Liveright Publishing.
Brenan, M. (2023). Americans' confidence in higher education down sharply. *Gallup.* https://news.gallup.com/poll/508352/americans-confidence-higher-education-down-sharply.aspx.
Brower, J. E., & Guilfoy, K. (Eds.). (2004). *The Cambridge companion to Abelard.* Cambridge University Press.
Brown, A. M. (2021). *Holding change: The way of emergent strategy facilitation and mediation.* AK Press.
Brown, W. (2015). *Undoing the demos: Neoliberalism's stealth revolution.* MIT Press.
Brownlee, W. E., & Graham, H. D. (Eds.). (2003). *The Reagan presidency: Pragmatic conservatism and its legacies.* University Press of Kansas.
Butler, J. (2020). *The force of nonviolence: An ethico-political bind.* Verso.
Caetano, C., Caetano, G., & Nielsen, E. (2024). Are children spending too much time on enrichment activities? *Economics of Education Review, 98,* 102503, 1–19.
Cantwell, B., & Kauppinen, I. (Eds.). (2014). *Academic capitalism in the age of globalization.* JHU Press.
Casey, P. J. (2024). Why aren't college grads "job-ready"? *Inside Higher Education.* https://www.insidehighered.com/opinion/views/2024/07/29/why-arent-colleges-getting-students-job-ready-opinion.

Cavanagh, S. R. (2019). *Hivemind: The new science of tribalism in our divided world*. Grand Central Publishing.
Cross, S. E., Gore, J. S., & Morris, M. L. (2003). The relational-interdependent self-construal, self-concept consistency, and well-being. *Journal of Personality and Social Psychology, 85*(5), 933–944. https://doi.org/10.1037/0022-3514.85.5.933.
Cunningham, W. G. (1983). Teacher burnout—solutions for the 1980s: A review of the literature. *The Urban Review, 15*(1), 37–51.
Damasio, A. (2021). *Feeling & knowing: Making minds conscious*. Little.
Davidson, C. N. (2017). *The new education: How to revolutionize the university to prepare students for a world in flux*. Basic Books.
Droege, R. C. (2003). Correcting the SAT's ethnic and social class bias. *Harvard Educational Review, 73*(1), 1–43. https://doi.org/10.17763/haer.73.1.8465k88616hn4757.
Eyler, J. R. (2018). *How humans learn: The science and stories behind effective college teaching*. West Virginia University Press.
Gaither, G. H. (Ed.). (1995). *Assessing performance in an age of accountability: Case studies*. Jossey-Bass.
Garza, A. (2021). *The purpose of power: How we come together when we fall apart*. Random House.
Germani, A., Buratta, L., Delvecchio, E., & Mazzeschi, C. (2020). Emerging adults and COVID-19: The role of individualism-collectivism on perceived risks and psychological maladjustment. *International Journal of Environmental Research and Public Health, 17*(10), 3497.
Giroux, H. A. (2014). *Neoliberalism's war on higher education*. Haymarket Books.
Giroux, H. A. (2015). *University in chains: Confronting the military-industrial-academic complex*. Routledge.
Gramsci, A. (2000). *The Gramsci reader: Selected writings, 1916–1935*. NYU Press.
Gretzinger, E., & Hicks, M. (2024). The chaos of compliance: How public colleges in two states are actually responding to DEI bans. *The Chronicle of Higher Education*. https://www.chronicle.com/article/the-chaos-of-compliance.
Guzzardo, M. T., Khosla, N., Adams, A. L., Bussmann, J. D., Engelman, A., Ingraham, N., & Taylor, S. (2021). "The ones that care make all the difference": Perspectives on student-faculty relationships. *Innovative Higher Education, 46*, 41–58.
Hari, J. (2018). *Lost connections: Uncovering the real causes of depression—and the unexpected solutions*. Bloomsbury Publishing.
Hartung, W. (2024, October 1). The military showers universities with hundreds of millions of dollars. *Responsible Statecraft*. https://responsiblestatecraft.org/2024/10/01/pentagon-divestment/.
Intelligent. (2023). Nearly half of all companies plan to eliminate Bachelor's degree requirements in 2024. *Intelligent*. https://www.intelligent.com/nearly-half-of-companies-plan-to-eliminate-bachelors-degree-requirements-in-2024/
Jagodics, B., & Szabó, É. (2023). Student burnout in higher education: a demand-resource model approach. *Trends in Psychology, 31*(4), 757–776.
Jaschik, S. (2011). Florida GOP vs. Social Science. *Inside Higher Education*. https://www.insidehighered.com/news/2011/10/12/florida-gop-vs-social-science.
Kim, A. Y., Sinatra, G. M., & Seyranian, V. (2018). Developing a STEM identity among young women: A social identity perspective. *Review of Educational Research, 88*(4), 589–625.
Kirschenbaum, M., & Raley, R. (2024). AI and the University as a Service. *PMLA, 139*(3), 504–515.
Klein, N. (2007). *The shock doctrine: The rise of disaster capitalism*. New York: Picador.
Kreighbaum, A. (2019, August 19). Persistent partisan breakdown on higher ed. *Inside Higher Ed*. Retrieved from https://www.insidehighered.com/news/2019/08/20/majority-republicans-have-negative-view-higher-ed-pew-finds

Lemon, J. (2021, April 27). Fox host Tucker Carlson says college education "diminishes" you, everyone should opt out. *Newsweek*. https://www.newsweek.com/fox-host-tucker-carlson-says-college-education-diminishes-you-everyone-should-opt-out-1586212.

Levinthal, D. (2015). How the Koch Brothers Are Influencing U.S. Colleges. *Time*. https://time.com/4148838/koch-brothers-colleges-universities/

Martin, R. (2019). The high price of efficiency. Harvard Business Review. https://hbr.org/2019/01/the-high-price-of-efficiency

Marzia, A. (2024). After Texas's DEI Ban, College Students Are Reconsidering State Schools. *The Nation*. https://www.thenation.com/article/society/university-texas-sb17-dei-ban-abbot-college-students/

Miller, A. C., & Mills, B. (2019). 'If They Don't Care, I Don't Care': Millennial and Generation Z Students and the Impact of Faculty Caring. *Journal of the Scholarship of Teaching and Learning*, 19(4), 78–89.

Mas, K. (2023). Why everything you buy is worse now. *Vox*. https://www.vox.com/videos/2023/2/9/23592998/consumerism-quality-decline-technology-fashion.

Øversveen, E. (2022). Capitalism and alienation: Towards a Marxist theory of alienation for the 21st century. *European Journal of Social Theory*, 25(3), 440–457.

Palast, G. (2014, April 24). Koch Foundation proposal to college: Teach our curriculum, get millions. *Public Integrity*. https://publicintegrity.org/politics/koch-foundation-proposal-to-college-teach-our-curriculum-get-millions/.

Parker, K. (2019). The Growing Partisan Divide in Views of Higher Education. *Pew Research Center*. https://www.pewresearch.org/social-trends/2019/08/19/the-growing-partisan-divide-in-views-of-higher-education-2/

Pasquarella, L. (2022). *What we value: Public health, social justice, and educating for democracy*. University of Virginia Press.

Pope-Ruark, R. (2022). *Unraveling faculty burnout: Pathways to reckoning and renewal*. JHU Press.

Roldán, S. M., Maurauri, J., Aubert, A., & Flecha, R. (2021). How inclusive interactive learning environments benefit students without special needs. *Frontiers in Psychology*, 12, 661427.

Ramírez, Andrés, & Hyslop-Margison, Emery. (2015). Neoliberalism, Universities and the Discourse of Crisis. *Journal for Critical Education Policy Studies*, 13(2), 272–299.

Sharma, S. (2024). How the self-care industry made us so lonely. *Vox*. https://www.vox.com/even-better/350424/self-care-isolation-loneliness-epidemic

Slaughter, S. & Leslie, L. (1997). *Academic capitalism: Politics, policies, and the entrepreneurial university*. JHU Press.

Slaughter, S., & Rhoades, G. (2004). *Academic capitalism and the new economy: Markets, state, and higher education*. JHU press.

Sawyer III, D. C., Torres, J.T., & Hudd, S. (eds.) (2024). *How to Incorporate Equity and Justice in Your Teaching*. Edward Elgar Publishing.

Szadkowski, K. (2019). An Autonomist Marxist Perspective on Productive and Un-Productive Academic Labour. TripleC: Communication, Capitalism & Critique. *Open Access Journal for a Global Sustainable Information Society*, 17(1), 111–131.

Tronto, J. (1993). *Moral boundaries: A political argument for an ethic of care*. Routledge.

Twenge, J. M. (2020). Increases in depression, self-harm, and suicide among US adolescents after 2012 and links to technology use: possible mechanisms. *Psychiatric Research and Clinical Practice*, 2(1), 19–25.

Twenge, J. M., Campbell, W. K., & Freeman, E. C. (2012). Generational differences in young adults' life goals, concern for others, and civic orientation, 1966–2009. *Journal of personality and social psychology*, 102(5), 1045.

Ubell, R. (2022, August 24). The political right is slamming the door on college access. *EdSurge*. Retrieved from https://www.edsurge.com/news/2022-08-24-the-political-right-is-slamming-the-door-on-college-access

Vassallo, S. (2020). *Neoliberal selfhood*. Cambridge University Press.
Wilder, D. A., & Shapiro, P. N. (1989). Role of competition-induced anxiety in limiting the beneficial impact of positive behavior by an out-group member. *Journal of Personality and Social Psychology, 56*(1), 60.
Xiang, P., Zhang, H., Geng, L., Zhou, K., & Wu, Y. (2019). Individualist–collectivist differences in climate change inaction: The role of perceived intractability. *Frontiers in Psychology, 10*, 187.
Yosso, T. J. (2005). Whose culture has capital? A critical race theory discussion of community cultural wealth. *Race Ethnicity and Education, 8*(1), 69–91.
Zeeble, B. (2024). Texas universities cut jobs after Texas bans DEI programs. *National Public Radio*. https://www.npr.org/2024/04/24/1246780909/texas-universities-cut-jobs-after-texas-bans-dei-programs

3

CARE BETWEEN TEACHERS AND CONTENT

Chapter Contents
Curiosity: Or, Caring With Content   55
Care as Pedagogy   56
The Science of Curiosity   59
Curiosity Entails Interdependence   62
Care Kit: Validate Backstories   65
References   68

A charming anecdote many educators like to share is this: *When someone asks me what I teach, I say, I teach students.*

The anecdote subverts the idea that teaching is all about the subject matter—the content—by emphasizing the relational power of teaching. Despite the importance of the quote's implied meaning, we do not have to hide the fact that many of us truly love *what* we teach, not just *who* we teach. I, for one, am passionate about learning theory, writing studies, and literacy. I feel most alive as a teacher when I can share that passion with my students. Conversely, nothing breaks my heart more than hearing a student lament having to write or, much worse, hearing a student claim they cannot write. It has always been difficult for me to imagine the possibility that not everyone values the field of study I deeply value. Content not only defines us (e.g., "I'm an English professor"), but it also forms the foundation of many possible relationships (e.g., academic departments and programs and majors that inform student course selection). Content, however, has recently developed a bad rep in educational research.

Accreditation agencies, curriculum designers, and program administrators continue to pack courses with more content. Teachers at all levels feel the

DOI: 10.4324/9781003591009-4

increased pressure to include more topics, books, texts, issues, and information in their lessons. The most frequent response I receive from educators when discussing the incorporation of care and community in their classrooms is, "Well I just don't have time with everything we have to cover."

They are not wrong.

For more than a decade, studies have suggested the counterintuitive finding that teachers covering content likely prevents students from learning content. In Petersen et al.'s (2020) review of several studies, the evidence supporting active learning environments, in which students engage with content in dynamic ways combined with continuous reflection, has become more convincing. Despite the growing evidence, the pressure to cover an ever-growing body of content results in more teachers choosing to lecture. As a method, lecture is not inherently a flawed pedagogical strategy. If lectures were so ineffective, *TED* videos would not receive 1.65 billion views across the globe each year (Ceiplak-Mayr von Baldegg, 2012). And shows like *Last Week Tonight with John Oliver* would not maintain decades-long runs of prestige and viewership. Dynamic lectures do work. The problem arises when it is the *only* strategy used in a learning environment, as lectures can position learners as passive individuals (Deslauriers et al., 2019). In general, it is always more difficult for community to form when there is only one person with a voice.

The challenge to creating community, or an interdependent classroom, goes beyond the content coverage pressures teachers face. Students have normalized passive, individualized classrooms to the point they often do not even recognize learning. Deslauriers et al. (2019) designed a study to assess how well students' perceptions of learning aligned with their actual learning. They recruited undergraduate students taking introductory physics courses at Harvard University. In the experimental group, teachers minimally lectured with chalkboards and relied more heavily on demonstrations, interactive quizzes, and conceptual questions. Students worked in groups, formed teams, and engaged conceptual questions with the care and support of others. In the control group, teachers relied only on chalkboard lectures. Other than those differences, the instructional materials (e.g., slides, handouts, rubrics, tests) remained identical, both teachers had comparable experience and training, and students were randomly assigned to either group. After each class, students completed a survey measuring their "feelings of learning" as well as a "test of learning."

Surprisingly, Deslauriers et al. (2019) found a highly significant negative correlation between students' feelings of learning and the results of their tests of learning. In other words, students in the active learning experimental group performed much better on tests of learning than the students in the passive learning control group. When it came to the feelings of the learning survey, however, students in the passive learning control group felt they learned much more than the students in the active learning experimental group. Deslauriers et al. (2019) propose three possible explanations: (1) students have been conditioned to think exposure to content is the same thing as learning, (2) novice students inherently have poor metacognition in general, and (3) the cognitive struggle required in active learning can signal a lack of learning (p. 19254). This is why educational researcher Stephen DiCarlo (2009) claimed that "how we teach is more important than what we teach" (p. 185). When so many of us have normalized passivity as learning, emphasizing care, engagement, and community can certainly feel like the wrong method.

One of the first teaching observations I received, when I was a graduate student in a Master of Fine Arts program at Georgia College & State University, highlights just how wrong such methods can appear. As part of my teaching assistantship, graduate students were paired up to perform observations for one another. During my observed class, students worked in groups as they performed social annotations. They discussed their questions, thoughts, and comments as they annotated the same essay. I used the time to visit with each group to guide their thinking and direct them toward the eventual individual analysis they would later complete. From the observer's view, students spoke to one another in their groups while I walked around and engaged in small talk.

About 30 minutes into my one-hour class, my observer asked me, "So when do you start teaching?"

When content is not the explicit focal point of a classroom, it can be hard to tell when teaching or learning happens.

I do not intend to reassert content as the most important aspect of teaching by beginning the book's Care Kit with our relationship with content. Rather, I hope to assert that *content* informs the *context* for the possible relationships that can emerge in a learning environment. In other words, while content remains a very important question of *what* we teach, our relationship with content can illuminate the *how* and *why* of our teaching. Importantly, how and why we teachers came to care with content has more to do with curiosity than mastery. Of course, curiosity and mastery are not competing goals. Cultivated curiosity often entails mastery, as any professional hobbyist will attest. Thus, this chapter will develop curiosity as a method for caring with content.

Based on current research, I will provide strategies for designing a college course that begins with and emphasizes curiosity, care, and emotional connection with the content. One example: I model the use of "backstories," drawing from our personal stories of falling in love with our content in order to prompt students to reflect on and narrate any prior knowledge or lived experience that might help them relate to the content. The chapter will contribute to our Care Kit by providing strategies for reflecting on our own intellectual backstories and creating opportunities for students to do the same. We can then share those reflections as models for other aspects of our Care Kit described in later chapters. By calling attention to our own stories of cultivated curiosity, we can remember how we fell in love with our content in the first place and how we nurtured that love into a profession.

Curiosity: Or, Caring With Content

Most of us become teachers because we are really good at school, meaning we have mastered our content and have become expert enough to teach it to others. Ironically, the impressive level of expertise we have achieved might actually work against our ability to communicate it to others, a phenomenon known as the "curse of knowledge." Chip and Dan Heath (2007), the authors of the book *Made to Stick*, define "the curse of knowledge" as the cognitive bias where someone, once they know something, finds it difficult to imagine not knowing it. This makes it hard for experts to communicate effectively with others who lack that same knowledge because they assume the information is obvious or easily understood. As an aside: the curse of knowledge is one of the barriers climate scientists have long faced in trying to communicate the very real dangers of an otherwise seemingly invisible threat.

In their research, Chip and Dan Heath found that experts with in-depth knowledge of a subject may struggle to explain it in simple terms. When explaining complex ideas, experts use jargon, technical terms, or take for granted their own expertise. In probably the most well-known example, the Heath brothers cite Elizabeth Newton's 1990 Stanford University PhD dissertation, known as the "tappers and listeners" experiment.

Participants were divided into two groups: "tappers" and "listeners." Tappers were asked to pick a well-known song (like "Happy Birthday") and tap out the rhythm by knocking on a table. Listeners had to guess the song based solely on the tapping. Before tapping, tappers were asked to predict how likely it was that the listeners would correctly identify the song. Tappers generally predicted that the listeners would recognize the song about 50% of the time. In reality, listeners were able to guess the correct song only about 2.5% of the time—far lower than the tappers predicted. Most listeners had no idea what song was being tapped. Once the tappers knew the song, they found it extremely difficult to imagine how the rhythm would sound to someone who didn't know it. In their minds, the melody was clear, and they couldn't understand why the listeners weren't picking up on it. From the listener's perspective, however, all they heard were disjointed taps without the necessary context of the song.

Try replicating the study with students. They enjoy the challenge, and I always enjoy watching their minds blown when no one can guess their tapped songs. Also, the study once more validates Freire's critique of the banking concept of education. What good is the narrating subject, regardless of the expertise, when the passive listening objects only hear disjointed jargon and terms?

The Heath brothers suggest that effective communicators need to "unlearn" their expertise and view the situation from the perspective of a novice. They recommend the use of analogies, storytelling, breaking down information into simple steps, and asking for feedback to gauge understanding. In short, they suggest promoting students' curiosity and equipping them with the skills to pursue their curiosity, in effect developing expertise similarly to how we did. In developing our own intellectual backstories, I frequently encourage teachers to ask themselves, Why do I care about this content so much? What are the most interesting questions in my field? Who inspired me to pursue this content, and *how* did they inspire me?

In support of the opening anecdote as well as DiCarlo's assertion that "how we teach is more important than what we teach," studies find that students are more likely to learn from instructors who are enthusiastic about teaching and learning than instructors who are only enthusiastic about the content. In one ethnographic study, Sybing (2019) found that learning can be dramatically enhanced simply by validating students' pursuits of their curiosity, especially when they experience challenges. In another study, Miller and Mills (2019) found that one of the most effective ways teachers can motivate students is by demonstrating care for students.

Care as Pedagogy

I used to believe that all I had to do was share my excitement about my content and my students would also be excited. Early in my professional teaching career, when I taught academic writing at the University of Alaska Anchorage, I had become obsessed with Jacques Derrida and his notion of deconstruction. So obsessed that I could not wait to teach my first-year students, many of whom were nontraditional in age, background, and cultural identity, deconstruction as an approach to reading and writing academic texts. I remember almost jogging to class the day I had assigned his essay "Plato's Pharmacy." How can anyone not love the complex ambiguity of language and the instability of meaning, I ambitiously wondered?

Specifically, I could not wait for students to share my excitement over Derrida's concept of the pharmakon, a paradox in which something is both the "remedy" and the "poison." Derrida uses this ambiguity to challenge the idea of binary oppositions (such as good/evil and truth/falsehood), which dominate Western philosophical thought. In Plato's Pharmacy, Derrida argues that the term pharmakon destabilizes the traditional opposition between remedy and poison, revealing that what is often seen as beneficial can also be harmful, depending on context and interpretation. For example, in Phaedrus, writing is described as both a cure for forgetfulness and a poison that weakens memory by making people rely on external signs instead of internal recollection. Derrida uses pharmakon to demonstrate the instability of meaning and to critique the idea that any concept or sign can be completely pure or fixed. Instead, meaning is always deferred and depends on its relational context—a key aspect of Derrida's theory of deconstruction. In Plato's Pharmacy, Derrida uses a metaphor of family relationships to describe the status of writing as compared to speech. In *Phaedrus*, Plato, through the character of Socrates, makes the comparison between speech and writing, likening speech to a "legitimate son" and writing to a "bastard" or illegitimate offspring. Plato argues that writing is an inadequate form of communication because it cannot defend itself or clarify meaning in the absence of its author, much like an orphaned child who lacks parental guidance. In this metaphor, speech is considered the "legitimate son" of knowledge or truth, while writing is the "bastard" or "illegitimate son." In Plato's view, speech is seen as the direct and authentic heir to knowledge or truth. When we speak, we are thought to be directly expressing our thoughts, ideas, and intentions. In the metaphor of family relationships, speech is like the "legitimate son" of the father (truth personified), meaning it is the rightful, natural, and direct descendant. In this sense, speech is given a privileged position because it is seen as connected to the speaker's mind and presence. Writing, on the other hand, is seen as disconnected from the original source of truth. Plato compares it to an illegitimate child or "bastard" because it lacks a direct, living connection to its origin. When words are written down, they lose the ability to respond, clarify, or defend themselves. They are "orphaned" or left to exist on their own, detached from the speaker. In Plato's hierarchy, this makes writing inferior—like a child born outside of marriage, without the same rights or status as the legitimate son. The metaphor continues by describing writing as an orphan because, once written, the words are no longer supported or accompanied by the author's presence. They are left to stand alone without the ability to adapt or engage in dialogue, as speech can. Plato sees writing as something that might spread knowledge but in an unreliable way, since the written text can't defend or explain itself further, unlike speech. Derrida, however, challenges this hierarchical family metaphor that privileges speech over writing. He argues that this distinction between speech as "legitimate" and writing as "bastard" is not natural or fixed. Both speech and writing involve deferring meaning, misunderstanding, and interpretation. Just as writing can be misinterpreted or incomplete, so can speech, which also relies on signs and symbols to convey meaning. By using the family metaphor, Plato is trying to make speech seem more authentic, but Derrida shows that both speech and writing are forms of representation that cannot fully capture truth or presence. Both are subject to the same limitations of meaning and communication. This metaphor illustrates the hierarchy that Plato establishes between speech and writing: speech is seen as closer to the original, living truth, while writing is a mere copy, detached from the source of meaning. Plato, through the voice of Socrates, argues that writing is inferior because it lacks the directness and immediacy of spoken dialogue. Writing cannot respond to questions or clarify its meaning, much like an "orphan" left without its parent to defend or explain it. Speech, in contrast, is associated with presence, vitality, and the ability to convey truth directly through dialogue, making it the preferred mode of communication. Derrida, however, critiques and deconstructs this family metaphor, showing that writing is not simply a secondary or corrupted form of communication. He argues that writing has its own generative power and that speech itself relies on forms of repetition and inscription. Derrida's larger point is that the distinction between legitimate (speech) and illegitimate (writing) is a false opposition—both forms of communication involve deferral and interpretation, and neither can fully capture nor can represent pure truth. This idea fits within Derrida's broader project of deconstructing hierarchical binary oppositions.

Be honest: how many of you read that entire paragraph with sincere excitement? (To this day, I still hope the majority of readers respond with a resounding, "I did!")

In my experience at the University of Alaska, students' eyes glazed over, no matter how enthusiastically I broke down the idea that language becomes its own thing and therefore we should take extra care as writers to consider all the possible meanings of the words we choose. When I shared my disappointment with my faculty mentor at the time, he laughed. "Same thing happened when I started teaching," he said. "You have to care about what *they* want to read. Then they will care about what you want them to read."

Of course I cared about my students, I assured myself. But was I curious enough about their social worlds to want to consume what they consumed? My mentor caused me to reflect hard on that question. I began to realize I could not have it both ways, claiming to care without modeling curiosity, for both care and curiosity are entangled concepts.

The English word *curiosity* originates from the Latin root *cūra*, meaning care or concern. From this, the Latin adjective *cūriōsus* emerged, meaning both "careful" and "inquisitive," suggesting that the more careful one is, the more attentive they are to details. This passed into Old French as *curios* and later into Middle French as *curiosité*, which referred to the desire for knowledge. Middle English borrowed the term, evolving into the modern *curiosity*, which was used to describe intellectual pursuits as well as emotional engagement with a subject of study. We have all heard the proverb, "curiosity killed the cat." The phrase, however, originated as "care will kill a cat." Its first appearance occurs in Ben Jonson's (1780) *Every Man in His Humour*, a comedic play first performed in 1598. Set in London, the play unfolds through a Coen-Brothers-esque series of misunderstandings, deceptions, and reconciliations, satirizing the era's prevailing preoccupation with status, appearances, and the admiration of the social elite. The line appears in Act III, when Cob, a water-carrier, waxes poetic about living a life without commitment to others. He says, "Helterskelter, hang sorrow, care'll kill a cat, up-tails all, and a louse for the hangman." As the phrase evolved to the contemporary proverb we know today, the meaning generally held stable. To care is to be deadly curious.

In that particular semester, my students frequently talked about their favorite National Football League (NFL) teams, mostly the Seattle Seahawks. I came into class one Monday morning and shared my curiosity as to why the NFL is so fraught with war metaphors. The defense blitzes the quarterback, hoping for a sack. Meanwhile, the secondary tries to intercept every pass. The offensive strategy depends on winning in the trenches so that the air raid has time to develop, resulting in a touchdown in the opponents end zone.

The returning veterans became engaged, making connections with other metaphors they had learned during their service. My athletes shared their experiences, making connections with the veterans. I scrapped my lesson plan for the day, which was supposed to introduce methods for rhetorical analysis. Instead, we created a concept map of war metaphors in the NFL and then discussed how the metaphors operate within a rhetorical context. What used to be a lecture became a student-led activity, in which they arrived at the content as if it were their own conclusion.

I invited students to bring new questions in following classes for us to rhetorically analyze. One student asked why dogs are associated with men ("man's best friend") while cats are associated with women ("cat lady"). Another student asked why the show *Friends* presents such a "white" version of New York. And yet another student asked why nursery rhymes tend to tell such creepy stories, like witches and wolves eating children or egg men falling and splattering on the street.

We asked question after question, and I noticed my role as the teacher began to change. Rather than being a source of content, I became a spark of curiosity, providing students a process for directly engaging the content by directing their questions. When students began deconstructing their own social worlds, they became excited. In other words, when I moved from deconstruction-as-content-to-be-memorized to deconstruction-as-playbook-for-exploring-curiosities, I could almost feel students move to the edge of their seats.

The Science of Curiosity

Curiosity is the engine that propels all of us toward learning. Its fuel is care. When we care about something, we want to know as much about it as possible. When the extreme happens and we obsess over our curiosities, we can even become addicted. Dr. Anna Lembke (2021) explains how we have long misunderstood the impact social media and smartphone use have had on our brains. The conventional wisdom had been that the devices and platforms themselves created an irresistible craving that resulted in increased use. For a long time, that discussion had been about the dangers of "screen time," as if the physical screen presented the allure. Rather, because humans have brains that are easily stimulated by information-seeking impulses, social media and smartphones provide immediate access to the information we seek, satisfying our FOMO (fear of missing out) and interests as soon as we feel them. When we try to recall information or when we ask questions that we care about, our brain yearns for the answer. Many of us know the feeling we experience when we have an epiphany or Eureka moment, the wonderful euphoria that spreads throughout our bodies the moment our brains become a turned-on lightbulb. Satisfying curiosity results in the release of dopamine, a neurotransmitter associated with reward and motivation. In the days prior to smartphones and social media, satisfying curiosity took some time, meaning we did not live in a constant state of euphoria. Maybe we had to read some books to have an epiphany, or maybe we had to travel across the world before we could feel enlightened. Today, our devices offer a gateway for immediate satisfaction, providing the perfect "dopamine hit" (Lembke, 2021, p. 8). Over time, our brains become dependent on the instant gratification and pleasure boost that comes with checking emails, text messages, or Instagram (Tams et al., 2018). In recent years, more individuals have reported experiences known as nomophobia, overwhelming feelings of dread, anxiety, or depression when one cannot use a smartphone (Notara et al., 2021). A defining feature of nomophobia is the general fear of losing contact with information shared via social networks, a sense of having one's curiosity dramatically rejected.

If curiosity did in fact kill a cat, it did so with an iPhone.

Healthy relationships with curiosity, on the other hand, offer many positive effects. Gruber et al. (2014) show that curiosity activates the brain's reward system, specifically the dopaminergic pathways, including the ventral striatum and prefrontal cortex, meaning that learning results from satisfying curiosity. They used functional magnetic resonance imaging technology (fMRI's) to measure brain activity in participants who answered trivia questions about which they were curious. Participants also completed delayed memory tests. Not only did the participants display higher levels of attention while answering the trivia questions when their curiosity was activated, but they also performed significantly better than the control group, who answered trivia questions about which they were not curious, on the delayed memory tests. Gruber et al. (2014) also found that the participants did not just remember the information that sparked their curiosity but also unrelated information they encountered in the same context.

The brain relies on curiosity as a motivational force—we want to feel more of that pleasurable sensation associated with figuring something out—to make sense of the world. Our brains encounter innumerable stimuli in our environments, channeled through all of our senses, activating internal thoughts. Curiosity serves as a filter, motivating us to pay attention to select stimuli (Wojtowicz et al., 2022). As we compress information into mental representations of the world, our brains reward us each time we encounter new knowledge that supports our mental representations. Curiosity could be understood as part of what Damasio (2019) calls "homeostatic regulation"—the brain's way of maintaining a stable internal state (p. 66). When we're curious, the brain seeks information to either confirm or adjust its understanding of the world, aligning with its drive for balance and coherence, essentially testing how predictive our mental representations of the world actually are. The ongoing adjustment of mental representations in part defines consciousness, as it drives the exploration and learning that shape our self-awareness and understanding of our environment. To say all of this as simply as possible: Once a hungry human experiences the pleasure of a satisfying fruit, they will care about and for the particular fruit over inedible fruit. Their curiosity might direct them to seek more of the fruit's kind or to just learn more about it in general.

Sakaki et al. (2018) find that curiosity and aging are co-relational. As we age, we tend to become less curious. At the same time, the less curious we become, the faster we age. Sakaki et al. (2018) reviewed decades of studies across various fields, such as neuroscience, psychology, and behavioral studies, to ask how lifelong learning can benefit older adults. From a motivational perspective, older adults prioritize emotional well-being over seeking new information, consistent with socioemotional selectivity theory. Neurologically, age-related declines in dopamine and norepinephrine systems, which are critical for curiosity, contribute to reduced exploratory behavior and interest in novelty. Ironically, the decline in curiosity accelerates aging by limiting engagement in cognitively stimulating activities, which are crucial for maintaining mental and physical health. Reduced curiosity impacts brain health by lowering the neuroprotective benefits of dopamine and norepinephrine, leading to increased inflammation and neural degeneration.

Generally, curiosity wanes from childhood to adulthood, but these shifts might be caused more by social forces than biological factors. Drawing upon Carstensen's (2021) socioemotional selectivity theory, which explains older adults' considerations of end-of-life scenarios on their behavior, Sakaki et al. (2018) posit that the awareness of time left on earth might encourage the prioritization of positive emotional states and stable social connections, which might discourage exploratory behaviors. Acting as something of a self-fulfilling prophecy, the concern of old age might reduce opportunities to be curious despite the fact that such opportunities can stave off old age.

On the other hand, Sakaki et al. (2018) point out that "higher curiosity predicts a better 5-year survival rate in older adults even after controlling for risk factors" like age and education level (p. 111). As people age, they should remain curious, finding that engaging curiosity can accurately predict physical health outcomes, like reduced mortality and improved functional abilities. Higher curiosity levels in older adults were associated with better survival rates over a five-year period. This correlation remained significant even after controlling for other health risk factors like age, education level, and smoking behaviors. Conversely, patients with mild cognitive impairment (MCI) who showed higher levels of apathy (defined as the lack of care or curiosity about the world) were more likely to develop dementia (Sakaki et al., 2018). The health benefits of a curious mind extend beyond humans. Sakaki et al.'s (2018) review also included studies finding that rats who displayed higher exploratory behavior benefited from healthier cognitive function at all ages.

How curiosity cultivates such a healthy brain is still a topic of investigation. At the moment, researchers believe that caring about learning throughout one's life instills a kind of cognitive resilience, helping the brain adapt to stress, anxiety, and the panic of new environments and challenges. In fact, Kashdan and Roberts (2004) found that curious individuals are better able to tolerate uncertainty and approach new experiences with an open mind, which can reduce stress and improve emotional well-being. Since chronic stress negatively affects the brain and cognitive function, this resilience can support long-term brain health. Besides these individual benefits, curiosity also keeps us healthy by keeping us connected.

Curiosity Entails Interdependence

In general, curiosity is a process of connection. Dezza et al. (2022) frame it as an "interdependent system of knowledge composed of relations among informational units, which grows over time by relation-finding actions" (p. 265). It is not that we seek information to fill a blank slate; rather, we seek information to close gaps in our mental representation or connect previously unconnected information in our memory. As an interdependent process, curiosity often stems from the ability to make connections between seemingly disparate ideas. For example, in a course on environmental science, students who are encouraged to consider not just the scientific aspects of climate change but also its social, economic, and ethical implications might become curious to explore how the knowledge in the course impacts broader contexts, sparking questions about how different systems interact. Inherently, curiosity operates as a social phenomenon, becoming activated via the social bonds that drive individuals to seek out and understand new knowledge by opening ourselves to others' thoughts, feelings, experiences, and fields of knowledge.

When people are curious about one another, they ask questions, engage in conversations, and actively listen, which helps people learn about shared interests, values, and backgrounds, and build trust. When someone shows curiosity toward another person, it signals interest and investment that, over time, leads to greater relationship satisfaction and stronger bonds. Kashdan et al. (2013) highlights that curiosity is linked to greater social engagement and stronger interpersonal relationships. The study suggests that curious individuals are more likely to initiate open conversations as opposed to defensive debates. As might be implied by now, curiosity and empathy depend on one another. Cassini Nazir and Meah Lin (2023) demonstrate how curiosity fosters care by asking us to step into the shoes of others and understand them, which "requires an abiding curiosity about what life may be like outside of our own experiences" (p. 588). Physicians, therapists, social workers, surgeons, and other care-related professions who are trained in empathic curiosity have improved relationships with patients that, in some cases, even result in improved patient recovery (McEvoy, 2013; Kurtz et al., 2020; Bugaj et al., 2024).

Not only can curiosity promote care for one another, but it might also be a key ingredient for addressing political polarization and bringing diverse communities together. If we are to solve any of the significant challenges we face, such as climate change, we need to find ways to shift our minds from defensive to curious. It is not just celebratory rhetoric to say that curiosity about the world and different perspectives can lead to collaborative problem-solving and shared discovery. Research continues to demonstrate that when we teach others how to care about particular issues by encouraging their curiosity as well as their care for others, collective action becomes possible (Cohen-Chen & Van Zomeren, 2018). Studies on collaborative problem-solving and group dynamics have shown that curiosity drives cooperative behavior. Hardy III et al. (2017) demonstrate that diversive curiosity, an association of curiosity with an individual's interest in learning something unfamiliar, can strongly predict creative problem-solving. Their results show that achieving academic outcomes at the end of a course can be positively influenced by encouraging collective interest and information-seeking behavior from one another at the beginning. Other studies with similar results support the idea that one of the most effective strategies a teacher can use is inspire collective awe in their students (Piff et al., 2015).

The word *collective* is important in considerations of awe. While awe is often defined as a nonsocial emotional response to stimuli that is so vast it makes us feel small (Piff et al., 2015), like the Grand Canyon-sized room of injustice I conjured in Chapter 1, experiencing awe has notable prosocial effects (Perlin & Li, 2020). This might explain why so many viewers prefer to experience films, sporting events, or plays as part of an audience rather than alone. Because awe has a tendency to shrink our sense of individual self—when I stand before the majesty of a towering mountain, I literally feel tiny—we might become more open to our connections with others—when I cower in fear during a horror movie, I feel assured that I am part of an audience. As we experience awe, we accommodate our mental representations of the world in ways that might both humble us and, possibly due to being humbled, call attention to interdependence (Keltner & Haidt, 2003). As Perlin and Li (2020) argue, "awe may enhance attention not to other-oriented concerns but rather to interdependence concerns, which balance the interests of self and other" (p. 293). In the context of a college classroom, collective awe is an effective way to begin any course, unit, or learning experience.

In their study, Anderson et al. (2020) explored the relationship between awe, curiosity, and academic outcomes. Their methods involved three key studies.

Study 1 tested the relationship between dispositional awe and self-reported curiosity in a sample of 1,005 individuals. Participants completed personality and emotion measures, including the Curiosity and Exploration Inventory (CEI-II) and dispositional awe scales. Researchers controlled for factors like Openness to Experience and other positive emotions to isolate the unique impact of awe on curiosity. Study 2 used peer ratings of curiosity to validate findings from Study 1. In this study, 100 college students nominated peers to rate their curiosity. The relationship between awe and peer-rated curiosity was assessed, again controlling for other personality traits and emotions. Finally, study 3 examined the indirect relationship between awe and academic outcomes (behavioral engagement, work ethic, and academic self-efficacy) through curiosity. The sample included 447 high school students. Structural equation modeling was used to assess whether awe influenced academic outcomes via its effect on curiosity, controlling for emotions like joy and pride. Remarkably, Anderson et al.'s (2020) results provide a clear pathway for teachers: begin a course with awe, encourage students' curiosities, and enjoy the improved academic outcomes. The participants in Anderson et al.'s (2020) studies shifted attention outward and opened them to gaps in their knowledge. This sense of wonder drives curiosity, encouraging individuals to seek new information and experiences. Over time, as people pursue curiosity-driven exploration, they build cognitive and academic skills, leading to improved academic outcomes. Awe's ability to orient individuals toward curiosity and exploration fosters intellectual engagement, enhances work ethic, and boosts academic self-efficacy.

Cultivating curiosity in college requires intentional strategies from both educators and students. By creating supportive environments, encouraging open-ended inquiry, promoting autonomy, integrating interdisciplinary learning, and fostering a growth mindset, curiosity can become a central part of the learning experience. In turn, this curiosity not only enhances academic success but also prepares students to become lifelong learners who approach the world with inquisitiveness and a desire to explore.

Whenever I meet with students, teachers, or community and organizational leaders for the first time, I always begin with curiosity. I try to keep these introductory conversations focused on their personal motivations for engaging in a particular space. While the topic of goals almost always emerges in this stage, what I want to mostly learn is what people care about and why. When working with college teachers in particular, I tend to begin consultations by homing in on their relationship with the content they teach. During these conversations, I frequently hear things like, "Math is wonderful. It is the universal language that makes sense of the universe," or "History is absolutely critical to maintaining our democracy and understanding our options for the future." As the conversations unfold, insights into individual interests crystallize. When I hear something like, "I first moved to the U.S. as a young adult and Math was the only way I could navigate this new world," I know we are on the way to developing powerful experiences for students. Curiosity helps improve cognitive flexibility, the ability to switch between thinking about different concepts or to think about multiple concepts simultaneously. This skill is crucial not just for problem-solving and creativity but also for thriving in an increasingly unstable and uncertain world.

Cultivating curiosity in college classrooms is a critical part of fostering a rich and dynamic learning environment. Researchers suggest several strategies that both teachers and students can employ to stimulate and nurture curiosity, promoting a culture of inquiry and exploration that is essential for deep learning. The recommendations focus on creating supportive environments, using open-ended questions, encouraging interdisciplinary thinking, and allowing for autonomy and self-directed learning. Next, we will apply these recommendations to our first Care Kit entry.

Care Kit: Validate Backstories

Broadly speaking, this chapter's Care Kit focuses on sharing the personal stories of how we pursued our curiosities as a strategy for initiating a learning environment. Beginning with such a strategy sets a foundation consistent with current research. Sharing personal stories indicates a safe and supportive classroom environment where students feel free to express their curiosity. When students fear judgment, embarrassment, or failure, they are less likely to ask questions or engage deeply with course material. For curiosity to flourish, educators must cultivate a culture of intellectual safety. Creating such an environment involves both pedagogical and interpersonal efforts. Educators should encourage risk-taking in thinking and inquiry by reinforcing the idea that failure is a natural and important part of learning. They can model this by sharing their own experiences of curiosity-driven learning, including the missteps and mistakes that often accompany discovery.

As teachers, we each have our particular backstories that guided us into relationships with our content. In my case, despite being raised in a primarily Spanish-speaking household, I was expected to primarily use English. These challenges led to an obsession with language as a cultural gateway. As a student, I felt most engaged when given the opportunity to question and critique language use in particular contexts. I always introduce myself to students by sharing this story, a strategy that is likely to result in empathy and engagement. Students immensely benefit from hearing that their teachers' relationships with content aren't always perfect. Stories of struggle humanize one another, resulting in empathy and compassion.

Remedy

Not every student has my story. Thus, if I assign activities that require questioning and critiquing language, I will likely only engage students who share a similar backstory and consequently exclude everyone else. The first goal then is to create space for all students to make their own connections based on their backstories.

Let's start with our own backstories. Feel free to keep a journal, write in the margins, or meditate on the following questions.

1. When did you first feel like a valued member of your disciplinary, professional, or intellectual community? What did you do to perform in ways consistent with others in the community? What did others do in recognition of your performance that validated the fact that you belonged to the community?
2. List out the burning questions in your life that compelled you to seek answers. What kept you up at night? What dominated conversations with your friends, colleagues, and family? What curiosities motivated you throughout your educational career?
3. Reflect on or write out a brief story of a time when you attempted to answer an important question and arrived at an unexpected answer. What happened? How did you respond to the change in trajectory? What new questions emerged?

Think about how you can share the story or stories that emerge from your reflection. Rather than beginning with policy, procedures, or other formal necessities when you first meet students, can you introduce yourself with a story about a learning journey in which students can see themselves? Can you introduce an assignment at some other point in the course by sharing how you have completed or continue to complete similar assignments?

Root

By setting the foundation and modeling curiosity and care with personal stories, teachers establish that important safe space, encouraging students to bravely share their own stories. Consider how the following structure might be integrated with an assignment or activity. Identify a specific content-related learning goal. An example might be to research, analyze, and evaluate political data and information. Learning goals provide two important elements that might evoke care, a verb and content/context. Some might care about the action (e.g., "I love researching anything"), while others might care about the content/context (e.g., "Political data excite me").

Create two sets of possible questions, one for the action students will take and one for the content that frames the context for the action. These questions should encourage students to tell their related backstories.

1. Research, analyze, and evaluate: How did you decide what college to attend? How do you know if someone you just met will make a good friend?
2. Political data: How did you vote in your first election? How did you resolve a political debate with a friend or family member?

Stories of curiosity are all about the pursuit, the journey, its struggles and failures, and the persistence necessary to stay with the trouble. In some ways, stories of curiosity can not only introduce a learning environment but also form the structure for the entirety of the course. The best example of this is problem-based learning (PBL). In PBL, students are presented with a complex, real-world problem and tasked with finding a solution. These problems are often ill-structured, requiring students to formulate questions, seek out new information, and think critically about possible solutions. Because there is no single "correct" answer, students must navigate uncertainty, which naturally engages their curiosity. PBL invites students to take control over their own learning. Providing opportunities for autonomy, such as allowing students to choose their own research topics or projects, can significantly enhance their engagement and curiosity. Put simply, providing students with choices that influence their learning invites them to author their own stories of curiosity.

Another model that can be used to structure an entire course as a story of curiosity is inquiry-based learning (IBL). In IBL, educators act as facilitators rather than knowledge dispensers, guiding students as they develop their own questions, conduct research, and arrive at conclusions. Class time tends to revolve around discussions that follow probing, open-ended questions, with the teacher providing possible next steps rather than answers so that students have to think on their feet and explore multiple perspectives, fostering a deeper sense of curiosity as they engage with complex ideas.

By emphasizing personal experience, care and empathy frame the kind of learning that can be anticipated. Just as teachers often center their enthusiasm and passion about a topic when teaching, students need the chance to realize that their enthusiasm and passion, even if different than their teachers' experiences, have a place in the learning environment. In other words, with prior knowledge and care activated, relational bonds rooted in experience begin to form and we are reminded that we do not just teach content, we teach students how to engage content. In the next chapter, we will build on these relational bonds based on an affinity for content to establish care between us and our students.

References

Anderson, C. L., Dixson, D. D., Monroy, M., & Keltner, D. (2020). Are awe-prone people more curious? The relationship between dispositional awe, curiosity, and academic outcomes. *Journal of Personality, 88*(4), 762–779.

Bugaj, T. J., Schwarz, T. A., Friederich, H. C., & Nikendei, C. (2024). The curious physician: Exploring the role of curiosity in professionalism, patient care, and well-being. *Annals of Medicine, 56*(1), 2392887.

Carstensen, L. L. (2021). Socioemotional selectivity theory: The role of perceived endings in human motivation. *The Gerontologist, 61*(8), 1188–1196.

Ceiplak-Mayr von Baldegg, K. (2012). 1 billion views: The viral rise of TED talks in one chart. *The Atlantic.* https://www.theatlantic.com/video/archive/2012/11/1-billion-views-the-viral-rise-of-ted-talks-in-one-chart/265152/.

Cohen-Chen, S., & Van Zomeren, M. (2018). Yes we can? Group efficacy beliefs predict collective action, but only when hope is high. *Journal of Experimental Social Psychology, 77,* 50–59.

Damasio, A. (2019). *The strange order of things: Life, feeling, and the making of cultures.* Vintage.

Deslauriers, L., McCarty, L. S., Miller, K., Callaghan, K., & Kestin, G. (2019). Measuring actual learning versus feeling of learning in response to being actively engaged in the classroom. *Proceedings of the National Academy of Sciences, 116*(39), 19251–19257.

Dezza, I. C., Schulz, E., & Wu, C. M. (Eds.). (2022). *The drive for knowledge.* The Science of Human Information Seeking. Cambridge University Press.

DiCarlo, S. E. (2009). Too much content, not enough thinking, and too little FUN! *Advances in Physiology Education.* https://journals.physiology.org/doi/full/10.1152/advan.00075.2009.

Gruber, M. J., Gelman, B. D., & Ranganath, C. (2014). States of curiosity modulate hippocampus-dependent learning via the dopaminergic circuit. *Neuron, 84*(2), 486–496.

Hardy III, J. H., Ness, A. M., & Mecca, J. (2017). Outside the box: Epistemic curiosity as a predictor of creative problem solving and creative performance. *Personality and Individual Differences, 104,* 230–237.

Heath, C., & Heath, D. (2007). *Made to stick: Why some ideas survive and others die.* Random House.

Jonson, B. (1780). *Every man in his humour: A comedy.* As it is acted at the Theatres-Royal in Drury-Lane and Covent-Garden. Written by Ben Johnson. printed for Harrison and Co. No 18, Paternoster-Row; and sold, likewise, by J. Wenman, Fleet-Street; and all other booksellers.

Kashdan, T. B., & Roberts, J. E. (2004). Social anxiety's impact on affect, curiosity, and social self-efficacy during a high self-focus social threat situation. *Cognitive Therapy and Research, 28,* 119–141.

Kashdan, T. B., DeWall, C. N., Pond, R. S., Silvia, P. J., Lambert, N. M., Fincham, F. D., Savostyanova, A., & Keller, P. S. (2013). Curiosity protects against interpersonal aggression: Cross-sectional, daily process, and behavioral evidence. *Journal of Personality, 81*(1), 87–102.

Keltner, D., & Haidt, J. (2003). Approaching awe, a moral, spiritual, and aesthetic emotion. *Cognition and Emotion, 17*(2), 297–314.

Kurtz, J., Steenbergh, K., Kessler, J., Vitous, A., Barrett, M., Sandhu, G., & Suwanabol, P. A. (2020). "What I wish my surgeon knew": A novel approach to promote empathic curiosity in surgery. *Journal of Surgical Education, 77*(1), 82–87.

Lembke, A. (2021). *Dopamine nation: Finding balance in the age of indulgence*. Penguin.

McEvoy, P. (2013). Empathic curiosity: Resolving goal conflicts that generate emotional distress. *Journal of Psychiatric and Mental Health Nursing, 20*(3), 273–278.

Miller, A. C., & Mills, B. (2019). "If they don't care, I don't care": Millennial and Generation Z students and the impact of faculty caring. *Journal of the Scholarship of Teaching and Learning, 19*(4), 78–89.

Nazir, C., & Lin, M. (2023). Beyond empathy: How curiosity promotes greater care. *Connectivity and Creativity in Times of Conflict*, 585–589. Academia Press. https://doi.org/10.26530/9789401496476-115.

Notara, V., Vagka, E., Gnardellis, C., & Lagiou, A. (2021). The emerging phenomenon of nomophobia in young adults: A systematic review study. *Addiction & Health, 13*(2), 120.

Perlin, J. D., & Li, L. (2020). Why does awe have prosocial effects? New perspectives on awe and the small self. *Perspectives on Psychological Science, 15*(2), 291–308. https://doi.org/10.1177/1745691619886006.

Petersen, C. I., Baepler, P., Beitz, A., Ching, P., Gorman, K. S., Neudauer, C. L., & Wingert, D. (2020). The tyranny of content: "Content coverage" as a barrier to evidence-based teaching approaches and ways to overcome it. *CBE—Life Sciences Education, 19*(2), ar17.

Piff, P. K., Dietze, P., Feinberg, M., Stancato, D. M., & Keltner, D. (2015). Awe, the small self, and prosocial behavior. *Journal of Personality and Social Psychology, 108*(6), 883–899.

Sakaki, M., Yagi, A., & Murayama, K. (2018). Curiosity in old age: A possible key to achieving adaptive aging. *Neuroscience & Biobehavioral Reviews, 88*, 106–116.

Sybing, R. (2019). Making connections: Student-teacher rapport in higher education classrooms: Student-teacher rapport in higher education classrooms. *Journal of the Scholarship of Teaching and Learning, 19*(5).

Tams, S., Legoux, R., & Léger, P. M. (2018). Smartphone withdrawal creates stress: A moderated mediation model of nomophobia, social threat, and phone withdrawal context. *Computers in Human Behavior, 81*, 1–9.

Wojtowicz, Z., Chater, N., Loewenstein, G., Cogliati Dezza, E. I., Schulz, E., & Wu, C. (2022). The motivational processes of sense-making. In *The drive for knowledge: The science of human information seeking*, 3–30. Cambridge University Press.

4

CARE BETWEEN TEACHERS AND STUDENTS

Chapter Contents

Creating Space in Busy Curricula for Relationships	71
Inclusive Teaching and the Science of Learning	74
Belonging and Positive Relationships	75
Culturally Sustaining Teaching	75
Benefits of Diversity for Cognitive Outcomes	76
Believing in Belief	77
Teachers as Relational Hosts	79
Care Kit: Thin-Slice	81
References	84

We might think that the best way to activate student learning is by jumping straight to content. This assumption, though, undercuts the power we hold as teachers. During my PhD program at Washington State University, my research focused on writing assessment. I also maintained a teaching fellowship, serving as an instructor of educational assessment for elementary and secondary pre-service teachers. When I first began teaching these courses, I held regular meetings with my advisor to reflect on my teaching and the courses' development. At the end of the year, we went over my student evaluation surveys together. One year, I happened to receive particularly positive results, often with very personal comments from students. One specific comment read:

> JT is the kindest, most approachable human I have ever met. I had serious reservations about a class on assessment, but JT added flavor to an otherwise boring topic.

DOI: 10.4324/9781003591009-5

Reading that comment with my advisor made me feel weightless. I could fly on those words. Sure, I was not the biggest fan of calling the content I love "boring," but that did little to deflate the ego boost I felt. My advisor probably detected my glow and, constructively critical as he was, asked me: "Did they develop a positive relationship with assessment or just with you?"

That question brought me right back down to earth. I believe my advisor meant for his question to motivate critical reflection about my instructional methods. It's one thing to be a likable person; it's another thing entirely to encourage students to care enough about content that they will learn it.

On the other hand, it's not always possible to tease apart one from the other, the teacher from the thing being taught. My advisor challenged me to consider how teachers serve as proxies, or even conduits, for their content. By building positive relationships with students, teachers can build positive relationships with content (Felten & Lambert, 2020). One of the most influential factors on whether students connect with content is how much they relate to their teacher (Allen et al., 2021), which likely explains the power of peer pressure (Prinstein & Giletta, 2020). Of course, this means that growing student diversity requires growing teacher diversity so that all student identities can benefit from representation (Redding, 2019). This does not mean, however, that teachers can only relate to students who share the same social identity markers. In the absence of shared race or gender, for example, some other genuine connection must be emphasized. The connections we make as humans become the gateway for learning the content. Unfortunately, higher education does not always make space for intentional relationship building.

Creating Space in Busy Curricula for Relationships

Frequently, I work with faculty undergoing review for tenure or promotion. Throughout this stressful process, which often incorporates some of the accountability pressures we reviewed earlier, faculty compile artifacts demonstrating that they provide the institution with undeniable value. In more than one case, faculty have shared with me emails they received from students thanking them for all the time they spent helping them throughout the semester. Other faculty shared cards, both store-bought and handmade, expressing sincere gratitude for, in the words of one card, "being the reason I stayed in college." The faculty member who received that particular card told me how frequently she met with the student outside of class. "I'm a Latina professor in a predominantly white institution, and the student is also Latina. She has no one else. Sometimes we'd meet until 9 or 10 at night." Despite the fact that the relationship between the professor and the student was genuine, the support provided to the student still constitutes labor and direct benefit to the institution. As Felton and Lambert (2020) show, these kinds of genuine relationships positively impact retention and graduation rates. And yet, neither the cards nor the additional meetings with the student warranted consideration during her official review. All student commentary had to come in the form of an institutionally distributed end-of-term evaluation. As a result, office hours, even when they extend beyond the times stated in the course syllabus, are baked into standard expectations of faculty performance. This one example serves as evidence that higher education lacks regular structures to promote relational practices, despite the overwhelming evidence of the importance of such structures (Osher et al., 2021). The traditional narratives around teaching and learning remain rooted in the history of higher education reviewed in Chapter 2.

Meanwhile, the familiar model of a classroom suggests students sitting quietly in rows upon rows, all facing forward to the teacher, a sage on the stage. The image evokes an assemblage of industrial order, religious authority, and a neoliberal deference to consumption. For the most part, only the teacher talks, because only the teacher has anything worth saying. These environments tend to produce the perception in students that they have little to offer in the relationship with their teacher, despite the fact that students benefit from a sense that their teachers value them (Cooper et al., 2017). In Paulo Freire's analysis of the familiar model, "the narrating Subject (the teacher)" explains reality to "patient, listening objects (the students)" (p. 57). Much like with lectures, dominant narration leaves little room for students to reflect on, interpret, or act upon the narrated reality. Their choice is only to accept the information (and be a "good student") or reject it (and be a "poor student"). Freire (2014) argued that this form of education is oppressive in that passive reception of knowledge prevents the freedom to critically think about the knowledge or use it in ways that improve students' social conditions. Even if the purpose of a lesson is simply to memorize factual information, we know from cognitive research that memory is an active operation. The more learners act upon new information via recall, elaboration, or application, the better their memory of the new information becomes (McDermott, 2021).

Freire called the education paradigm emerging from the familiar model (narrating Subject and passive listening object) the "banking concept of education" (p. 58). He describes this concept in more detail:

> Instead of communicating, the teacher issues communiques and makes deposits which the students patiently receive, memorize, and repeat.... The scope of action allowed to the students extends only as far as receiving, filing, and storing the deposits.
>
> (p. 58)

Freire contrasted this with his model of "problem-posing education," where teachers and students engage in dialogue and learn from each other. In this approach, knowledge is not something handed down from teacher to student, but rather co-created through inquiry and discussion. He believed this kind of education fosters critical consciousness, or *conscientização*—the awareness of one's social, political, and economic conditions, and the power to transform them. In short, Freire believed that literacy involved reading the word as well as the world.

Of course, Freire also lived within a particular ecology. The social tensions shaping his thinking are not so unlike the ones faced by the Western world today. Freire spent much of his early career teaching literacy to children and adults living in poverty in Brazil. Many of the adults living as peasants throughout rural villages lacked any kind of literacy. For the most part, they had been excluded from formal education and did not have any access to libraries. Freire's approach was unconventional: instead of merely teaching people the basics of reading, such as phonics or fluency, he used literacy as an opportunity to help his students think critically about their social conditions. Pretty explicitly, literacy became an opportunity to challenge the very systems that banished large portions of Brazil's population to a life of illiteracy and poverty. If they could read and write, they could question everything from legal discourse to cultural rhetoric, and they could organize. Freire employed a dialogical process, where both teacher and student engaged in mutual learning and exploration. By doing so, educators not only teach content but also empower students to explore it critically, make connections to their own lives, and become agents of change in society. By promoting a dialogical and participatory model of education, Freire challenged the traditional banking model and urged educators to view students as active agents capable of caring about the world and themselves.

Initially, Brazil celebrated Freire's success and planned to officially institute his method. Unfortunately, empowering the oppressed tends to disrupt social order. When Brazil's government fell to a military dictatorship in 1964, Freire became an enemy of the state and eventually went into exile. Clearly, Friere's methods proved too disruptive for those who preferred a disempowered people. After all, a typical method of dictators has been to restrict the public, often by attacking journalists and educators, from asking questions and critically reflecting. The banking concept of education can disempower students by requiring them to comport their own existence to meet the current social conditions rather than transform social conditions to improve their existence. In other words, the banking concept of education presupposes a teacher-student relationship founded upon obedience.

Both learning and liberation depend on a different kind of teacher-student relationship model. For Freire, when the teacher-student relationship emerges out of mutual humanistic care for one another, liberation becomes the outcome. "From the outset," Friere writes, the caring educator's efforts "coincide with those of the students to engage in critical thinking and the quest for mutual humanization," which is only possible when the teacher acts as a "partner of the students in [their] relations with them" (p. 62). This chapter contributes to the Care Kit by suggesting strategies for partnering teacher and student relations, priming students to love what teachers love about their content. The curiosity sharing of the prior Care Kit entry should extend throughout a course by continuously connecting with newly introduced or reinforced content. Since the teacher facilitates these connections, there needs to be a healthy sense of trust shared between teachers and students. Taking inspiration from Freire, when we begin with the formation of positive bonds, assuming the role of "student among students," we "undermine the power of oppression and serve the cause of liberation" (p. 62).

Inclusive Teaching and the Science of Learning

Pause for a moment and think about how you got here. Reflect on how you became a capital T-teacher. Why did you decide to devote your life to educating others? What and who guided your trajectory?

Focus on one person in particular. Describe them—on paper or in your mind. List their memorable features, not necessarily their physical attributes (in many cases, gender, race, etc. matter when it comes to representation), but also *how* they played a role in shaping your journey to become a teacher.

When I lead this activity in-person, I then encourage participants to share their stories with others by first forming groups of "shared experience" (matching with others who have similarly memorable mentors) and then reflecting together on the question: Why were these mentors so memorable?

By far, the majority of the responses explain mentors who cared for them, supported them, or challenged them in meaningful ways. Very rarely did a mentor stand out because of their content expertise, although many state that content expertise is a minimum requirement for a mentor. In my own journey, it mattered a great deal that my faculty mentor at Colorado Mountain College, Dr. Leticia Burbano de Lara, is not only Latina but also a scholar of translingualism and culturally and linguistically diverse education. What I will remember most, however, is how she regularly hosted me for dinner and provided feedback on my teaching and on my scholarship. I will also remember how she and her family even hosted my parents, splitting a dessert with my father while Leti explained to my very conservative parents the challenges undocumented students face in America.

"They are terrified they will be detained and so they are too stressed to do their best work," could be heard alongside, "[T]his banana foster is delicious."

Leti always made me feel like I belonged. And this was also true for her students.

Understanding that every class is a living community, she intentionally dedicated the first week of each course to getting to know everyone. She and her students engaged in activities like creating identity maps, sharing literacy stories, or assembling class banners—opportunities to work collectively on affirming each member of the classroom. In a perfect summary of interdependent classrooms, Leti once advised me that her students do not "*strive* because of a grade or attendance policy. They *thrive* because they know others in the room care about what they care about."

Inclusive teaching—encompassing students' sense of belonging, the inclusion of diverse perspectives, and equitable learning opportunities—has increasingly been recognized not only as fundamental to the science of learning but also as central to creating interdependent classrooms rooted in care. Research from educational psychology shows that when learners feel valued and supported in diverse, inclusive environments, their motivation, engagement, and achievement often improve (Goodenow, 1993; Johnson et al., 1981). At its core, inclusive teaching affirms that learning is a shared, relational process: one that flourishes through collaboration, mutual respect, and emotional safety.

Inclusive teaching builds on decades of pedagogical theory and research that position learning as a social and cultural act. Early 20th-century thinkers like John Dewey (1916) emphasized the importance of democratic, student-centered classrooms—spaces where all learners' experiences are valued. Mid-century research introduced the idea that contact across difference not only reduces prejudice but also enriches thinking by promoting perspective-taking (Allport, 1954). Later, cooperative learning research demonstrated the academic advantages of peer collaboration in diverse groups, where learners support each other and deepen understanding together (Johnson et al., 1981). Similarly, Goodenow (1993) found that students who feel accepted in their classroom communities are more academically motivated, underscoring that learning thrives in classrooms where care and connection across diverse groups are present (Antonio et al., 2004; Chang et al., 2006).

Belonging and Positive Relationships

A sense of belonging is foundational for interdependence. When students trust that they are accepted and supported, they are more likely to take intellectual risks and persist through academic challenges. In a seminal study, Walton and Cohen (2011) showed that even brief interventions affirming students' belonging led to improved grade point averages (GPAs), well-being, and engagement, particularly among students of color. Years later, those same students reported higher career satisfaction—demonstrating that fostering a sense of belonging can have durable effects on personal and academic development. A meta-analysis by Cornelius-White (2007) revealed that learner-centered relationships marked by empathy, encouragement, and trust correlated strongly with academic performance and classroom participation. Faculty mentorship and approachability are especially important for first-generation and underrepresented students (Walton & Cohen, 2011), affirming that inclusive teaching is inherently relational: it is built through consistent, affirming connections that, as Leti taught me, allow students to thrive with and because of one another. The growing evidence encouraged the proliferation of practices that respond to and sustain the diverse cultural assets students bring to a learning environment.

Culturally Sustaining Teaching

Culturally sustaining teaching (CST) promotes a classroom culture where students' identities are affirmed and their backgrounds are honored as sources of strength. Gay (2010) defines cultural responsiveness as using the cultural knowledge, experiences, and styles of diverse learners to make teaching more meaningful and relevant. Aronson and Laughter (2016) found that such approaches improve student engagement and achievement—particularly for those from historically marginalized communities. When instruction reflects students' lived experiences, as Dee and Penner (2017) demonstrate with their assessment of a culturally relevant ethnic studies curriculum, academic outcomes improve for all students, including those labeled at-risk.

Curriculum design does not have to be the only place to implement inclusive practices. At the classroom level, Abacioglu et al. (2020) showed that teachers with strong perspective-taking skills were more likely to use inclusive, socially attuned practices. Small moves teachers make can help students feel safe to learn and care for one another as members of a shared community. Even as we operate within the realms of our influence, Paris and Alim (2017), editors of the book *Culturally Sustaining Pedagogies*, remind us that it is not enough to simply respond to students' diverse cultural identities. In order to sustain diversity as a cultural aspiration, educators need to actively critique and transform systems of injustice that favor a hegemony of culture in schools. Doing so, as we will describe below, helps direct learning toward liberation as well as improve cognitive abilities.

Benefits of Diversity for Cognitive Outcomes

Diversity directly contributes to cognitive development. Learning alongside peers from different backgrounds promotes complex reasoning, critical thinking, and creativity. Gurin et al. (2002) found that diverse interactions in college consistently improved intellectual engagement and integrative thinking. Bowman (2010) echoed this in a meta-analysis, linking diversity experiences to measurable cognitive gains. Importantly, these benefits emerge through collaborative meaning-making. Antonio et al. (2004) found that students in racially and ideologically diverse groups demonstrated more integrative complexity in their thinking—suggesting that students learn more deeply when they collectively wrestle with perspectives that challenge preconceived beliefs. Diverse classrooms thus function as interdependent learning communities, where the richness of thought stems from respectful engagement and mutual influence.

Inclusive classrooms often rely on active learning approaches that emphasize collaboration and co-construction of knowledge. Freeman et al. (2014) found that active engagement in diverse experiences improved exam performance and reduced failure rates in undergraduate STEM courses. Theobald et al. (2020) showed how similar effects were especially pronounced for underrepresented students, helping to close long-standing equity gaps. McMaster and Fuchs (2002) found that students with learning disabilities gained significantly more when learning with peers in inclusive groups. These pedagogies cultivate interdependence by structuring opportunities for students to support each other's learning. Indeed, a long body of research by Johnson et al. (1981), Slavin (1995), and Kyndt et al. (2013) confirms that cooperative learning benefits students academically and socially. Chapter 5 will explore the benefits and strategies for developing relationships between students more deeply; for now, the point is that for students to develop relationships with each other, they must first relate to their teacher. The teacher serves not just as an intellectual proxy for content but also as a social emotional host for interaction. (More on being a host later in this chapter.)

Believing in Belief

Primarily, inclusive teachers help build students' belief in themselves. Ballen et al. (2017) found that underrepresented students in classes with teachers they trusted reported increased science self-efficacy, which mediated improved performance. This rise in confidence is more than a psychological gain; it reflects a shift in students' sense of belonging within academic spaces, further supporting the interdependent nature of learning environments where every student is seen as capable and essential.

Equity-focused interventions that address psychological barriers can further strengthen interdependent belief (in oneself and in others). Cohen et al. (2006) and Miyake et al. (2010) found that values affirmation interventions reduced stereotype threat and improved academic outcomes, particularly for women and students of color. By affirming students' identities, teachers can create classrooms where care is not only expressed but also part of a pedagogical routine, encouraging risk-taking, creative thinking, and persistence in challenging situations.

Perceived relevance offers another example. Harackiewicz et al. (2014) showed that when first-generation and underrepresented students were prompted to connect course content to their personal goals, their academic performance significantly improved. These interventions work because they honor the full personhood of students—acknowledging their aspirations, values, and sense of purpose. As we discussed earlier, what we care about directs our attention and other cognitive resources. Feeling valued in all the ways we exist is a prerequisite to learning anything at all.

Mentorship, learning communities, and inclusive research opportunities (Ballen et al., 2017) also function as teacher-directed, care-based structures that support success. When students are embedded in networks of support, they are more likely to persist, achieve, and, in turn, uplift others. Harackiewicz et al. (2014) demonstrated that interventions tailored to students at the intersection of multiple marginalized identities (e.g., first-generation and minoritized) had the greatest impact. One-size-fits-all strategies fall short; it is the intentional responsiveness to layered experiences that creates genuinely inclusive, supportive learning environments.

For women of color in STEM, intersectional programs—those that address both race and gender—have shown greater success in promoting retention than generic diversity efforts. Similarly, inclusive classrooms for students with disabilities benefit everyone, not just those receiving accommodations. Cole et al. (2004) found that universal design strategies enhanced academic outcomes for all students when those strategies fostered access and community support, for example, through accessible study groups or identity-based support spaces.

In these intersectional spaces, the caring-with gets amplified. Students are not required to fragment their identities to succeed. Instead, they are invited to bring their whole selves into the classroom and to participate in a learning process that directly connects them with their teacher through a shared interest and purpose. Across empirical studies, DEI-aligned teaching practices do more than boost academic metrics—they reframe the classroom as a site of interdependence and care. When students feel they belong, they are more motivated, resilient, and open to learning (Walton & Cohen, 2011; Cornelius-White, 2007). When educators affirm cultural identities and foster inclusive relationships, students are empowered to participate fully (Gay, 2010; Aronson & Laughter, 2016). When learning is active, collaborative, and attuned to identity, performance gaps narrow and communities of care flourish (Freeman et al., 2014; Theobald et al., 2020). And when interventions address psychological and structural inequities, they open space for every student to contribute and grow (Miyake et al., 2010; Harackiewicz et al., 2014), providing each student with their own memorable mentor.

Facilitating the strategies demonstrated in these studies, however, is not always easy. In general, translating scholarship of teaching and learning as well as the science of learning has long presented many challenges and setbacks. In *Nonviolent Response: Strategies for Responding to Writing*, Sheri Rysdam and I (2026) shared a story about Valorie Kondos Field, the hall of fame gymnastics coach for University of California Los Angeles (UCLA), that applies here. When Kondos Field first began coaching, she did what her coaches had done, which meant being "tougher and meaner and more of a bully."

In some instances, she mocked gymnasts if they had gained weight. In others, she called them "losers" or accused them of not deserving to be on the team. As a young coach, she believed these responses would motivate her athletes to try harder. For those two years, however, her gymnasts struggled. Tensions came to a head when the team called Kondos Field into a meeting and demanded a culture change. Kondos Field explains:

> They wanted to be supported, not belittled. They wanted to be coached up, not torn down. They wanted to be motivated, not pressured or bullied. It is

so much easier in any walk of life to dictate and give orders than to actually figure out how to motivate someone to want to be better. Being a dogmatic dictator may produce compliant, good little soldiers, but it doesn't develop champions in life. With awards and medals, athletes often leave their teams damaged—emotionally, mentally, not just physically. We have become so hyper-focused on that end result, and when the end result is a win, the human component of how we got there often gets swept under the proverbial rug, and so does the damage.

(Zomorodi, 2020)

Remarkably, Kondos Field was able to hear, consider, and reflect on the feedback from her team. She was then able to implement a new coaching style that focused on celebrating her athletes for every achievement, however small. Kondos Field noticed that they began trusting her, adopting her feedback, and improving beyond expectation.

When I began weightlifting as a hobby, I needed to find a trainer who could teach me safe and effective methods. Without a trainer, I had no idea which weights I should use, how to keep the correct form, and how to best develop strength. I found a good trainer who educated me so I could tell not only the difference between a bench press and an incline press but also the difference between bench pressing with dumbbells versus barbells. But my trainer went beyond gym weight room literacy. She built a relationship with me by asking about my goals, experiences, and health history. She also asked me about my motivation as well as my lifestyle habits. I noticed she used what she learned during these conversations to encourage me when exhaustion kicked in and caused me to question whether I could successfully complete the workout she had designed for me during a particular session. My fitness trainer always assures me, "I won't let the bar fall." Or, she'll say, "You can do this. You *will* do this. One more rep." I believe she is not going to send me to the hospital. I believe she wants me to get stronger, not injured. Without her, I am never able to lift as much weight or as many reps.

Teachers as Relational Hosts

Dr. Adrienne Jones, a sociology professor, once invited me to perform a classroom observation for her. She mostly wanted feedback about how she engaged the class, ensuring all students participated, even if they participated in different ways.

On the day of the observation, I took a seat in the corner, in the middle of groups of students scrolling through social media while Adrienne arranged her notes at the podium. As soon as she settled, she sparked something in the room. She asked one student if he was excited about his upcoming trip to North Carolina. He immediately put away his phone and told her about his plans to hang out with friends in Chapel Hill. Then Adrienne asked another student about her psychology class, referencing an earlier conversation they must have had about the psychology of social media. It just so happened that social media's influence on information sharing was the day's topic.

During class, Adrienne found ways to include students at what seemed like the perfect moment. She drew from students' backgrounds, interests, previous conversations, and any other insight she had gleaned. And by doing so, she drew students in. For instance, when describing the incentive for social media companies to reinforce users' strongly held beliefs, Adrienne cued the psychology student, who enthusiastically defined confirmation bias and applied the concept to the discussion.

Afterwards, after applauding the masterful performance, I asked Adrienne how she knew so much about her students. She explained that she had dedicated the first two weeks of the semester, as well as the first assignment, to opportunities for students to incorporate aspects of themselves. Not only did Adrienne find that the strategy led to higher motivation levels, but grading the assignments gave her valuable insight into who her students are. This means that students reflect on connections between lived experience and the content the course would cover early on, introducing students to content and introducing themselves to Adrienne.

At the time of the observation, Adrienne was a postdoc, teaching her own class for the first time. And yet, she shared with me during our post-observation debrief something that took me years to realize: "Teaching is much more about helping students navigate their socio-emotional development rather than actual instruction."

Teachers cannot just be vehicles for content. The position requires the emotional labor that can so often burn us out if institutions do not care for teachers. The position requires not just instruction but also coaching, counseling, mentoring, guiding, motivating, designing, and hosting. Remember from the Introduction that Cate Denial (2024) offered the theory of IEH, which defines instructors as critical hosts. Adding to this idea, Priya Parker (2020), in *The Art of Gathering: How We Meet and Why It Matters*, emphasizes that the host has a critical responsibility in creating meaningful gatherings. She describes hosting as a role that goes beyond just organizing logistics; it involves setting a purpose, fostering a safe environment, and guiding participants toward the intended outcome. In any other context, these descriptions would directly apply to any teacher. The comparison also calls attention to an important tension in many hosts. Most of the time, good hosts do not want to host. We might have gone to a party that felt incredibly awkward because everyone only interacted with the people with whom they came. Or, worse, everyone sat around a living room with a drink in their hand and a phone in the other. I have worked with many educators who wanted to incorporate equitable teaching practices. In several cases, these well-intentioned and very talented teachers offered students a radically open classroom, in which students could determine their grade, the amount of work they would complete, and even what they would learn. While none of these approaches are inherently ineffective—on the contrary, they should be the ideal—students (and, when it comes to social interaction, all of us) need direction about how to participate in an emerging community, such as a new course.

Parker (2020) believes the host should embody a "generous authority" (p. 81). This means that they need to balance welcoming warmth with firm direction, curating the experience to ensure guests are safe, engaged, and connected. Hosts should be clear about the gathering's purpose and be willing to make choices—even uncomfortable ones—to serve that purpose. For example, a host might intentionally introduce prompts or structure activities that draw people out, enabling deeper conversations and genuine connections. We might remember other parties in which the host prompted some game or activity that helped connect everyone present. Ultimately, Parker argues that a good host takes responsibility for shaping the space, mood, and interactions so the gathering can become something greater than a simple meeting—transforming it into a shared experience where participants feel they belong and contribute meaningfully.

Care Kit: Thin-Slice

This entry provides possible strategies for establishing trust and community early in a course, such as through the intentional use of thin-slicing. Ambady and Rosenthal (1992) brought attention to the power of first impressions. In particular, people make incredibly accurate judgments about one another based on brief displays of expressive behavior. "Much of this expressive behavior is unintended, unconscious, and yet extremely effective," Ambady and Rosenthal (1992) say. "For example, we communicate our interpersonal expectancies and biases through very subtle, almost imperceptible, nonverbal cues" (p. 256). Their results have extended to education, suggesting that many students make enduring determinations about their teachers within minutes. For instance, college students' first impressions of teachers are highly predictive of the final evaluations teachers receive (Begrich et al., 2021).

The first encounter between students and teachers is critical; unfortunately, first encounters are typically deadened by syllabus coverage or classroom policy agreements. Thin-slicing reminds us that humans make strong judgments about one another based on brief, narrow experiences. Even more impressive, these judgments tend to be accurate. If teachers make intentional use of this phenomenon, they can more effectively shape the desired learning environment than they could by mandating policies and procedures. Immediately beginning a semester, for instance, by asking students to share backstories hopefully thinly slices a teacher who prioritizes their students.

Remedy

The first Care Kit entry nurtures our love for learning and the content we teach through storytelling. Backstories help activate the power of curiosity, an intellectual and emotional caring-with other people and ideas. This Care Kit entry nurtures the positions teachers and students have in an interdependent classroom. First impressions especially determine how our positions shape the relationships that emerge in shared space. How teachers and students initially come into relationship with one another can impact the entire term.

Humans inherently begin any new endeavor with some apprehension. New experiences always include some sense of risk. Such tension could generate the perfect opportunity to promise students that even though learning is uncomfortable, they will be supported. Create an opportunity for students to take a low-stakes risk, and then immediately provide positive feedback, celebrating the risk. One possibility is to invite students to suggest and justify relevant questions or topics they would like to pursue during the course. This approach flips the script of the traditional syllabus day, asking students about their intentions as opposed to enforcing institutional intentions. Take the time to acknowledge each student's suggestion and justification. This is not the time for critical feedback or course correction. Let students lead as much as possible and praise them for doing so. Not only will students sense an environment that they can shape, indicating their agency in the course, but also the positive feedback will promise them encouragement and care.

Storytelling is a powerful, and ancient, method of connecting storytellers with audiences. You can borrow from the previous chapter's Care Kit by starting a course with an authentic, personal story about anything at all. The more appropriately vulnerable your story, the more likely you will draw in students (Pandolpho, 2018). I will always remember the first day of English in tenth grade because my teacher began the class with a story about how he ran out of gas driving through rural Canada and had to hitchhike. There was no real point to the story. But sharing his story ignited my interest and captured my attention. I was ready to listen and learn whatever followed. As David Brooks (2019) experienced in one of his classes at Yale, if students empathize with you, they are more likely to care about what you teach.

Thin-slicing who you are is one way to go. Another option is to thin-slice the kind of environment students can expect. The traditional opening act of reading a syllabus to students might communicate that the class will largely consist of lectures and require silent listening from them. In my educational assessment class, I often began the first day with a game. We randomly drew a social construct (e.g., love, joy, solidarity) from a hat. We then put that social construct on "trial," and students worked in breakout groups (both online and in-person, using AI as a thought partner) to present evidence in support of the social construct. The group that presented evidence that "could not be debated" (a difficult task) won. Rarely did a group win, since the very nature of a social construct entails subjectivity. The goal was to establish an expectation that the class would be interactive, playful, driven by their involvement, and open to uncertainty.

Root

You can also initiate a more structural learning environment by immediately asking students to co-design the environment. One strategy is to welcome students into the space by sharing the broad outcome of a course ("We will spend the year becoming academic writers") and then ask students to share their individual goals within that outcome. I have used surveys, word clouds, or—if the class is small enough—simple oral sharing to ask students things like, "What would you like to write about?" or "What would you like to read about?" or "What song playlist would you like for us to use to open each class with?" Again, the initial impression of such an approach hopefully communicates that students are front and center and that you, as the teacher, care about their input.

If this process becomes iterative, to the point of connecting each activity and assignment with the broader course assessment, teachers can promote a sense of ownership of the learning process. Over the course of the term, students have multiple chances to develop metacognitive skills as they reflect on the decisions they make to progress in the class. An entrepreneurialism professor with whom I consulted rooted the initial invitation to "build the course you want" at different moments throughout the term. She frequently deployed student check-in surveys, similar to end-of-term surveys distributed by the institution, but more focused on students' learning and needs. These surveys provided a chance for students to quickly express their care for the course and their perceptions of being cared for by the teacher. After each survey, the professor aggregated the results into anonymous charts that she displayed the following course. Based on the charts, they agreed on any changes the learning environment needed to remain positive.

> Creating intentional spaces to check in with students and incorporate their feedback into the course sends a strong message of care. It also roots the course in interdependence, as everyone participates in the learning process, individually and collectively. Encouragingly, research suggests that establishing care between teachers and students early and continuously highly predicts final grades (Lammers et al., 2017). To enjoy these documented benefits, though, caring-with must begin with the teacher.

Thin-slicing a supportive, encouraging learning environment can be an effective and affective introduction for students, immediately activating their participation and motivation. If students trust that they will not be punished for making mistakes, they will be more likely to take risks and stretch their learning. With trust and confidence activated, the classroom becomes fertile ground for community. As we expand these relationships into an ecology, the next step is to foster these connections laterally, between one another, as a complex network that centers the relational bonds as opposed to each individual student. In the next chapter, we will connect students to one another, forming a web of relationships across the learning environment.

References

Abacioglu, C. S., Volman, M., & Fischer, A. H. (2020). Teachers' multicultural attitudes and perspective-taking predict their inclusive educational practices. *Journal of Applied Developmental Psychology, 66*, 101084.

Allen, K. A., Slaten, C. D., Arslan, G., Roffey, S., Craig, H., & Vella-Brodrick, D. A. (2021). School belonging: The importance of student and teacher relationships. In *The Palgrave handbook of positive education* (pp. 525–550). Cham: Springer International Publishing.

Allport, G. W. (1954). *The nature of prejudice*. Addison-Wesley.

Ambady, N., & Rosenthal, R. (1992). Thin slices of expressive behavior as predictors of interpersonal consequences: A meta-analysis. *Psychological Bulletin, 111*(2), 256–274.

Antonio, A. L., Chang, M. J., Hakuta, K., Kenny, D. A., Levin, S., & Milem, J. F. (2004). Effects of racial diversity on complex thinking in college students. *Psychological Science, 15*(8), 507–510.

Aronson, B., & Laughter, J. (2016). The theory and practice of culturally relevant education: A synthesis of research across content areas. *Review of Educational Research, 86*(1), 163–206.

Ballen, C. J., Wieman, C., Salehi, S., Searle, J. B., & Zamudio, K. R. (2017). Enhancing diversity in undergraduate science: Self-efficacy drives performance gains with active learning. *CBE—Life Sciences Education, 16*(4), ar56.

Begrich, L., Kuger, S., Klieme, E., & Kunter, M. (2021). At a first glance–how reliable and valid is the thin slices technique to assess instructional quality? *Learning and Instruction, 74*, 101466.

Bowman, N. A. (2010). College diversity experiences and cognitive development: A meta-analysis. *Review of Educational Research, 80*(1), 4–33.

Brooks, D. (2019). People learn from people they love. *New York Times.* https://www.nytimes.com/2019/01/17/opinion/learning-emotion-education.html.

Chang, M. J., Denson, N., Saenz, V., & Misa, K. (2006). The educational benefits of sustaining cross-racial interaction among undergraduates. *Journal of Higher Education, 77*(3), 430–455.

Cohen, G. L., Garcia, J., Apfel, N., & Master, A. (2006). Reducing the racial achievement gap: A social-psychological intervention. *Science, 313*(5791), 1307–1310.

Cole, C. M., Waldron, N., & Majd, M. (2004). Academic progress of students across inclusive and traditional settings. *Mental Retardation, 42*(2), 136–144.

Cooper, K. M., Haney, B., Krieg, A., & Brownell, S. E. (2017). What's in a name? The importance of students perceiving that an instructor knows their names in a high-enrollment biology classroom. *CBE—Life Sciences Education, 16*(1), ar8.

Cornelius-White, J. (2007). Learner-centered teacher-student relationships are effective: A meta-analysis. *Review of Educational Research, 77*(1), 113–143.

Dee, T. S., & Penner, E. K. (2017). The causal effects of cultural relevance: Evidence from an ethnic studies curriculum. *American Educational Research Journal, 54*(1), 127–166.

Denial, C. J. (2024). *A pedagogy of kindness* (Vol. 1). University of Oklahoma Press.

Dewey, J. (1916). *Democracy and education.* Macmillan.

Felten, P., & Lambert, L. M. (2020). *Relationship-rich education: How human connections drive success in college.* JHU Press.

Freeman, S., Eddy, S. L., McDonough, M., et al. (2014). Active learning increases student performance in science, engineering, and mathematics. *Proceedings of the National Academy of Sciences, 111*(23), 8410–8415.

Freire, P. (2014). *Pedagogy of the oppressed.* Bloomsbury Publishing.

Gay, G. (2010). *Culturally responsive teaching: Theory, research, and practice.* Teachers College Press.

Goodenow, C. (1993). Classroom belonging among early adolescent students: Relationships to motivation and achievement. *Journal of Early Adolescence, 13*(1), 21–43.

Gurin, P., Dey, E. L., Hurtado, S., & Gurin, G. (2002). Diversity and higher education: Theory and impact on educational outcomes. *Harvard Educational Review, 72*(3), 330–366.

Harackiewicz, J. M., Canning, E. A., Tibbetts, Y., Priniski, S. J., & Hyde, J. S. (2014). Closing achievement gaps with a utility-value intervention: Disentangling race and social class. *Journal of Personality and Social Psychology, 111*(5), 745–765.

Johnson, D. W., Maruyama, G., Johnson, R., Nelson, D., & Skon, L. (1981). Effects of cooperative, competitive, and individualistic goal structures on achievement: A meta-analysis. *Psychological Bulletin, 89*(1), 47–62.

Kyndt, E., Raes, E., Lismont, B., Timmers, F., Cascallar, E., & Dochy, F. (2013). A meta-analysis of the effects of face-to-face cooperative learning. *Review of Educational Research, 83*(2), 644–680.

Lammers, W. J., Gillaspy Jr, J. A., & Hancock, F. (2017). Predicting academic success with early, middle, and late semester assessment of student–instructor rapport. *Teaching of Psychology, 44*(2), 145–149.

McDermott, K. B. (2021). Practicing retrieval facilitates learning. *Annual Review of Psychology, 72*(1), 609–633.

McMaster, K. L., & Fuchs, D. (2002). Effects of cooperative learning on the academic achievement of students with learning disabilities. *Exceptional Children, 68*(4), 437–452.

Miyake, A., Kost-Smith, L. E., Finkelstein, N. D., et al. (2010). Reducing the gender achievement gap in college science: A classroom study of values affirmation. *Science, 330*(6008), 1234–1237.

Osher, D., Cantor, P., Berg, J., Steyer, L., & Rose, T. (2021). Drivers of human development: How relationships and context shape learning and development. In *The science of learning and development* (pp. 55–104). Routledge.

Pandolpho, B. (2018). The power of sharing your stories with students. *Edutopia.* https://www.edutopia.org/article/power-sharing-your-story-students/.

Paris, D., & Alim, H. S. (Eds.). (2017). *Culturally sustaining pedagogies: Teaching and learning for justice in a changing world.* New York, NY: Teachers College Press.

Parker, P. (2020). *The art of gathering: How we meet and why it matters.* Penguin.

Prinstein, M. J., & Giletta, M. (2020). Future directions in peer relations research. *Journal of Clinical Child & Adolescent Psychology, 49*(4), 556–572.

Redding, C. (2019). A teacher like me: A review of the effect of student–teacher racial/ethnic matching on teacher perceptions of students and student academic and behavioral outcomes. *Review of Educational Research, 89*(4), 499–535.

Rysdam, S. & Torres, JT. (2026). *Nonviolent Response: Strategies for Responding to Writing.* U of Pittsburgh Press.

Slavin, R. E. (1995). *Cooperative learning: Theory, research, and practice.* Allyn & Bacon.

Theobald, E. J., Hill, M. J., Tran, E., et al. (2020). Active learning narrows achievement gaps for underrepresented students in undergraduate science, technology, engineering, and math. *Proceedings of the National Academy of Sciences, 117*(12), 6476–6483.

Walton, G. M., & Cohen, G. L. (2011). A brief social-belonging intervention improves academic and health outcomes of minority students. *Science, 331*(6023), 1447–1451.

Zomorodi, M. (2020). How can we reinvent the definition of Success? *Ted Radio Hour.* https://www.npr.org/transcripts/814990852

5
CARE BETWEEN STUDENTS

Chapter Contents
Group Work *Does* Work   89
When Disconnection Is the Norm   94
Teaching Connection   96
Care Kit: Cultivate a Learning Community   99
References   103

I know you might be thinking: When do we get to teach students the actual content?!

Almost. I promise.

In 2021, I first met the masterful facilitator Cindy Kern. Cindy is an award-winning science educator at both the college and high school levels. She founded and directs a program in Connecticut that provides high school students from diverse communities college readiness experiences, such as intensive mentorship relationships and community-based learning. Cindy served as a fellow for a grant-funded inclusive excellence teaching lab. I joined the lab after its formation as a co-director with Khalilah Brown-Dean, who founded the Inclusive Excellence Teaching Lab. The Lab organized and hosted several programs for educators to reflect on and share inclusive teaching practices, including an annual summer conference. Cindy and I also worked together on curricula for graduate education courses.

Cindy's presence is an experience. One might not notice her entering a room. She tends to make herself small, with hunched shoulders and head down, dressed often in a hoodie and jeans. The moment she begins speaking, especially as a facilitator, the air around her suddenly changes and becomes electric with joyful energy. She is an expert at conjuring audience participation because her presenter voice carries the perfect balance of encouragement and authority. In the five years I've observed Cindy present, I have never witnessed her ask for a volunteer from the audience only to stand before a silent crowd. Quite the contrary, I have observed Cindy many times not only asking for a volunteer but herself volunteering the most powerful person in the room with zero resistance. One time, during a faculty development presentation, she volunteered the dean to lead a karaoke session. Another time, during a college-wide event, she plucked the Provost from the audience to serve as her assistant.

At first, I could not get over the feeling that the pace of her approach to facilitation felt unnecessarily *slow*. I wondered why we conducted so many "icebreakers" and why we allowed so much discussion (even when it became small talk) before moving on. It was not until we received feedback from our participants that I recognized how much everyone actually accomplished. Even months after our program, I heard from the participants that the materials they developed resulted in grants, awards, and lifelong relationships with other participants.

Cindy used to tell me,

> If I begin Week 1 with Chapter 1, by the time we reach Week 10, I'm on Chapter 10. If I begin Week 1 with connection, we might not begin Chapter 1 until Week 2 or 3. But by the time we reach Week 10, I'm on Chapter 15.

When I give presentations, I share Cindy's quote, an important reminder that an interdependent classroom is a cultural shift that resists efficiency in favor of effectiveness and resists management in favor of maximalization. In *The Slow Professor: Challenging the Culture of Speed in the Academy*, authors Maggie Berg and Barbara Seeber (2016) provide a detailed analysis of the social-historical forces normalizing stress, overwork, status-seeking, and mental health crises in higher education. Unhealthy as these conditions may be, they have become firmly accepted. Slowing down and emphasizing community can certainly include a certain "discomfort of going against the grain of institutional cultures" (p. 89). It will feel uncomfortable at first, but the rewards are worth the change of pace. Following Cindy's wisdom, this chapter contributes to the Care Kit by offering ways we can form strong social networks and learning communities that not only help take the pressure off of the teacher of being the center of teaching, learning, and caring but also increase the impact.

Social interdependence learning theory (SILT) as a pedagogical concept is explored more deeply, providing more detailed examples from Johnson & Johnson's (2009) seminal work studying and articulating the theory in practice. The teacher cannot be everything to everyone, especially in large class sizes. The labor of care, as established earlier, needs to be shared equitably, not equally (Sawyer III et al., 2024). This chapter's Care Kit considers strategies for ensuring equity through the distribution of teams, roles, and shared affinities within various courses and modalities. Embedded learning communities cultivate networks of care and support that extend beyond the teacher, providing opportunities for everyone in the environment to sustain interdependence depending on each person's capacity, cultural capital, and privilege. These approaches deepen students' sense of care and their learning, but they also drastically reduce instructional or identity-based labor, such as time spent on assessment or the burden of care falling on those who identify as women (Van Aalst, 2013).

Group Work *Does* Work

Almost every time I introduce a group project in one of my classes, students initially express frustration. Fascinated every time, I point out that they live highly social lives and yet would rather work alone. Invariably, they offer similar objections:

"I always get stuck doing all of the work."
"It's too difficult to agree on things."
"Coordinating group meetings is impossible."
"It's easier to make my own decisions."

It probably does not surprise anyone to hear college students voice frustration over group work assignments. Nonetheless, the importance of teamwork skills in the professional world is undeniable. The *Future of Jobs 2023* report from the World Economic Forum highlights the growing demand for social skills in the modern workforce, with creative thinking and curiosity identified as among the most highly valued competencies. Analytical thinking remains the top priority for employers, but the ability to approach problems innovatively and think outside conventional frameworks is increasingly essential. Creative thinking is viewed as crucial for adapting to technological advances and driving innovation, while curiosity underpins lifelong learning and adaptability, both necessary in a rapidly evolving job market. Recalling Chapter 3, curiosity entails care. Indeed, curiosity thrives when individuals care deeply about the subject they are exploring and when they connect with others who share similar interests. Caring-with others provides collective emotional investment that drives sustained inquiry; it transforms distal goals into proximal possibilities. When social groups value a subject, they are more likely to achieve their goals than they would in isolation. Moreover, curiosity often flourishes in social contexts where individuals exchange ideas with others who are equally passionate. These interactions can inspire new perspectives, validate the importance of exploring the topic, and create a supportive environment for shared discovery.

Social learning theories, such as SILT, highlight how collaboration and dialogue with others who share common interests enrich individual understanding and motivate continued engagement. For example, in educational settings, group discussions and collaborative projects often heighten curiosity because students care about contributing to their peers and learning from them. Similarly, in professional contexts, curiosity-driven innovation often emerges when teams with diverse expertise work together, building on each other's ideas and fostering a culture of mutual intellectual excitement.

Employers consistently express a desire for graduates with strong teamwork and interpersonal skills. In today's job market, the ability to collaborate effectively is more critical than ever. Employers are looking for individuals who can work well in teams, communicate across different departments, and contribute to the collective success of the organization. As indicated by the World Economic Forum (2023, May), employers rank teamwork as one of the most important skills they seek in new hires because most industries are shifting toward collaborative models of problem-solving, where complex tasks require input from diverse perspectives. Workplaces increasingly rely on teams to innovate, manage projects, and drive growth. Employers value employees who can navigate group dynamics, handle conflict constructively, and contribute to a positive work environment. Therefore, the skills developed in cooperative learning environments, such as active listening, mutual accountability, and empathy, align closely with the competencies needed in professional settings. More importantly, these skills are crucial in addressing larger societal issues: coalition and community-building skills present the only effective option for confronting systemic injustices, whether at the organizational, community, or even global levels.

Complaining about group work is counterintuitive, yes, but it is also a biological contradiction. Human societies have traditionally relied on collaboration as a primary means of problem-solving. Neuroscientific research reveals that humans are biologically hardwired for social connection. Our brains are designed to thrive in cooperative environments where social bonds are strong. According to research in social neuroscience, the brain's reward systems activate when we experience positive social interactions, such as collaboration, empathy, and care. Oxytocin, often called the "bonding hormone," is released during interactions that foster trust and connection, creating a sense of belonging and safety. Dopamine, a neurotransmitter that facilitates bonding, also activates feelings of reward and pleasure (Barrett, 2019). Our brains are hardwired for social interaction and cooperation, which has been essential for our survival and success as a species. This neural wiring suggests that we are biologically inclined toward working with others, as cooperative behavior benefits the group and the individual alike. From an evolutionary standpoint, societies that thrived historically were those that fostered cooperation and shared labor. Group work isn't just an academic exercise; it's a practice that mirrors how we tackle complex challenges, such as climate change, social inequality, and global health crises. Social psychologists emphasize that while group projects can feel cumbersome in educational settings, they do cultivate resilience, negotiation skills, and a deeper understanding of collective responsibility—competencies that are indispensable in an interdependent world (Raidal & Volet, 2009).

In *Relationship-Rich Education*, Felten and Lambert (2020) provide an excellently detailed roadmap for how to build upon student connections in ways that translate into college success. They emphasize that building strong connections is not just a matter of chance but something that can be intentionally designed into the fabric of higher education institutions. They highlight the role of faculty in mentoring, advising, and creating inclusive classrooms where students feel seen and supported. They also explore the importance of peer relationships and how institutions can create opportunities for students to connect with one another across different backgrounds and experiences. Felten and Lambert (2020) explain that interdependent classrooms require more than "simply having students talk with peers" (p. 91). Consider that many students have been socialized into what Derek Thompson (2025) calls "the anti-social century," in which rigid social structures have isolated and disconnected us from one another. When Thompson (2025) writes about the mid-century sociological shifts that contributed to disconnection, one could substitute "phone" for "television" and "social media" for "TV," and the following passage would be immediately relevant for our times:

> Starting in the second half of the century, Americans used their cars to move farther and farther away from one another, enabling the growth of the suburbs and, with it, a retreat into private backyard patios, private pools, a more private life. Once Americans got out of the car, they planted themselves in front of the television. From 1965 to 1995, the typical adult gained six hours a week in leisure time. They could have devoted that time—300 hours a year!—to community service, or pickup basketball, or reading, or knitting, or all four. Instead, they funneled almost all of this extra time into watching more TV.

The only outstanding difference would be the fact that, as we addressed in Chapter 2, in the past 20 years, the typical adult has lost significant leisure time. The ultimate point is that, as Felten and Lambert (2020) suggest, "faculty need to both design and communicate about constructive and meaningful peer interactions," facilitating group work as frequently as possible while also clearly modeling how to engage others and the value of doing so (91). This might include stipulating "well-defined, rotating roles so that all students are required to take (and relinquish) the initiative, that schedule time to develop group cohesion, and that assign complex and open-ended challenges that will require collaboration to address successfully" (p. 93). While planning these activities can frontload a lot of instructional labor, the payoff is worth it.

Michael Ben-Avie realized the payoff of frontloading a course with care. Michael is the Assistant Provost for Learning Assessment and Research at Quinnipiac University. Prior to this role, he was a lecturer in the Yale Child Study Center. As a researcher in youth development, he understands how humans develop through moments of caring-with, when others who believe in us as well as share the labor of caring-for support us through zones of proximal development. Michael teaches undergraduate courses that require students to learn basic principles of coding and communication within information systems. He grew disheartened that so many of his students, in his words, "did not want to be there."

He decided to make a root-level change. Michael flipped the order of the semester, beginning, rather than ending, with the final assignment, a blueprint for an app. With the new order, his students first reflected on social problems that could potentially be addressed with a new app. Then, they formed groups based on similarities in the social problems. He provided class time for students to cultivate a collective identity around the social problem, such as by sharing their relevant lived experiences. During this time, Michael clearly communicated the expectations and processes for collaborating as professionals. By the time they reached the actual course content, four weeks had passed. Echoing Cindy Kern's promise that beginning with community means faster progress in the long-run, something extraordinary, happened week 10 of Michael's redesigned course.

He knocked on the door of my office one afternoon, eyes radiant with excitement. "Can I show you something?" he asked, smiling in a way that prevented any answer that wasn't, "Of course."

I followed him down the hall as he explained that his class was currently meeting. "I'm not even in the room," he said, as if just realizing it.

When we reached the class, I witnessed students diligently working in small groups of two to three. Each student seemed so "in the zone" that they barely noticed our entrance. Some students sketched notes while others tapped away at their laptops. All along, the steady hum of conversation sustained a calm but intentional energy throughout the room. The only thing that broke their rhythm was when Michael introduced me to each group.

"Please tell my colleague what you are working on," he prompted one group.

The student tilted her laptop to show me a map of "vacant" or "occupied" bathrooms across campus. "It's pretty hard living on campus and having to wait in line for the showers every day," she said. She demonstrated how the map collects data to provide users with peak usage times and "most likely available" times. "This will help students better time their bathroom needs."

Then Michael introduced me to another group.

"This app develops personalized study plans based on your daily schedule," the group representative explained. "We all," pointing to the students in the group, "struggle with attention deficit hyperactivity disorder (ADHD), so having something help us stick to a plan would be amazing."

Each group led with their caring-with, either shared experiences or shared interests in solving particular problems. The vehicle for accomplishing these collective goals: the course content, which could only serve as a vehicle if the interdependent pathways are first created.

"My biggest challenge at this point of the semester," Michael said, "is figuring out how to stay out of their way."

We both agreed: that's a great challenge to have. When students take ownership of their learning, learning feels autonomous.

Felten et al. (2023) created a student-friendly sequel to *Relationship-Rich Education*. Designed as a practical guide for students, *Connections Are Everything* translates the scholarship of relationship-rich education for students, emphasizing that college success isn't solely dependent on taking the right classes or pursuing the most marketable major. The irreplaceable value of college, according the Felten et al. (2023), depends on building strong personal and academic connections. The authors present strategies that students can use to cultivate these relationships, including seeking out mentors, participating in extracurricular activities, and engaging with diverse communities on campus. It also addresses the barriers that marginalized students may face in building such connections and provides insights into how institutions can support inclusive relationship-building practices. Felten et al. (2023) advocate for students to be proactive in forming meaningful connections, as these relationships can enhance academic motivation, personal development, and career preparation. They illustrate their points with stories of real students, highlighting the transformative effects of human connections in higher education. Both books convey the message that human connection is fundamental to the college experience, and they advocate for students and institutions alike to prioritize relationships as a pathway to academic success and personal growth.

For the most part, group work falls apart when students do not first have the chance to form the social bonds that cohere into groups. In my experience as an early educator, I frequently assigned students into groups and then immediately dove into their task. When I observed less than positive group dynamics, I switched the method to allow students to choose their own groups, thinking the freedom to choose along with the comfort of knowing at least one or two group members would enhance the experience. Still, I ran into the common outcome of some members doing all the work while other members completely disengaged. What I did not realize was that I needed to *teach* students how to function as part of a group. Famed educator James Lang (2022) made the strong claim:

> [I]f you are assigning and grading group projects and: (a) not giving your students any explicit guidance or resources for how to work together effectively, and (b) not checking in and intervening when groups show signs of dysfunction, then you are engaging in pedagogical malpractice.

Social connection needs to be an explicit instructional outcome. A lack of belonging can lead to social anxiety, disengagement, and even academic failure (Allen et al., 2021). Much of what we teach is social—the ironically named "soft skills," even though they are often the most difficult skills to practice. Students need guidance cultivating a sense of belonging as well as playing a part in maintaining an environment that promotes belonging of others. As we will see below, studies suggest that modeling social connection by explicitly guiding students through a process of forming social bonds, fostering consensus, exchanging role responsibilities, and holding one another accountable can significantly enhance learning outcomes.

When Disconnection Is the Norm

Technically, we all need help connecting with one another. The difficulty of connecting in a new social environment depends once again on the "generous authority" of an effective host (Parker, 2020, p. 81). Many traditionally aged students have not had the same social opportunities as previous generations. In *The Anxious Generation*, Jonathan Haidt (2024) argues that today's students, particularly those born after 1995 (Generation Z), are missing out on critical social experiences that are key to emotional and psychological development. Haidt (2024) correlates the rise of smartphones and social media, combined with overprotective parenting, with alarming outcomes particular to Generation Z, such as increased anxiety, depression, and social isolation. According to Haidt's (2024) argument, instead of engaging in face-to-face interactions, young people spend more time online, where their social experiences are often shallow, mediated by screens, and dominated by social comparison and cyberbullying.

This shift in how young people interact has reduced opportunities for them to develop essential social skills, like conflict resolution, emotional regulation, and empathy. Haidt (2024) emphasizes that students are missing out on the everyday challenges of social life, such as dealing with difficult situations or making new friends, because much of their socialization is now virtual. As a result, many young people struggle with real-life social interactions, contributing to a rise in mental health issues like anxiety and depression. As he has done in this book and others (see Lukianoff & Haidt, 2019), Haidt (2024) suggests that American parents in particular act overly protective when it comes to in-person interaction, preventing, for example, children from playing outside with other children, while encouraging risky behavior, like interacting online without supervision under the misguided belief that online is safer than in-person. Haidt's (2024) analysis highlights the urgent need for educators and parents to encourage more in-person, unstructured social experiences to help students learn how to care for one another in real time, sustaining connections that benefit their intellectual and social development.

Just before the 2024 election, a college faculty member requested a consultation with me to reflect on a particularly troublesome interaction between two students in her class. The faculty member, a journalism professor, had been facilitating a discussion on privacy rights. The discussion centered around a recent case in which the elected president of a student organization had been exposed, via a student-run newspaper, as transgender. The professor wanted students to debate whether a violation of privacy had been committed by the newspaper. One student in the class spoke at length about the needs to protect the privacy of especially vulnerable populations, suggesting that laws ensuring privacy should consider context as opposed to blanket applications. While this student spoke, another student packed up their things and stormed out of the classroom.

The professor scheduled a one-on-one with the student, during which the student shared that they had felt so offended by the fact that someone would "defend a trans person" that they had to leave before "saying something that could get me in trouble." As the professor learned that classroom discussion presented the first time in the student's life that they heard a perspective in defense of trans people. Consistent with current research, the fact that many students primarily interact online can often mean they are only exposed to perspectives they already maintain, creating a closed information circuit that limits, if not eliminates, their exposure to challenging or contradictory ideas (Metzger et al., 2015). This reality dramatically emphasizes the difficulty students might have interacting with others, but it also explicitly demands that teachers teach care and connection, especially across different identities, viewpoints, and backgrounds.

To better understand the challenges and opportunities of helping students learn to connect with one another, Jean Twenge et al.'s (2012) research on Generation Z is especially enlightening. In her studies, Twenge finds that Gen Z, those born after 1995, are far less likely to engage in typical adolescent social activities, such as going out with friends, dating, and even having sex. She attributes much of this shift to the rise of smartphones and social media, which have replaced face-to-face interactions with virtual ones. Twenge's (2012) research shows that Gen Z spends far more time alone, interacting through screens rather than in-person. This trend has led to fewer opportunities for building deep, personal relationships and social skills. Interestingly, the decline in sexual activity is part of this broader pattern of reduced social engagement. Twenge suggests that this lack of physical and emotional closeness may stem from both increased screen time and a greater focus on safety and risk-avoidance behaviors, such as delaying driving and drinking alcohol. Overall, Twenge's findings indicate that Generation Z's social life is more isolated and less experiential, which gives even more reason to explicitly teach students how to maintain healthy group dynamics.

Whether in-person or online, college teachers must prioritize teaching students how to interact meaningfully with one another. The urgency of this task has grown in light of the COVID-19 pandemic and the rise of social media, both of which have stunted students' social development. More and more students are entering college without having had the opportunity to practice the nuanced social interactions that are essential in academic and professional environments. Furthermore, social interaction is highly contextual; how engineers communicate with their peers is vastly different from how artists exchange ideas. This means teachers must also help students understand the social norms of their particular fields. For instance, many faculty from across disciplines have consulted with me because they want to utilize more effective peer review. In their view, students do not provide useful feedback to one another when reviewing each other's work. Many faculty want their students to analyze, critique, and interrogate the work of others, pointing out flaws in composition and gaps in logic. One faculty member even posed the question, "How do I get them to stop being so nice?"

Given the fact that many young students spend the majority of their time in online environments, which tend to be more aggressive and negative than in-person environments, this question feels somewhat ironic. Research shows that social media, where negative content tends to go viral more often than positive, encourages a culture of meanness (Hari, 2018). Studies have found that Twitter posts designed to provoke anger or outrage are more likely to spread, and Facebook users are more likely to share derogatory posts about those they politically disagree with than complimentary ones about allies (Rathje & van der Linden, 2023). This cultural shift reveals a troubling binary: on the one hand, faculty cringe at the niceties that pervade the margins of student work in peer review sessions, while on the other hand, the same faculty are horrified by the hostility that pervades online discourse. The two extremes—excessive politeness in peer review and aggressive hostility online—highlight the difficulty of finding a balance between constructive critique and destructive communication.

Given these realities, educators are left to grapple with the question of how to engage students when they have learned throughout their lives to disengage. Online learning, in particular, amplifies this challenge, as the digital space can make it harder to build the empathy and trust that are essential for meaningful learning. Although we know that community and relationship building enhance personal instruction, the impersonal nature of online settings makes this difficult. Without the ability to feel, sense, or connect with one another as fully human, empathy becomes harder to cultivate. This raises critical questions: How do we create a sense of community in physically disconnected spaces? And as online learning continues to expand, how can educators foster genuine connection and belonging among their students despite the physical and emotional distances?

Teaching Connection

Translating SILT into practice is not the daunting task it once was, thanks to the emergence of several helpful strategies. Cooperative learning is a well-researched instructional strategy in which students work in small groups to achieve shared learning goals. Cooperative learning in higher education emphasizes structured collaboration among students to achieve shared academic goals. Central to this approach is positive interdependence, where students rely on each other to succeed, often through complementary roles or tasks that require collective effort. For example, one student might research a topic while another synthesizes findings, ensuring that all contributions are essential for group success. At the same time, individual accountability ensures that each member is responsible for their portion of the work and their understanding of the material, which might be assessed through individual quizzes or reflective submissions. Equally important is group processing, where students regularly reflect on their teamwork, discussing what went well and identifying areas for improvement. This reflection fosters growth in collaboration skills and strengthens group dynamics. Finally, face-to-face promotive interaction requires students to engage directly with one another, sharing resources, supporting ideas, and offering constructive feedback, creating a supportive environment that enhances learning outcomes. Together, these elements ensure that cooperative learning is both academically rigorous and personally enriching.

In my research methods course, I designed a cooperative learning project centered around creating a mini-research proposal. I divided the class into small groups of four and assigned each member a specific role: the literature reviewer, the data analyst, the project manager, and the presenter. Each role was crucial to the success of the group, ensuring positive interdependence. For example, the literature reviewer gathered relevant studies to frame the research question, while the data analyst focused on identifying appropriate methods for collecting and analyzing data.

To promote individual accountability, I required each student to submit a reflection on their role and how it contributed to the group's overall progress. Additionally, I conducted a short quiz at the end of the project that tested their understanding of all aspects of the proposal, not just their specific role. This ensured that each student engaged with the entire research process.

Throughout the project, I facilitated group processing by incorporating regular check-ins where students reflected on their collaboration. These sessions often revealed insightful strategies for improving teamwork, such as redistributing tasks when one member fell behind or refining communication channels. During class time, I also encouraged face-to-face promotive interaction by having groups meet in-person to work on their projects, share resources, and give one another feedback in real time.

The final presentations were a highlight. Each group shared their proposal, and every member participated in the presentation. Not only were the proposals thoughtful and creative, but the students also demonstrated a deeper understanding of the research process. More importantly, I observed a sense of pride and ownership in their work, along with stronger connections among classmates. It was rewarding to see the principles of cooperative learning come to life in such a meaningful way.

Collaborative grading takes this concept further by involving students in the assessment process, promoting shared responsibility and reflection. Students often engage in peer review or group-based evaluations, which fosters a deeper understanding of course content and the assessment criteria. Drawing upon SILT, collaborative grading suggests that learning is enhanced when students see their success as intertwined with that of their peers. This interdependence encourages students to care for one another, as they assess themselves in relation to the peers with whom they collaborate in order to achieve group success.

In my current scholarship, my colleagues and I investigate student perceptions on various grading systems. By comparing methods like labor-based grading, ungrading, specs-based grading, and collaborative grading, we ask which methods of grading create a sense of equity and fairness. By far, our data suggest that students are more likely to endorse a grading system in which they had a say. Collaborative grading allows students to share responsibility for assessing their learning, fostering a sense of ownership and transparency in the grading process. One approach is involving students in co-creating rubrics, where they discuss and define the standards for assignments, clarifying what constitutes exemplary work. For example, in a writing-intensive course, students might collaboratively decide that an A paper must include a clear thesis, well-supported arguments, and polished prose, while also agreeing on acceptable levels of grammatical leniency. Another strategy is self-evaluation, where students reflect on their work using a rubric and assign themselves a preliminary grade, encouraging them to critically assess their strengths and areas for growth. Peer evaluation is also effective, as students provide feedback to one another on drafts or projects, often resulting in higher-quality submissions and a stronger understanding of grading criteria. To maintain consistency, the instructor can guide these processes and offer final oversight, ensuring fairness while honoring students' input.

Establishing clear group norms is essential for fostering effective collaboration in higher education settings. Setting expectations around respect, active listening, and shared responsibility creates a foundation for productive teamwork. Collaboratively developing these norms with students can enhance their buy-in and accountability, as they are more likely to adhere to guidelines they have helped create. This collaborative approach not only sets the tone for group dynamics but also empowers students to take ownership of their interactions.

Assigning specific roles within groups, such as facilitator, note-taker, or timekeeper, ensures that every student has a meaningful responsibility and that tasks are distributed equitably. These roles provide structure to group activities and help mitigate imbalances in participation. Rotating roles throughout the course further supports skill development and encourages students to engage with different aspects of collaborative work, fostering a sense of fairness and inclusivity.

Fostering positive interdependence is another key element of successful group work. Activities should be structured so that students rely on one another to achieve their goals, requiring each member to contribute unique knowledge or skills. This approach ensures that everyone plays an integral role in the learning process, promoting collaboration and mutual support. Regular reflective dialogue is critical for maintaining healthy group dynamics. Check-ins and reflections allow students to discuss how their group is functioning, whether members feel supported, and how the group can improve. These conversations build self-awareness and emotional intelligence, equipping students with the tools to navigate interpersonal challenges and enhance their teamwork.

Providing training in peer feedback equips students to offer and receive constructive, developmental input. By modeling and practicing this skill, instructors can reduce the anxiety often associated with peer review and ensure that feedback is both supportive and actionable. Effective feedback processes help students view critique as an opportunity for growth rather than as criticism. Creating a safe emotional climate further strengthens group collaboration. Building trust through icebreakers, sharing personal experiences, and normalizing mistakes as part of the learning process encourages students to be open and vulnerable. When students feel safe to express their ideas and emotions, they are more likely to take intellectual risks and engage deeply with the material.

Incorporating collaborative assessment, such as peer and self-evaluation, fosters accountability and self-regulation. By reflecting on their contributions and those of their peers, students develop a greater awareness of how their actions impact group dynamics and outcomes, cultivating caring-with as a shared process for learning.

Care Kit: Cultivate a Learning Community

For the remedy, I will provide a "workshop" approach for guiding individuals into an interdependent community. I usually employ a variation of this approach for single sessions or checkpoints. For the root, I will describe a multi-step strategy that helped organize a learning environment into student communities that can be sustained over multiple meetings.

Remedy

The "PowerPoint Improv" activity provides an exciting way for educators to simulate high-stakes environments where students must work under pressure, think critically, and rely on each other's support. It's an excellent method for building resilience in the classroom, helping students develop 21st-century skills while fostering a caring, supportive learning environment. By using humor and unexpected challenges, this method helps students become adaptable, creative, and resilient in navigating unforeseen challenges, which is an essential skill for the modern world.

Instructors can create an environment that invites students to embrace risk-taking and failure by incorporating high expectations and providing opportunities for students to make mistakes and learn from them. A key aspect of this is ensuring that the learning space is caring and supportive. Just like in the "PowerPoint Improv" activity, where students pitch a topic without knowing the content of the slides, the classroom can be a space where students take on unexpected challenges and practice resilience. By doing so, students will gain the confidence to handle curveballs and adapt to changing circumstances, which is an important skill both in and outside the classroom.

In "PowerPoint Improv," students are placed into teams where they rely on each other for feedback and creative problem-solving. As they work together to meet the non-negotiable goals of their pitch—despite the randomness of the PowerPoint slides—they develop teamwork skills and learn how to support one another. By fostering an environment where collaboration is key, instructors can help students navigate uncertainty and build resilience. Teachers can replicate this method by having students work together on spontaneous tasks or simulations, offering feedback that encourages creativity and critical thinking, rather than rigidly scripted assignments.

The "PowerPoint Improv" activity invites students to reflect critically on their presentations, considering what they could have done differently and where they demonstrated care, vulnerability, and risk-taking. These reflections help students develop an awareness of their own decision-making processes and learn how to adjust their thinking in real time. Teachers can adapt this by creating activities that push students to think on their feet, requiring them to make quick decisions based on limited information. These activities can be tailored to any course content and can support a wide range of student outcomes, including enhancing communication skills, flexibility in thought, and the ability to engage in critical self-reflection.

One of the most critical components of "PowerPoint Improv" is the emphasis on risk-taking. By creating an environment where students are encouraged to take risks—knowing they have the support of their peers—they learn that mistakes are not failures but opportunities for growth. The underlying premise is that the higher the risk, the more care needs to be present in the environment. Educators can adopt this strategy by acknowledging that taking risks is an essential part of learning and supporting students when they venture outside their comfort zones. Care, in this context, means offering support without judgment, assuming the best intentions, and believing in each student's ability to succeed, regardless of the outcome.

Instructors who embrace this method must be open to the unexpected, allowing room for creativity and spontaneous challenges. Like the curveballs thrown in "PowerPoint Improv," educators should be ready to adapt their teaching strategies and support students as they navigate these unpredictable moments. This flexibility in teaching can create a dynamic and engaging learning environment, one in which students feel empowered to think critically and adapt to new challenges.

Ultimately, the "PowerPoint Improv" activity is more than just a fun classroom game; it's a way to prepare students for the complexities of modern life. It cultivates essential 21st-century skills such as adaptability, teamwork, critical thinking, and creativity—all within the framework of care and support. Educators can replicate this type of activity in their own classrooms, creating explicit opportunities for students to develop these skills while building resilience through care. By making space for risk-taking and team collaboration, teachers provide students with the tools they need to succeed in an unpredictable world.

Root

First, determine a grouping strategy that has symbolic import without being too explicitly connected to the course content. Because I am an avid lover of *Avatar the Last Airbender*, I draw my inspiration from the series. Other possibilities include replicating *Harry Potter's* sorting hat or athletic teams.

Due to cognitive biases, humans tend to group with others with whom they feel some familiarity. Maybe they already know the others in the group or maybe they share some identity marker, like race or gender. To disrupt this tendency, symbolic interpretations can help.

I read for students an explanation of the elements provided by an important character in the series—Uncle Iroh—in an episode titled "Bitter Work" (Nickelodeon, 2006). A paraphrase of the explanation goes something like:

Fire

Fire is the element of power, representing the Fire Nation's desire, will, energy, and drive.

Earth

Earth is the element of substance, representing the Earth Kingdom's diversity, strength, persistence, and endurance.

Air

Air is the element of freedom, representing the Air Nomads' detachment from worldly concerns and their finding of peace and freedom. Air Nomads also have a great sense of humor.

Water

Water is the element of change, representing the Water Tribe's ability to adapt to many things and their deep sense of community and love.

Based on these explanations, I invite students to choose the element that best represents them at this moment in their life. (In truth, I assure them, we are multiple elements at once.) If online, I create breakout rooms with the elements as titles so that students can self-enroll. If in-person, I direct them to certain areas of the room. Students tend to equally distribute, since these groups are not inherently superior to one another. If a particular group needs additional members, I'll ask members from a more popular group to consider their second-best option.

Once we have group parity, I provide large flipchart paper if in-person or a visual design application like Padlet or DALL-E. I ask them to create a logo that represents their collective identity. I provide questions like:

- What do each of you bring to this group in the context of this class? In a writing class, they might mention favorite genres in which they are an "expert" or communication skills they bring as assets to the class.
- How can the logo symbolize your connections to one another? Students might share that water symbolizes their ability to "go with the flow" or that fire represents their "anger at climate injustice."

- How might the logo indicate the intersection of your individual goals, both within this class and beyond? Do they all share a fiery anger at climate injustice? Will they all promise one another to be easy-going and adaptive like a river? Or will they remain grounded like earth?

The goal is for them to introduce themselves in a directed activity that emphasizes interdependence. They might each have interest and expertise, but in the composition of a logo, they blur their individual boundaries as they imagine a collective identity.

Throughout the duration of the course, these groups function as a learning community. When I use this strategy, I even create groups in the learning management system that reflects the elements and ask them to sign up so that their group submissions honor their collective identities. They complete some projects together, meet together at certain moments to reflect on their progress in the class and share challenges, and develop a group support plan (e.g., if anyone is confused, a representative from the group will email the instructor). With the roots of interdependence, individual students are less likely to feel isolated in their learning. We develop some of Tronto's (1993) elements of care, notably attentiveness and responsibility. They become responsible for one another by learning how to check in with others, support others, and provide continuous feedback. At a macro level, I also commit to Tronto's elements by ensuring the class a portion of regular time to meet with their teams and check in with me, giving me the chance to help guide groups as they face emergent challenges. Best of all, this strategy creates systems of support that resemble more of a hub and spoke model of care, in which the labor of care becomes distributed throughout the class rather than positioning the teacher as the sole source of support.

With interdependent roots, we can finally introduce content as the context for the relational bonds to develop. With time and care, students will be more likely to extend their openness and curiosity to learn what we love to teach.

References

Allen, K. A., Slaten, C. D., Arslan, G., Roffey, S., Craig, H., & Vella-Brodrick, D. A. (2021). School belonging: The importance of student and teacher relationships. In *The Palgrave handbook of positive education* (pp. 525–550). Springer International Publishing.

Barrett, L. F. (2019). *How emotions are made*. Macmillan.

Berg, M., & Seeber, B. K. (2016). *The slow professor: Challenging the culture of speed in the academy*. University of Toronto Press.

Felten, P., & Lambert, L. M. (2020). *Relationship-rich education: How human connections drive success in college*. JHU Press.

Felten, P., Lambert, L. M., Artze-Vega, I., & Tapia, O. R. M. (2023). *Connections are everything: A college student's guide to relationship-rich education*. JHU Press.

Haidt, J. (2024). *The anxious generation: How the great rewiring of childhood is causing an epidemic of mental illness*. Random House.

Hari, J. (2018). *Lost connections: Uncovering the real causes of depression—and the unexpected solutions*. Bloomsbury Publishing.

Twenge, J. M., Campbell, W. K., & Freeman, E. C. (2012). Generational differences in young adults' life goals, concern for others, and civic orientation, 1966–2009. *Journal of personality and social psychology, 102*(5), 1045.

Johnson, D. W., & Johnson, R. T. (2009). An educational psychology success story: Social interdependence theory and cooperative learning. *Educational Researcher, 38*(5), 365–379.

Lang, J. (2022). Why students hate group projects (and how to change that). *Chronicle of Higher Education*. https://www.chronicle.com/article/why-students-hate-group-projects-and-how-to-change-that.

Lukianoff, G., & Haidt, J. (2019). *The coddling of the American mind: How good intentions and bad ideas are setting up a generation for failure*. Penguin.

Metzger, M. J., Flanagin, A. J., Markov, A., Grossman, R., & Bulger, M. (2015). Believing the unbelievable: Understanding young people's information literacy beliefs and practices in the United States. *Journal of Children and Media, 9*(3), 325–348.

Nickelodeon. (2006). *Bitter work* (Season 2, Episode 9) [TV series episode]. In M. DiMartino, & B. Konietzko (Creators), *Avatar: The last airbender*. Nickelodeon Animation Studio.

Parker, P. (2020). *The art of gathering: How we meet and why it matters*. Penguin.

Raidal, S. L., & Volet, S. E. (2009). Preclinical students' predispositions towards social forms of instruction and self-directed learning: A challenge for the development of autonomous and collaborative learners. *Higher Education, 57*, 577–596.

Rathje, S., & van der Linden, S. (2023). Shifting online incentive structures to reduce polarization and the spread of misinformation. In *Research handbook on nudges and society* (pp. 91–108). Edward Elgar Publishing.

Sawyer III, D. C., Torres, J. T., & Hudd, S. (Eds.). (2024). *How to incorporate equity and justice in your teaching*. Edward Elgar Publishing.

Thompson, D. (2025, February). The anti-social century. *The Atlantic*. https://www.theatlantic.com/magazine/archive/2025/02/american-loneliness-personality-politics/681091/.

Tronto, J. (1993). *Moral boundaries: A political argument for an ethic of care*. Routledge.

Twenge, J. M., Campbell, W. K., & Freeman, E. C. (2012). Generational differences in young adults' life goals, concern for others, and civic orientation, 1966–2009. *Journal of Personality and Social Psychology, 102*(5), 1045.

Van Aalst, J. (2013). Assessment in collaborative learning. In *The international handbook of collaborative learning* (pp. 280–296). Routledge.

World Economic Forum. (2023, May). Future of jobs 2023: Skills for the future. https://www.weforum.org/stories/2023/05/future-of-jobs-2023-skills/.

6
CARE BETWEEN STUDENTS AND CONTENT

Chapter Contents
How Can Teachers Design Classrooms Like *Ark*?	108
The Value of Play in Adult Learning	110
Playing With Content	112
Caring About and Situational Interest	113
Caring for and Self-Regulated Learning	114
Caring With Others	115
Play Entails Tricky Relationships	118
Care Kit: Adopt a Concept	120
References	122

A colleague of mine, Justin Peterson, has coordinated residence life at multiple institutions across the country. He designed and coordinated Living Learning Communities at Utah State University and Southern Maine University. A Living Learning Community (LLC) is a specialized residential program that integrates students' campus environments with their academic and personal interests to create sustained connections throughout the college experience. Each LLC is centered on a shared focus or theme, such as sustainability, leadership, STEM, the arts, global issues, or health and wellness. These communities are often tied to academic programs or interdisciplinary topics, providing students with opportunities to engage deeply with their interests outside the classroom. Justin directs programming tailored to a variety of community themes, including workshops, group projects, and events like guest lectures or field trips. Justin also coaches faculty and staff who serve as mentors or affiliates with LLCs. These collaborations

DOI: 10.4324/9781003591009-7

create a seamless connection between academic and residential life, fostering closer relationships rooted in care between students, their peers, and faculty.

At a macro-root level, LLCs operationalize the approach expressed in this book, fostering interdependent care centered on shared interests and experiences. Given the evidence in support of opportunities like an LLC (Felten & Lambert, 2020), I have been very interested in how such spaces have adapted to recent disruptions in higher education. I reached out to Justin in 2023 to inquire about how his programming, which had always prioritized in-person interaction, fared during the height of the COVID-19 pandemic in the United States. Rather than answering my question directly, he invited me to play an online video game with him.

Justin studies games, especially the influence they can have on socialization and community building. He has long told me that the history games have had not only on civilization, such as the use of games to develop military strategies (Clancy, 2024), but also on human development in the form of play (Huizinga, 1955). The video game, *Ark: Survival Ascended*, generally centers on trying to survive as a human in a prehistoric world. The publisher, Studio Wildcard (2024), provides an immersive summary:

> You awake on a mysterious island, your senses overwhelmed by the blinding sunlight and brilliant colors bouncing off every surface around you, the azure waters of a verdant Island lapping at your bare feet. A deep roar echoes from the misty jungle, jolting you into action, and you stand up—not afraid, but intrigued. Are you ready to form a tribe, tame and breed hundreds of species of dinosaurs and other primeval creatures, explore, craft, build, and fight your way to the top of the food-chain?

At the start of the game, you create an avatar and appear randomly in a lush landscape defined by towering mountains, dramatic rock formations, diverse vegetation, and glistening lakes and rivers. Your avatar starts with nothing more than a loin cloth, rock bottom of the proverbial food-chain. *Ark* utilized one of the steepest learning curves I had ever experienced. As a vulnerable human, everything from the weather to the flora and fauna can spell instant death. And I mean that literally. Early on, I was lucky if my avatar lasted 30 seconds without dying and having to start over—it was that brutal.

It is up to the player to make sure the avatar has access to food, water, clothes, and anything else that might contribute to a longer life. "The only way to survive," Justin explained over my Playstation 5 headset, "is to cooperate." The general goal of *Ark* is to work together with other human players to collect enough resources within an unforgiving environment in order to craft shelter from the resources. Cutting down a tree, for example, provides wood, which players can use to construct a house. For the most part, however, cutting down a tree exposed my avatar to aggressive dinosaurs also scavenging the land for resources.

"I can't even operate, let alone *co*operate," I said. "What does getting devoured by dinosaurs have to do with student connections during quarantine?"

"Keep playing," he said. I could almost hear him grin through the headset.

During the first ten minutes of playing *Ark*, my avatar died of heat exhaustion, a carnotaurus attack, hunger, an oviraptor attack, dehydration, an Allosaurus attack, and intoxication. Each time my avatar died, he respawned somewhere at random, which meant any time Justin's and my avatar finally found one another in the impressively large open world and ended up dying, we would start from scratch and have to relocate one another all over again. At one point, we had managed to gather enough thatch, wood, and fiber to construct a small hut. My sense of helplessness started to give way to a feeling of accomplishment. Never did Justin explicitly instruct me on how to play or what we should be doing, other than sticking together and not dying. To go from repeated failure to actually building a virtually livable structure from scratch felt pretty rewarding—especially since I am not an engineer nor even a crafty enough person to build a physically livable structure in real life. Just as I began to celebrate this emotional turn, a pack of oviraptors tore through the thatch walls and ended our avatars' run. What had taken almost an hour was undone in seconds.

"This is ridiculous," I complained, the frustration evident in my tone.

Justin laughed. Then he wanted to make two points. Justin's first point: even though the hut was destroyed, because we successfully built it, we had acquired the blueprint to rapidly build the next hut. In other words, because we successfully learned how to do something, the game rewarded us with the privilege of employing that skill more frequently and with much greater ease. The enhanced ability to build allowed us to cooperate in different ways. "Now," Justin added. "One of us can rebuild the hut while the other collects resources."

Justin's second point: technically, there is zero punishment for failing—when the avatar dies, they simply respawn. Sure, there is the inconvenience of having to relocate one another, but even that becomes easier once we established a more permanent hut, which eventually became a compound, and then a town for other human players to join, creating a community that felt organic and immersive. Soon, three other human players from around the world joined, pitching in to secure the town as we talked and got to know one another.

Throughout the experience playing *Ark*, I thought of all the students with whom I had worked who were terrified of making a single mistake. When I taught at a community college or as part of a bridge program serving students outside of the dominant norm, I frequently heard students express self-limiting beliefs. Each semester, students confessed to me that they "could not write," or that "reading is not something I've ever been good at." When I taught at a private liberal arts university with high selectivity rates, meaning they specifically admitted the dominant norm, I frequently heard students express anxiety over their academic performance. Each semester, students stressed that they "could not afford to mess up an assignment" or that "nothing I do will ever be good enough." At all levels of academic preparedness, a deep fear of failure defines the college experience.

Unfortunately, deep-rooted fears of failure condition the kinds of relationships students have with content. Some students avoid majors, programs, or courses if they perceive them to be too difficult (Martin et al., 2008). Some students associate entire disciplines with unpopular instructional experiences (e.g., "I wanted to major in Chemistry, but I hate taking tests") (Watkins & Mazur, 2013). This chapter will contribute to the Care Kit by providing a strategy for activating shared affinities as a method for connecting students with content. I will explain how all of the work teachers commit to creating a caring environment and socially supportive relationships between teachers and students, as well as between students, helps establish the foundation for engaging content. The previous chapters cultivate resilient relationships, and Chapter 6 directs those relationships toward the essential learning outcomes and material that students need to master.

How Can Teachers Design Classrooms Like *Ark*?

While many educational researchers extol the benefits of gamification, instructors do not need to turn every learning activity into a game. Instead, gamification offers a valuable reminder: immersing students into a structured and well-defined context—whether or not it includes explicit game elements—encourages them to care deeply about the work and the people within that context. The best way to explain how *Ark* works so well as an example of an interdependent classroom might be to consider Griffin and Butler's (2005) *Teaching Games for Understanding*. With their book, Griffin and Butler intend to provide a framework for how physical education instructors can better teach students how to participate in particular games. In the context of an interdependent classroom, I believe that their book also provides an argument for teaching students how to participate in content as if it were a particular game.

In the below passage, when Griffin and Butler (2005) define "game" as a concept, one could easily substitute the word "discipline" or "disciplinary" without distorting the passage's meaning:

> Games are governed by rules. Rules not only regulate game play, but also dictate or define the skills needed to play the game. We often consider only the regulatory function of rules, but rules do much more. . . . For example, specific rules define how to move the ball between players and how to shoot on goal. Thus, the rules of the game not only regulate play, court dimensions, ball size, and so on, but also dictate the skills needed to play the game . . . and the form the skills take within game contexts.
>
> *(p. 129)*

Just as basketball requires players to master dribbling—a skill that has an entirely different meaning and purpose in soccer—each discipline requires students to learn and apply distinct skills. For instance, biologists must master observation and hypothesis testing, while historians must navigate and analyze primary sources. Viewing disciplines as games helps instructors clarify these conventions for students, immersing them in the rules of the game so they can understand not only *what* to learn but also *how* to think and act within a particular domain.

Griffin and Butler (2005) encourage physical education instructors to teach students rules as routines, conditioning students to employ newly learned skills in different game contexts (e.g., dribbling a basketball versus dribbling a basketball while a defender tries to steal the ball), echoing much of the research on teaching for transfer (Perkins & Salomon, 2012). As stated in the well-known book, *How People Learn: Brain, Mind, Experience, and School*, students need multiple opportunities to practice skills in comparative contexts, helping them develop the ability to transfer their learning to novel situations (NRC, 2000). Research on enclothed cognition provides further support for teaching content as a game with clear rules: in one study, science students who wore lab coats demonstrated higher levels of self-efficacy than students who learned the same material without the identity cue of wearing a lab coat (Jones et al., 2019). The simple clothing rule created a meaningful context that encouraged students' confidence in themselves as scientists, which boosted their engagement and performance. Instructors can create similarly effective learning experiences by immersing students in the conventions and practices of a discipline, much like a game teaches players its conditions for success. Whether or not explicit gamification is used, teaching the rules and routines of a discipline can foster a sense of belonging and purpose.

Framing disciplines as games can also encourage students to collaborate and cooperate, just as team sports require players to work together under shared rules and objectives. Games simulate interdependence when students begin to view learning as a collective effort. In a biology lab, for example, when students discuss hypotheses before an experiment, they direct their care toward one another as they compose a hypothesis, but they also foster a collective care for the lab experience, developing an appreciation for the generation of scientific knowledge. These shared experiences cultivate a sense of community, reminding students that their success is tied not just to their own skills but also to their ability to work within a larger system.

Mikki Brock, a professor of History at Washington & Lee University, has spent her career designing college history courses as immersive games. In particular, she draws from Reacting to the Past (RTTP), a collaborative of educators who create role-playing experiences to learn about history. Because of her approach, Mikki is not too worried about recent disruptions like AI and increasingly disengaged students. "It seems to me that if students are using ChatGPT in ways that are deemed unethical by the parameters of the class, it's because they don't care about the assignment enough to do it themselves," Mikki told me over email from Wellesley University, where she completed her sabbatical research.

All of which is to say that in my dream world, I would run all of my classes as either literary salons or using RTTP-type projects that engage students. The magic ingredients in this dream world would be care and curiosity and confidence.

We can join Mikki's dream world by immersing students in the rules, practices, and identities that define their academic game. In adult learning environments, creating a classroom that feels like a space for play has increasingly been recognized as a significant factor in fostering engagement, creativity, and deeper learning (Van Leeuwen & Westwood, 2008). While the psychological study of play has been traditionally relegated to child development, play is also critical for healthy adult lives (Tonkin & Whitaker, 2016). By fostering a classroom atmosphere that encourages exploration, creativity, and risk-taking without fear of failure, instructors can create a space where students are more open to learning, willing to take intellectual risks, and able to collaborate more effectively with their peers.

The Value of Play in Adult Learning

Play remains a central component throughout the human journey. Johan Huizinga, in his classic work *Homo Ludens*, described play as a fundamental aspect of culture and society. According to Huizinga, play stretches beyond childhood in its ability to help adults reflect on their relationships and activities in relation to their social context. Huizinga (1955) offers a definition of play that closely resembles my rendering of an interdependent college classroom. Huizinga (1955) describes play as

> a free activity, experienced as make-believe and situated outside of everyday life, nevertheless capable of totally absorbing the player; an activity entirely lacking in material interest and in utility. It transpires in an explicitly circumscribed time and space, is carried out in an orderly fashion according to given rules, and gives rise to group relationships which often surround themselves with mystery or emphasize through disguises their difference from the ordinary world.
>
> *(p. 13)*

For adults, play offers a strategy for engaging in learning that feels intrinsically motivated and enjoyable. Many adult learning environments can easily become so task-oriented that they lose contextual value. Adults are experts at sniffing out busy work, leading to questions like, "Why is it important for me to learn or do *this*?" Once an experience is questioned, adults become skeptical and safeguard their limited cognitive resources, making learning more challenging. Reflecting back on Chapter 3, curiosity is not a given; it needs cultivation and activation. When curiosity is nurtured, however, rigor becomes flow (Nakamura & Csikszentmihalyi, 2009) and work becomes play.

In *Drive: the Surprising Truth About What Motivates Us*, *New York Times* best-selling author Daniel Pink (2011) succinctly differentiates between work and play: "Work consists of whatever a body is obliged to do. Play consists of whatever a body is not obliged to do" (p. 34). Everything else is interchangeable. Rather than viewing work and play as opposites, they differ only in the mindset the worker or player maintains in relation to the activity. The important distinction Pink (2011) emphasizes is that play, by definition, operates via intrinsic motivation rather than external demands, which can have a profound impact on how adults approach learning. Creating a classroom that feels like a space for play involves rethinking the traditional social order defining higher education. As stated throughout this book, the majority of students have been institutionalized to operate within the power structure of a top-down epistemology (i.e., the banking concept of education), in which teachers deliver knowledge to passive students. In contrast, an interdependent classroom encourages students to care about their learning and actively engage in co-constructing knowledge through interaction, experimentation, and collaboration. Bob Black (1986) offers a humorous take on Pink's work/play divide that directly challenges education's traditional social order. In "the Abolition of Work," Black (1986) highlights the oppressive nature of work when it is imposed: "What might otherwise be play is work if it's forced." Adult learners, in particular, often juggle multiple responsibilities—work, family, and other commitments—and may approach formal education with a sense of obligation rather than enthusiasm. If classroom activities feel like additional work, learners are less likely to engage deeply or enjoy the process. By contrast, when classroom activities are framed as play—voluntary, engaging, and intrinsically motivated—they can transform the learning experience.

Psychologist Stuart Brown, a leading researcher in adult play, notes that play is essential for the development of emotional regulation, creativity, and resilience (Brown & Vaughan, 2009). For adults, play provides a space where they can step outside of the rigid structures and expectations of work or other formal obligations and engage in activities that feel self-directed, creating a sense of autonomy in a world that otherwise feels rigidly structured by external forces. Both schools and corporations can easily institutionalize human activity to the point where everything feels like (busy) work. When rules and routines become the sole focus without any meaningful connection to context or purpose, both children and adults easily become disengaged. Compliance can easily overshadow, or even silence, creativity, as following orders can turn working and learning into tasks that ultimately preserve a social order. On the other hand, when learning is framed as a form of play, it opens up opportunities for playful disruption. Encouraging students to own the learning experience means encouraging them to take risks, explore possible perspectives, make decisions, and consider novel conclusions without worrying about being a "threat to the existing order" (Brown & Vaughan, 2009, p. 139). Thus, it is not enough to simply gamify a classroom and expect the rules and routines of an activity to automatically become meaningful. Students need explicit guidance in both participating in play and critically thinking about the learning associated with play (Rashid & Qaisar, 2017). John Dewey, a prominent figure in educational philosophy, argued that play enables learners to engage more fully with their environment only when play is paired with reflection. Dewey (2024) also differentiates play from work by emphasizing the necessity of reflection:

> In play, the interest is more direct—a fact frequently indicated by saying that in play the activity is its own end, instead of its having an ulterior result. The statement is correct, but it is falsely taken, if supposed to mean that play activity is momentary, having no element of looking ahead and none of pursuit. Hunting, for example, is one of the commonest forms of adult play, but the existence of foresight and the direction of present activity by what one is watching for are obvious. When an activity is its own end in the sense that the action of the moment is complete in itself, it is purely physical; it has no meaning. The person is either going through motions quite blindly, perhaps purely imitatively, or else is in a state of excitement which is exhausting to mind and nerves. Both results may be seen in some types of kindergarten games where the idea of play is so highly symbolic that only the adult is conscious of it. Unless the children succeed in reading in some quite different idea of their own, they move about either as if in a hypnotic daze, or they respond to a direct excitation.
>
> (p. 92)

The idea that learning should feel playful aligns with broader theories of social interdependence. Play, in this context, encourages collaboration, dialogue, and the exchange of ideas among peers. In an interdependent classroom, activities that simulate play, such as role-playing, gamification, or problem-based learning, can make complex concepts more accessible and create a sense of shared discovery among students.

Playing With Content

Play can take many forms in adult learning environments. In the attempt to distill theories and scholarship of play into pedagogical strategies, I will focus on two salient features: (1) play motivates students by fostering interdependent care and (2) play contextualizes the rules and routines of a situated activity (e.g., a game). Stated simply, play inspires, and play clarifies. Instructors can incorporate game-like elements—such as points and rewards—or design entire courses around frameworks such as project-based learning (PBL), which encourages students to work collaboratively on complex, real-world problems. The overall goal is to maintain an environment in which students can experiment, take risks, think creatively, reflect on processes and ideas, and engage with content in imaginative and innovative ways. Driven by play, an interdependent classroom normalizes failure by encouraging novelty and maintaining belonging so that all students feel connected and supported. Creating a playful classroom environment involves giving students a sense of autonomy and choice in their learning. When learners have control over what they are doing, they are more likely to approach it with enthusiasm and curiosity. This autonomy can be fostered by allowing students to choose their own projects, collaborate on designing assessments, or take the lead in classroom discussions. In this way, the classroom becomes a space where learning is not only meaningful but also joyful.

The two salient features drawn from theory on which I will focus below align with two evidence-based practices in adult learning: (1) Play motivates students by activating situational interest, and play connects us with others who share in our situational interest and (2) play contextualizes and clarifies rules, routines, and processes by promoting self-regulated learning. Caring-about/for/with provides a powerful lens for understanding how instructors can cultivate situational interest and self-regulated learning in college students. Both situational interest and self-regulated learning hinge on emotional and cognitive engagement, which can be nurtured through intentional strategies rooted in care.

Caring About and Situational Interest

In Chapter 1, I reviewed Nel Noddings' framework of caring-about. As a quick refresher, caring-about signifies one's attention to relational needs. When we care about someone or something, we spend a lot of time thinking about that person or thing, considering how we might deepen our connections. When we become engrossed, care takes root in our hearts. Noddings (2013) asserts that foundationally "all caring involves engrossment" (p. 17). She describes engrossment as the palpable presence of a caring person, one who is aware of a need for care and attentive to those needs. When I meet with a student or instructor who shares a story of a challenging experience with me, I can almost feel the world beyond the storytelling individual wash away. The office walls fade into an indistinguishable blur. The whir of campus commotion vanishes so that the only thing I can hear is the storyteller's voice. It is like the individual speaking to me becomes the only being in existence. I become engrossed. Similarly, when I care about an issue, such as climate justice, I can get lost in a rabbit-hole of engrossment that lasts days, weeks, or even months, during which I consume everything from climate fiction films to recently published studies and reports from climate scientists and panels. Noddings' use of engrossment, especially as it forms the foundation for caring-about, intersects with educational research on situational interest.

Different from individual interests, which refer to interests that remain somewhat stable from context to context—a student athlete probably remains interested in athletics regardless of the situation—situational interest depends on context, emerging within particular moments of curiosity or fascination. Researchers define situational interest as socially situated due to the social and relational factors that induce engrossment (Schraw et al., 2001). While a student athlete might remain interested in athletics across contexts, they might become momentarily fascinated by a discussion in a history class because of their teacher's enthusiasm or approachability, two of the strongest predictors of activating students' situational interest (Quinlan, 2019).

Despite the term's implication that this form of interest is ephemeral in nature, research suggests that situational interest can act as an entry point to deeper, sustained engagement. In Noddings' terms, caring-about, and in particular engrossment, is foundational to activating situational interest because it involves instructors helping students make meaningful connections between course content and their preexisting passions or curiosities. For example, when a student who cares deeply about sports is tasked with analyzing rhetorical appeals through sports commentary, they experience situational interest because the content feels relevant to their world. This relevance creates an emotional hook that heightens curiosity, attention, and engagement. As students deepen their understanding of rhetorical appeals in the context of sports, they can then learn to transfer this knowledge to new contexts, such as analyzing political speeches. This transfer expands their capacity for caring-about into new domains, fostering a more generalized interest in the subject matter.

Situational interest is often triggered by novelty, relevance, or emotional connection and can evolve into individual interest when students repeatedly see the value and application of their learning in diverse contexts. Instructors play a crucial role here by designing assignments and learning experiences that align with students' existing passions, thereby helping move students from concern (caring-about) to action (caring-for).

Caring for and Self-Regulated Learning

While caring-about focuses on sparking interest, caring-for involves ongoing, relational support to nurture that interest and guide students in managing their learning processes. Building on the discussion on Noddings in Chapter 1, caring-for signifies the actions taken to address the needs of a cared-for subject. Caring-for differs from caring-about when concern turns to practice, becoming what Judith Butler (2020) calls a "force" (p. 12). In the context of education, when students care-about a subject, they are interested in learning more about the subject, or they desire to know how they can address the needs related to the subject. When students care-for a subject, they actively practice and engage in the subject, taking ownership of their learning.

Self-regulated learning refers to a learner's active management of their cognitive, emotional, and behavioral processes to achieve personal learning goals. It involves setting clear objectives, monitoring progress, and adapting strategies based on instructor feedback and guidance. In my scholarship, I have argued to consider self-regulation as inherently collective, as these processes are relational and depend on positive student-teacher relationships (Torres, 2022). While traditional self-regulated learning emphasizes individual goal-setting, monitoring, and adapting strategies, these processes require interactions with peers, instructors, and the broader social environment. Co-regulation highlights how learners draw on external guidance, feedback, and collaboration to develop and refine their self-regulatory skills (Hadwin et al., 2011). Learning is not an isolated act but a shared experience where individuals engage in dialogue, model strategies, and provide mutual support. By framing self-regulated learning as an interdependent practice, we recognize the essential role of relationships in fostering metacognitive awareness, sustaining motivation, and building the capacity to adapt and grow in diverse learning contexts. In other words, we learn to care-for ourselves, our world, and the diverse others who shape our world and ourselves.

From the perspective of educational researchers, students thrive when they perceive themselves as agents of their own education. This agency can be cultivated through scaffolding that balances autonomy with support—guiding students to apply their interests while providing tools to manage challenges. When students learn to care for their own learning, they are better able to adapt to new contexts, persevere through difficulties, and internalize a sense of responsibility for their academic growth.

Caring With Others

Caring-with brings together these concepts into an interdependent classroom. By first fostering situational interest through caring about, instructors create a foundation of engagement. Then, by caring-for students—providing personalized feedback, modeling reflective practices, and encouraging adaptive learning strategies—instructors help students sustain that interest and apply it in new ways.

Sustaining situational interest via self-regulated learning depends on interdependent processes that connects the new context/content with students' prior knowledge and experience. This process is often referred to as perceived relevance. In my work developing general education programs, I am always heartbroken when I hear from students that their required, general education courses are irrelevant, especially when they do not pertain to their major. I always have to remind myself: this mindset is not their fault. We taught them to only care about their own specific individual needs, however myopic, and check off boxes on the way to their linear life goals. When I evaluate general education programs across the country, I find that students are often disengaged in large lecture-based first-year classes. Remembering the spark that inspired each of us to become a teacher, I always ask how we can create moments for students to have their own spark, how we can become less like bankers of information and more like "architects of task design" (Griffin & Butler, 2005, p. 134). In order to immerse students in content in ways that activate interest and ownership of the learning process, students need to perceive the content as relevant.

Fedesco et al. (2017) found that simply altering course assignments can positively impact student perceptions and motivation for participating in introductory courses. In their study, assignments contextualized public speaking content within contexts that mattered to students. They chose topics about which to formulate speeches and they utilized their speeches in other courses as well as with authentic audiences. Such assignment alterations preclude the ill-fated perception that "I will never use content outside of this course." Perceived relevance is an instructional strategy that turns "just in case" learning into "just in time" learning.

Whether students perceive something as relevant or not depends on culture. For far too long, classrooms have been monocultures that favor Western middle-class white ideologies (hooks, 2000). As facilitators, we must work to ensure learning environments welcome and center multiple cultural identities, giving everyone a chance to establish relational relevance with content. Gloria Ladson-Billings (1995) provides three propositions for encouraging such facilitation: (1) Teachers and students share in the learning process, which requires understanding of one another's social and cultural histories up to and beyond the learning encounter; (2) relationships are fluid, always in process, and interdependent on one another; the more diverse a community, the healthier the relationships; and (3) knowledge is also fluid, always in process, and shaped by those within the learning community. Connecting caring-for (situational interest) and caring-about (self-regulated learning) with perceived relevance helps address one of the biggest challenges to learning: cognitive load.

Learning requires a lot of cognitive resources. A student's cognitive capacity must also take into account relatively challenging processes like navigating a learning management system, interpreting class notes, recalling information, or making sense of assignment instructions. By the time students get to think meaningfully about content, they are often cognitively exhausted. In our everyday lives, we can probably reflect on several occasions during which we experience cognitive load. Let's say I order a bookshelf with the intent of building one for the first time. The bookshelf arrives and the instructions are so poorly written that I spend an hour just trying to figure out what the arrows are pointing to and whether I have all the right pieces. After this hour, I probably feel a bit overwhelmed and defeated and question whether I should have majored in something more tangible, like carpentry, over learning theory. Also after this hour of scanning confusing instructions and tallying foreign pieces, I did not enjoy any sense of "development," a feeling that

I was getting better at bookshelf building. I didn't learn anything that I can transfer to new situations, unless installation instructions are standardized—which they aren't. This is extraneous load, the demands on cognition that do not directly correlate with the learning task (Sweller, 2011). Struggling with extraneous load is more likely to result in learned helplessness, burnout, or disengagement.

At some point, I start assembling the bookshelf for the first time. I focus on leveling the shelves, marking for nails, building from the foundation, etc. I am not only building *this* bookshelf, but I am also building a schema for building bookshelves in general, what is called germane load (Sweller, 2011). Germane load is probably more cognitively taxing than interpreting instructions, but it is permanent, useful, and develops our ability to think about similar situations (maybe I apply this learning to building a coffee table next). Struggling with germane load is more likely to induce a feeling of flow, self-efficacy, and self-regulation (Nakamura & Csikszentmihalyi, 2009). Germane load tends to be the kind of struggle we want for our students. However, since working memory is a very limited resource, we should always think about how we are cognitively "loading" students. Here is what we know from current research: the more we eliminate extraneous load, more we can ask of germane load.

One fascinating feature of *Ark* is that, despite my initial frustration playing with Justin, the game was designed to teach me how to survive, even as it kept trying to kill my avatar. This is an amazing feat that can feel counterintuitive to the design of a game. By nature, video games want to be a challenge, but not so much of a challenge that players give up and stop playing.

Frustration in video games can actually play a key role in keeping players engaged, as it often motivates them to push through challenges. Some games deliberately frustrate players to evoke a sense of revenge or determination, which can lead to greater satisfaction when the challenge is overcome. In fact, measuring frustration—rather than just the absence of satisfaction—can offer valuable insights, especially in games designed to be transformative or thought-provoking (Kosa & Uysal, 2022). These types of games may include intentional frustrations in their mechanics or storytelling to shift players' perspectives or inspire personal growth. Interestingly, many players enjoy emotional challenges in games alongside traditional tests of skill or strategy. However, frustration isn't always beneficial. Research shows that in cases where players do not have a passion for games (i.e., they do not care much about games), frustration can lower confidence and hurt their loyalty to a game (Mills et al., 2018). In games that are played frequently, excessive frustration can become demotivating, leading players to quit altogether. For game designers, understanding frustration is a powerful tool. It helps them identify areas where players may have negative experiences and adjust their games accordingly. For researchers, studying frustration offers a way to explore both the challenges and rewards of gaming. Developers strike a very delicate balance between keeping players at a threshold of difficulty that is both frustrating and pleasurable.

That balance depends on how much the player cares about the game context. In the case of *Ark*, the context of trying to live and survive as a fragile human in a prehistoric world populated by realistic dinosaurs not only justifies the frustration but also contextualizes the frustration. I cannot recount how many times Justin remarked, "Well, this is what it would actually be like to try to build a home where dinosaurs roam." Drawing from renowned game designer Raph Koster, Stuart (2013) explains how game design choices have to both teach and challenge players in ways very similar to course or curriculum designers. "Pacing and variation are the necessary components in a compelling experience that doesn't frustrate," Stuart says.

> The human brain enjoys learning patterns, but if it finds the process too easy or too hard, it quickly becomes bored. And boredom leads to frustration and anger. I think one of the reasons the real-time strategy genre has been so enormously successful is that it cleverly telegraphs what you need to do—unlock more powerful units—and then provides whole new strata of gameplay when you have them. The compulsion loop is perfect—both predictable and expansive.

That same loop makes sense in an interdependent college classroom. First, the learning context should invite engagement and interest. Through clear models—from professionals in a field, the instructor, or other students—the learning task should be exceptionally clear. As students become more proficient in the learning task, a whole new strata of knowledge, ability, and skill application becomes available. Infusing meaningful challenges, such as "desirable difficulties" (Bjork & Bjork, 2020), in an interdependent learning environment can be tricky.

Cultivating such a relationship between students and content requires teachers to be both an antagonist—the dungeon master who creates difficult challenges for students—and a mentor, who swoops in with wisdom the moment the challenge becomes overwhelming. How can teachers effectively play both roles at once?

Play Entails Tricky Relationships

Beyond science, we can find inspiration in folklore: the teacher-as-facilitator is witch, conjurer, and trickster (Garrison, 2009). No matter what mythological archetype we use to describe the profession, teaching already feels like magic. Our learning outcomes tend to be social constructions that do not have inherent tangible markers indicating when or how they have been met. Think for a moment how you define things like "critical thinking," "creativity," or "reflection." Usually, depending on who is asked, these definitions can vary widely. I have hosted many workshops with participants from across disciplinary settings in which lively debates about these definitions consumed a good amount of time. When I step into the debate and ask the assessment question of, "Well, how do you *know* when students demonstrate critical thinking (or any other socially constructed outcome)?"

The most common response: "It just happens."

Magic!

Experience divides humans from knowledge. One does not know what heat really is until they feel a flame. But a facilitator can ensure that the experience is reflective. We interact with the world, reflect on our interaction, and then modify our interaction based on our reflection. The more difficult the interaction, the deeper the reflection, and the more significant the learning. Thus, good facilitators antagonize students by pushing them to the point of failure, only to swoop in with encouraging feedback to help them overcome failure.

In *Trickster Makes the World*, Lewis Hyde (2008) defines the trickster archetype as a boundary-crossing, culture-creating figure, present across many mythologies. Tricksters like Hermes, Loki, and Coyote transgress norms, using cunning and disruption to reveal hidden truths and unsettle conventions. Hyde argues that tricksters catalyze creativity and cultural growth by moving fluidly between domains—right and wrong, and sacred and profane—and forcing society to confront contradictions and ambiguities. By embodying paradoxes, tricksters challenge static worldviews and encourage transformation, revealing the limitations of binary thinking and stimulating growth through disorder. Free from social restrictions, the trickster offers insights most of us cannot detect. Hyde (2008) writes of the trickster's agency: "where someone's sense of honorable behavior has left him unable to act, trickster will appear to suggest an amoral action, something right/wrong that will get life going again" (p. 7). As such, the trickster archetype served many purposes for cultures across history, from facilitating healing rituals to entertaining crowds. Trickster's most important role, however, is teaching. "Coyote not ought to do things more than four times," Hyde (2008) writes.

> He ought to have proper humility; he ought to have proper respect for his body. Part of the entertainment derives from his self-indulgent refusal of such commands, of course, for there is vicarious pleasure in watching him break the rules, and a potentially fruitful fantasizing, too, for listeners are invited, if only in imagination, to scout the territory that lies beyond the local constraints (what does Coyote see from that high tree?).
>
> (p. 12)

Thus, Coyote teaches both the dangers of defying social order and the promise of freedom. The trickster approach can only be effective if it is underpinned by strong trust and care between the teacher and students. Trust is essential because it allows students to take risks and embrace the uncertainty that is inherent in a challenging task (Davis & Weeden, 2009). If students feel that their teacher genuinely cares about their growth and is committed to their success, they are more likely to persevere through difficulties (Hensley, 2018). For a teacher to "trick" students into learning, they must build a safe environment where students are encouraged to fail forward, knowing that mistakes are part of the learning process. The Care Kit for this chapter offers some suggestions for striking that careful balance.

Care Kit: Adopt a Concept

The importance of creating a classroom that feels like a space for play cannot be overstated. Play is a powerful tool for fostering engagement, creativity, and deep learning, particularly for adult learners who benefit from environments that encourage exploration and intrinsic motivation. Drawing on the work of scholars like Vygotsky, Dewey, and Brown, as well as insights from thinkers like Bob Black and Daniel Pink, it is clear that when learning feels playful, it becomes a source of joy and curiosity rather than a chore. As educators, our challenge is to create classrooms that feel less like work and more like play, where students are free to explore, experiment, and engage with the material in meaningful and imaginative ways.

Remedy

Just as we began the Care Kit by reflecting on our affinities (i.e., the potential of shared love of content and what we teach), I have found it effective to create a foundation of relationships between students based on a similar potential. Distribute post-it notes to students and ask them to identify one "passion" per post-it. (Padlet works great for online post-it note activities, but they can also use Yuja or Flip to create video introductions of their passions.) I encourage them to create as many post-its as possible, but they only need a minimum of one per student. Of course, they need some explanation of "passion"—hobbies, interests, desires, or any activity that fills them with joy. When I run this activity with first-year students, many of them are surprised that I care if they play video games, write songs, or play instruments. In other words, they are surprised that even if there is not an apparent connection between their whole selves and the content of the course, I still care.

Once they have exhausted all possible passions, we create a post-it note or Padlet gallery. Then, I affirm the importance of curiosity and ask them to peruse the gallery and draw one passion that piques their curiosity in some way. The reason for drawing the passion can be a shared affinity, as in a student realizing that someone else is interested in video games. Or, the reason can be pure curiosity—a passion includes something that the student *wants* to know more about but has no prior experience in the passion. The only rule is that they cannot draw their own contribution to the gallery.

In the final stage, students share their drawn passions and form a networks based on overlapping passions. Perhaps someone with a "mountain biking" post-it groups with students who have "hiking" and "camping," forming an "outdoor recreation team." Perhaps a students with "gardening," "cooking," and "mixology" form a "culinary arts team." This stage can become very exciting and messy, as human interactions tend to be. The teacher's role here is to perform impromptu thematic analysis, helping people identify connections and come together. I have actually found it easier to run this activity online, especially asynchronously, since it provides me time to perform the thematic analysis of students' interests. Discussion boards and learning management systems' announcement pages work really well for organizing students into their networks.

Once in groups, students can perform particular tasks related to the course and, importantly, connect their affinity with the course in some way. Perhaps in the writing class, the culinary arts team work on individual rhetorical analyses of the food industry.

Note: this activity can be used to mix up prior grouping strategies. Depending on the learning environment, it might be beneficial to keep students in the same groups throughout the duration of a course or offer them a creative way to form new relationships.

Root

This strategy comes from educational philosopher Gert Biesta (2015) can help frame an immersive assignment in which students "live with content" (p. 236). This approach closes the time gap between what students are learning and when/how they apply the learning. In other words, teachers can avoid the "when will I use this" question by designing experiences in which students actually "use this." Assign students the opportunity to, using educational philosopher Gert Biesta's (2015) words, "adopt a concept" in their lives (p. 238). When students have the chance to incorporate their learning in their lives and reflect on how the learning enhances their everyday interactions, they deepen their connections to the content.

Ask students to create a list of their daily non-academic activities (e.g., doing laundry, grocery shopping, exercising, dating, playing video or tabletop games). Then ask them to identify the activity that currently poses a challenge (e.g., "I'm trying to only shop for non-processed foods but the labels are confusing"). Provide students either with a specific topic or with a range of topics relevant to the content. A biology teacher, to provide a simplistic example, might assign "carbohydrates." Students could then create a list of the items they purchase and analyze the ingredients with their newly forming knowledge of carbohydrates. Importantly, ask students to reflect on how the content influenced their behavior, driving the point home that the content knowledge enhances their lives. In this case, students might say, "this biology course helped me become a healthier shopper and eater." As a term-long assignment, students can advance their relationship with the content by adding new elements, layers, or concepts. Frequent check-ins can make for engaging class discussion as well as provide valuable insight into their understanding of content. The prompts provided to direct them to "live with content" do not matter as much as the fact that they are continuously thinking about the content in different contexts across long periods of time.

Drawing from similar aims of fostering and developing relationships between students, the next chapter directs these strategies toward teachers, academic staff, and other educators in our ecologies, reframing self-care as a collective effort.

References

Biesta, G. (2015). Freeing teaching from learning: Opening up existential possibilities in educational relationships. *Studies in Philosophy and Education, 34*, 229–243.

Bjork, R. A., & Bjork, E. L. (2020). Desirable difficulties in theory and practice. *Journal of Applied Research in Memory and Cognition, 9*(4), 475.

Black, B. (1986). *The abolition of work and other essays*. Loompanics Unlimited.

Brown, S., & Vaughan, C. (2009). *Play: How it shapes the brain, opens the imagination, and invigorates the soul*. Penguin.

Butler, J. (2020). *The Force of Nonviolence: An Ethico-Political Bind*. New York: Verso.

Clancy, K. (2024). *Playing with reality: How games shape our world*. Random House.

Davis, K. W., & Weeden, S. R. (2009). Teacher as trickster on the learner's journey. *Journal of the Scholarship of Teaching and Learning, 9*(2), 70–81.

Dewey, J. (2024). *Democracy and education*. Columbia University Press.

Fedesco, H. N., Kentner, A., & Natt, J. (2017). The effect of relevance strategies on student perceptions of introductory courses. *Communication Education, 66*(2), 196–209.

Felten, P., & Lambert, L. M. (2020). *Relationship-rich education: How human connections drive success in college*. JHU Press.

Garrison, J. (2009). Teacher as prophetic trickster. *Educational Theory, 59*(1), 67–83.

Griffin, L. L., & Butler, J. (2005). *Teaching games for understanding: Theory, research, and practice*. Human Kinetics.

Hadwin, A., Järvelä, S., & Miller, M. (2011). Self-regulated, co-regulated, and socially shared regulation of learning. In B. Zimmerman, & D. Schunk (Eds.), *Handbook of self-regulation of learning and performance* (pp. 65–86). Routledge.

Hensley, N. (2018). Transforming higher education through trickster-style teaching. *Journal of Cleaner Production, 194*, 607–612.

hooks, b. (2000). Learning in the shadow of race and class. *The Chronicle of Higher Education, 47*(12), B14–B16.

Huizinga, J. (1955). *Homo Ludens: A study of the play-element in culture.* Beacon Press.

Hyde, L. (2008). *Trickster makes this world: Mischief, myth, and art.* Canongate Books.

Jones, M. G., Lee, T., Chesnutt, K., Carrier, S., Ennes, M., Cayton, E., . . . & Huff, P. (2019). Enclothed cognition: Putting lab coats to the test. *International Journal of Science Education, 41*(14), 1962–1976.

Kosa, M., & Uysal, A. (2022). Need frustration in online video games. *Behaviour & Information Technology, 41*(11), 2415–2426.

Ladson-Billings, G. (1995). But that's just good teaching! The case for culturally relevant pedagogy. *Theory into Practice, 34*(3), 159–165.

Martin, J. H., Hands, K. B., Lancaster, S. M., Trytten, D. A., & Murphy, T. J. (2008). Hard but not too hard: Challenging courses and engineering students. *College Teaching, 56*(2), 107–113.

Mills, D. J., Milyavskaya, M., Mettler, J., Heath, N. L., & Derevensky, J. L. (2018). How do passion for video games and needs frustration explain time spent gaming? *British Journal of Social Psychology, 57*(2), 461–481.

Nakamura, J., & Csikszentmihalyi, M. (2009). Flow theory and research. In C. R. Snyder, & S. J. Lopez (Eds.), *Oxford handbook of positive psychology* (pp. 195–206). Oxford University Press.

National Research Council. (2000). *How people learn: Brain, mind, experience and school.* J. D. Bransford, A. L. Brown, & R. R. Cocking (Eds.). National Academy Press.

Noddings, N. (2013). *Caring: A relational approach to ethics and moral education.* University of California Press.

Perkins, D. N., & Salomon, G. (2012). Knowledge to go: A motivational and dispositional view of transfer. *Educational Psychologist, 47*(3), 248–258.

Pink, D. H. (2011). *Drive: The surprising truth about what motivates us.* Penguin.

Quinlan, K. M. (2019). What triggers students' interest during higher education lectures? Personal and situational variables associated with situational interest. *Studies in Higher Education, 44*(10), 1781–1792.

Rashid, S., & Qaisar, S. (2017). Role play: A productive teaching strategy to promote critical thinking. *Bulletin of Education and Research, 39*(2), 197–213.

Schraw, G., Flowerday, T., & Lehman, S. (2001). Increasing situational interest in the classroom. *Educational Psychology Review, 13*, 211–224.

Stuart, K. (2013). Is frustration an essential part of game design? *The Guardian.* https://www.theguardian.com/technology/gamesblog/2013/feb/14/frustration-in-game-design.

Studio Wildcard. (2024). *ARK: Survival Ascended* <Video Game>. Snail Games. PlayStation 5.

Sweller, J. (2011). Cognitive load theory. In *Psychology of learning and motivation* (Vol. 55, pp. 37–76). Academic Press.

Tonkin, A., & Whitaker, J. (Eds.). (2016). *Play in healthcare for adults: Using play to promote health and wellbeing across the adult lifespan.* Routledge.

Torres, J. T. (2022). Feedback as Open-Ended Conversation: Inviting Students to Coregulate and Metacognitively Reflect during Assessment. *Journal of the Scholarship of Teaching and Learning, 22*(1), 81–94.

Van Leeuwen, L., & Westwood, D. (2008). Adult play, psychology and design. *Digital Creativity, 19*(3), 153–161.

Watkins, J., & Mazur, E. (2013). Retaining students in science, technology, engineering, and mathematics (STEM) majors. *Journal of College Science Teaching, 42*(5), 36–41.

7

CARE BETWEEN TEACHERS

Chapter Contents
Confronting Burnout in Higher Education   126
Permission to Care for Ourselves   129
Sound Advice From the Federal Aviation Administration   132
Collective Care Empowers Us All   133
Redefine Work–Life Balance   134
Care Kit: Support Communities of Practice   135
References   140

I will never forget the moment we went into quarantine. That moment simultaneously felt like an unimaginable disruption and, somehow, a familiar crisis. When my iPhone notified me of the breaking news, as well as emails from my university that read like passages from a dystopian novel, I was waiting for my partner, Erin, at Yale University. Erin worked for Yale New Haven Hospital as a nurse, but on that day, she was there as a patient. For the past few weeks, she had been experiencing heart palpitations and chest pains. Her doctor had attached a heart monitor to her that she had to wear for five days. I had come directly after my class to meet her. The day felt both ordinary and momentous.

    Spring 2020, a threshold that has permanently changed society, did not seem all that sudden. In 2019, Erin's mom passed away after a long battle with pancreatic cancer. Erin's mom had been her only parent, and Erin had been her mom's only child. The loss hit Erin hard. I expected the emotional symptoms to be a challenge for both of us. But for Erin, all kinds of physical symptoms emerged—hair loss, breathlessness, and the chest pains. Erin has thick black curls that reach her waist. She works out every day and has always been athletic. The symptoms became increasingly concerning. We became more focused on Erin's wellness than the international news of COVID-19's spread across countries, states, and now the U.S. Northeast. When Erin and I met on Yale's Old Campus Courtyard, an eerie silence had already fallen across campus. Even the students seemed so withdrawn that approaching them at all could be construed as threatening.

Erin quickly shared that despite irregularities in her heart rhythm, her doctor was not too concerned. The symptoms were attributed to anxiety and stress. Then she immediately switched to the news about quarantine. We huddled over my iPhone. The plan had been to go to dinner in New Haven, but stores had already begun locking up.

I say this with sincere acknowledgment of the implicated privilege: quarantine was exactly what Erin and I needed. Yes, the disruption closed the surgery center where Erin worked, meaning she lost employment. Yes, the disruption led to layoffs at my university and a rapid conversion to online that resulted in the worst teaching I've ever experienced. Yes, the disruption included personal tragedies, including my mother spending three weeks in ICU with COVID-19. But the disruption also meant that "business as usual" was no longer possible. The imposition of shelter in place, requiring Erin and I to stay home, not work, grieve, breathe, and heal came at a climax of tragedy in our lives.

During quarantine, Erin and I learned how to garden, we rescued our husky, Kenai, and for the first time in our relationship, we learned about each other, our needs, boundaries, and emotional rhythms. We walked every morning with Kenai before tending to our garden. On one walk, we marveled at the silence of the world. The roads had no cars. No honking horns, sirens, or screeching tires. The parks were closed and therefore empty. It was like we were the only family that existed. It felt lonely, but it also called our attention to one another. In other words, by necessity we learned how to care for one another.

I share this story because, beyond the particulars, I have found that others share similar experiences. While quarantine certainly had inequitable effects, especially for those who did not have shelters in which to "shelter in place," the pausing of compulsory labor introduced something that many felt had been lost.

America has been and still is a nation of overworked citizens, with American workers clocking in more hours per year than workers in other developed nations. On average, Americans work about 1,791 hours per year, compared to workers in Germany, who average 1,386 hours, and those in France, who work 1,490 hours per year. Additionally, 55% of Americans do not use paid time off, leaving them with less opportunity for rest and recovery (Giattino et al., 2020). The COVID-19 pandemic has worsened these trends. A 2022 Gallup poll reported that 76% of American workers experience burnout at least sometimes, with 28% reporting they feel burned out "very often" or "always" (Wigert, 2020). While long hours, job insecurity, and economic instability have combined to push many workers to the brink, burnout is also associated with feelings of disconnection, a loss of purpose, and a misalignment between personal values and institutional demands. People do not simply feel tired. Many express losing touch with themselves.

Perhaps that is why so many people in America and across the world initiated what became known as "the great resignation," when record numbers of workers (around 4.4 million just in America during 2021) left their jobs (Tessema et al., 2022). The pandemic in general highlighted structural inequities in labor markets and called into question Western lifestyles, especially around work–life balance. Even before the pandemic, people felt burned out, tired, and overworked (Brewer & Shapard, 2004). Rising costs of living and increased income inequality required more people to work multiple jobs while simultaneously being able to afford fewer necessities like food and rent. The pandemic not only highlighted these issues, but it also introduced another possible way of life: working from home, spending more time with family, and refusing the constant barrage of external demands that benefit only those with political and economic power.

Confronting Burnout in Higher Education

As we explored in Chapter 2, higher education currently exists in an ecology of stress that foments burnout at multiple levels—students, faculty, administration, and staff. Treating burnout as an individual issue will more likely exacerbate the phenomenon as systemic drivers of the present reality seem relentless. Increased competition between colleges and universities for the shrinking number of traditional students lead to increased workloads and more frequent calls for innovation. The advancement of new technologies like AI lead to more fervent calls for faculty to redesign their curricula and instructional methods. The decreasing mental health rates in students (and everyone else!) lead to more responsibility to provide care and support beyond delivering content. The latter case especially impacts diverse educators as their shared identity with diverse students often means they are the only person students can trust with personal challenges. A female student of color who faces a setback particular to her and not the dominant white, straight, male student population will likely want to confide in someone who looks like her and has experienced similar setbacks. As important as these connections are, they present additional labor and demands on already vulnerable educators.

Care professionals, which includes both nurses and teachers, had long reported higher levels of burnout than professionals in fields that do not require the emotional labor of care (Skovholt & Trotter-Mathison, 2010). Sustaining relationships, helping others with emotional, physical, or intellectual challenges, and practicing genuine empathy on a daily basis can rapidly deplete one's capacity to care, such as compassion fatigue (Sinclair et al., 2017). In *Unraveling Faculty Burnout*, Rebecca Pope-Ruark (2022) explains how, as care professionals, "good teachers build personal relationships with students that are grounded in looking out for their welfare" (p. 119). Despite the importance of these relationships, overworked and undervalued teachers struggle to maintain "wells of compassion from which we recognize and want to relieve stress or fear in others" (p. 119). If someone has exhausted their capacity to care, then they cannot even care for themselves.

Teachers are often burdened with heavier teaching loads, administrative duties, and service expectations, leaving less time for research and personal development. The shift toward online or hybrid teaching during the pandemic has added to these responsibilities. COVID-19 required a dramatic revolution in teaching, pivoting to remote learning, increased student needs, and managing health concerns. Many faculty felt unprepared for these shifts, which significantly increased stress. Meanwhile, institutions have not increased support or resources to match the growing demands on faculty. Budget cuts, hiring freezes, and lack of professional development opportunities exacerbate feelings of isolation and overwork. For adjunct and non-tenure-track faculty, low pay, minimal benefits, and a lack of stability create additional layers of stress. Finally, remote work and technological advances have made it harder for faculty to maintain boundaries between work and personal life, as constant connectivity means many feel the need to be available to students and colleagues around the clock.

Teachers follow the implied expectation that they should prioritize caring for others above their own well-being, perpetuating a dynamic where self-care is devalued and burnout becomes an endemic challenge. This expectation creates an environment where emotional labor, moral dilemmas, cultural expectations of sacrifice, lack of institutional support, devaluation of self-advocacy, blurred work–life boundaries, and societal pressure to accept overwork coalesce to undermine the well-being of these professionals. Addressing this paradox requires a deeper understanding of the systemic challenges faced by those in caring professions.

Teachers and nurses perform intense emotional labor, requiring them to constantly manage their own emotions while addressing the needs of those in their care. For teachers, this often includes supporting students both academically and emotionally, while nurses are tasked with providing compassionate care to patients. Emotional labor is largely invisible and not accounted for in workload metrics, leaving little room for professionals to prioritize their own emotional or mental health. For example, a survey by the National Education Association (2021) found that 55% of U.S. teachers planned to leave the profession earlier than expected due to stress and burnout, much of which stemmed from excessive workloads. A similar percentage of nurses entertain the same consideration. Dangerously, rates of nurse burnout seem to correlate with decreased patient safety outcomes (Li et al., 2024), meaning that burnout in caring professions can harm those depending on caring professionals. Unfortunately, public discourse tends to ignore this relationship.

When teachers strike or nurses protest unsafe working conditions, they are often accused of abandoning those they are supposed to care for, which can create moral dilemmas and feelings of guilt. Public opinion frequently pressures these professionals to accept substandard conditions for the sake of their students or patients, reinforcing the notion that caring for others must take precedence. During the 2018 teacher strikes in West Virginia, Oklahoma, and Arizona, for instance, educators faced backlash from critics accusing them of neglecting students. However, public support for their demands was strong, with more than 70% of respondents endorsing better pay and working conditions (Iasevoli, 2018). Similarly, nurses advocating for better protective measures during the COVID-19 pandemic were bullied for allegedly leaving patients vulnerable (Serafin et al., 2022), despite 89% of Americans ranking nursing as the most ethical profession in 2020 (Brenan, 2022). When care professionals advocate for themselves, they are often perceived as selfish or lacking dedication to their roles. This devaluation discourages them from demanding fairer conditions, perpetuating environments detrimental to their well-being. For instance, inflation-adjusted teacher salaries declined by 4.5% between 2010 and 2020 (Allegretto, 2022), yet teachers striking for better pay were frequently portrayed negatively in the media. Similarly, 2020 Bureau of Labor Statistics data indicated that registered nurses earned 18% less than the national average for professionals with similar education levels, underscoring systemic undervaluation.

Societal narratives often frame caring professions as callings rather than jobs, implying that teachers and nurses should willingly endure long hours and poor conditions without complaint. This perception can easily become weaponized, complicating efforts to assert professional rights to fair working conditions, as any act of resistance risks being interpreted as neglect of their core responsibilities. The pervasive cultural expectation demands that public service professionals demonstrate selflessness by prioritizing others' needs over their own. Teachers often work beyond contracted hours to grade, prepare lessons, and address students' personal concerns, while nurses endure long shifts with minimal breaks. These expectations normalize the idea that caring professions require personal sacrifice rather than fostering sustainable work conditions.

Despite policy initiatives in England aimed at supporting teachers by reducing overnight and weekend labor, trends of overwork and burnout hold steady over two decades (Allen et al., 2021). Meanwhile, despite new measures meant to prioritize patient safety in U.S. hospitals, nurses continue to work around the clock, sometimes going more than 24 hours without sleeping (Stimpfel et al., 2020). Even when policy attempts to shift practice, culture can remain stubborn. As the saying goes, "culture eats strategy for breakfast." Budget constraints, understaffing, and an institutional focus on efficiency often result in insufficient support for teachers and nurses. In education, larger class sizes and fewer support staff escalate teachers' workloads, while nurses face high patient-to-nurse ratios that limit their capacity for self-care. Research pinpoints institutional culture or organizational structure as the primary driver of both nursing burnout and unsafe patient care (Lasater et al., 2021) as well as teacher burnout and unsafe student care (Rizvi Jafree et al., 2023). The expectation that teachers and nurses prioritize others' well-being while neglecting their own creates a systemic paradox that fuels burnout. Such a dynamic underscores the necessity for structural change, emphasizing the importance of institutional and societal support to sustain the well-being of public service professionals. Without such changes, these professions will continue to grapple with high turnover rates, diminished morale, and declining quality of care.

As Rebecca Pope-Ruark (2022) highlights in *Unraveling Faculty Burnout: Pathways to Reckoning and Renewal*, faculty burnout often stems from overcommitment, lack of boundaries, perfectionism, isolation, and emotional labor. Faculty members frequently juggle teaching, research, service roles, and administrative duties, often without clear boundaries. The academic culture's emphasis on perfectionism and high expectations compounds this stress, while the solitary nature of research and limited institutional support exacerbate feelings of isolation. Addressing these systemic issues through self-reflection, community building, and institutional change is essential for fostering healthier work environments.

Permission to Care for Ourselves

When Erin received the notification that she was being laid off due to the quarantine, the news hit her differently than I had anticipated. Considering the grief she had carried with her for a year and the stability her identity as a nurse provided her, I worried a great deal about her mental health. At the same time, nursing had long capitalized on her care and empathy. She worked multiple 12-hour shifts, followed by weekends on call. She shared stories with me about getting yelled at by desperate patients and ignored by despondent doctors. We spent countless dinner conversations deriding a "sickcare" system that keeps patients in an often fatal loop of dependency and confusion. "It's hard to care," she said once, "when the system is designed to prevent care." From time to time, she considered a career change, but never fully pursued the option. When she received the layoff notice in early summer 2020, she expressed a sense of liberation.

"I have always been a nurse," she said to me that day. "I never knew I did not have to be one until now."

Through disappointment and crisis, we learned the hard way what Pope-Ruark (2022) succinctly stated, that "self-care and self-compassion aren't necessarily synonymous with self-indulgence," but care and compassion for oneself do mean no longer offering the whole of ourselves to external demands (p. 130). We need our wells to be full if we want to offer wells to others. In many ways, tending our first garden together became a ritual in which Erin and I tended new selves. We just needed permission, tragic as that permission was.

The collectively authored (2015) article "For Slow Scholarship: A Feminist Politics of Resistance through Collective Action in the Neoliberal University" provides a model for change, granting readers not just permission but also a blueprint. As a quick note, while the official reference entry for "For Slow Scholarship" credits "Mountz et al.," the collaborative authorship, which includes 11 total authors, is itself a rejection of traditional academic hierarchies that privilege individual achievement and position educators and scholars in exhausting competition. Authorship emerged from the Great Lakes Feminist Geography Collective, a group formed during a 2013 workshop in Ontario. The authors initially shared personal narratives to explore the embodied effects of academic labor. Over time, these individual accounts were synthesized into collective themes, reflecting a feminist ethics of care. They describe their approach as "our version of refusal, our attempt to act in-against-and-beyond the university" and as an effort to resist "the isolating effects of work conditions" that perpetuate neoliberal academia (p. 1240). They model a praxis of scholarship that both keeps scholars' wells filled and produces sound knowledge. In reverence to their approach, I'll refer to them using "the authors (2015)."

The authors (2015) extend Hartman and Darab's (2012) call for slow scholarship by examining how the neoliberal transformation of universities has accelerated academic life, creating a work environment that prioritizes efficiency and metrics over intellectual and personal well-being. The neoliberal university, shaped by market-driven values, demands high productivity in compressed timelines, resulting in isolating and unsustainable working conditions for academics. These pressures include expanded workloads, constant evaluations through metric-based systems, and a culture that devalues slower, reflective intellectual work, even though "good scholarship requires time: time to think, write, read, research, analyze, edit, and collaborate" (p. 1236). Time pressures of the neoliberal university act as a mechanism of oppression, disproportionately affecting those already burdened with care responsibilities or institutional inequities. By advocating for "slow scholarship," the authors challenge the masculinist and capitalist valorization of speed, productivity, and efficiency, which has historically undermined the value of feminized work, such as caregiving and community building (p. 1248). As teachers find themselves accumulating increased administrative tasks while competing for diminishing public funding and eroding job stability, they also try to continue "good scholarship" and reflect on and improve their pedagogy.

The authors (2015) foreground care as central to their argument, echoing feminist theories that challenge the devaluation of care work in capitalist and patriarchal systems. They explicitly draw on feminist thinkers, like Sara Ahmed and Joan Tronto, to assert that "care work is work" and that fostering care within academia is a political act (p. 1239), opposing the neoliberal dehumanization of academic labor, which reduces scholarship to metrics and productivity while sidelining relational and emotional labor often disproportionately carried by women and marginalized groups. Academic life divides the university (and the universe) not only by discipline but also often by gender, race, class, sexual orientation, and ability. Degree programs like Women and Gender Studies tend to compartmentalize female and LGBTQ+ faculty. Others hold the misconception that topics of race and class only apply to Sociology. These divisions, the authors point out, further marginalize knowledge bearers who would otherwise infuse academic culture with the charge to "make the university a place where many people . . . can collectively and collaboratively thrive" (p. 1240).

Rather than framing slow scholarship as an individual choice or privilege, however, the authors (2015) emphasize the need for structural changes within the academy. This includes creating supportive policies, valuing diverse forms of labor, and fostering communal spaces. They argue that feminist interventions must address both personal and systemic dimensions of care and labor, aiming to dismantle hierarchies that perpetuate exclusion and burnout (p. 1252). Taking a both/and approach means organizing spaces for collaboration, such as workshops and writing groups, to foster solidarity and challenge individualization; pushing back against narrow productivity measures by recognizing diverse forms of academic contributions, such as mentorship and community engagement; encouraging academics to prioritize self-care and collective care, emphasizing that "care work is work" and is essential to resisting neoliberal pressures (p. 1239); and advocating for a reimagining of academic timelines to support thoughtful and meaningful scholarship, rather than merely producing outputs for evaluation systems. The feminist intervention illustrated by the authors (2015) calls for a recalibration of academic culture to prioritize intellectual and personal well-being while addressing systemic inequities, creating a university environment where diverse voices and slower, more reflective scholarship can thrive.

Maggie Berg and Barbara Seeber (2016) continue those calls in their book *The Slow Professor*. They draw from Frank Martela's research into nursing homes to find that organizations that emphasize the healthy cultivation of a "holding environment," an interconnected socially supportive space as opposed to requiring individuals to manage their own "baggage," can lead to the explicit acknowledgment that "our work has a significant emotional dimension" that cannot be accurately measured by quick metrics or mediated by task or time management (p. 83). Both time and collaboration, according to Berg and Seeber, need redefinition to align with complex human needs, especially within organizations that provide care as a service. In the neoliberal model of higher education, individualism remains the defining feature of the model academic—someone who is the first or only author of published work, aloof and unreachable, self-reliant, and therefore never in need of support. Berg and Seeber (2016) encourage us to remember that a holding environment that promotes collaboration "can allow us to challenge neoliberal models of higher education and the remasculinization of the academy" not only by creating sustainable systems of labor but also by inspiring one another through the sharing of new ideas and perspectives (p. 89).

Such a holding environment calls attention to the ways in which spaces both constitute and are constituted by individuals, existing within interdependent networks of relationships that determine agency and being (Martela, 2014). We will almost definitely burn out if we treat every act of care, even for ourselves, on an individual basis. Adding a spa day to your calendar to help you unwind can easily become another task on top of all the other work and life commitments. Interdependent classrooms are holding environments, but so too should our professional development spaces incorporate networks of caring relationships that restore and inspire. Relationships define the foundation of any holding environment or interdependent space. Pouring our energy into relationships, either through professional collaboration or through social support networks, also means pouring energy into ourselves.

Sound Advice From the Federal Aviation Administration

The airplane safety message, "Place your own oxygen mask on before helping others," is a powerful analogy for the conversation about teachers being overburdened by caring for students at the expense of their own well-being. The oxygen mask message emphasizes that you cannot effectively help others if you are in distress or incapable of functioning yourself. This analogy counters the guilt many teachers feel when they advocate for better working conditions or take time for themselves. It reframes self-care as not selfish but necessary, showing that professionals are not abandoning their responsibilities by focusing on their own well-being. Just as you wouldn't be expected to ignore your oxygen mask to help others on a plane, teachers shouldn't be expected to neglect their needs to care for students. Both situations recognize that effective care requires balance.

While the message technically refers to emergency situations, as an analogy it affirms Skovholt and Trotter-Mathison's (2010) argument that self-care should be "an essential component of our professional identities" (p. 166). If teachers neglect their own physical, mental, and emotional health, their ability to care for students diminishes. In fact, student learning outcomes can directly depend on teachers' self-efficacy and psychological well-being (Zee & Koomen, 2016). Just as oxygen is essential to remain conscious and helpful in an emergency, self-care is vital for educators to sustainably fulfill their teaching roles. Burnout, stress, and exhaustion reduce their capacity to provide quality instruction.

Putting on your oxygen mask first ensures that you are physically capable of helping others over the long term. For teachers, engaging in self-care or advocating for better conditions (like smaller class sizes, more support staff, or adequate teaching resources) is essential for avoiding burnout and remaining effective in their roles. When their own needs are met, they can continue to provide high-quality instruction and support over the long term, rather than burning out and leaving the profession. In teaching, professionals serve as role models. By taking care of themselves first, they model the importance of boundaries and self-care for students. Just as putting on your own oxygen mask demonstrates to others how to respond effectively in an emergency, showing a commitment to self-care teaches students the value of personal well-being, encouraging a culture of care that includes the caregiver.

The airplane analogy also implicitly points to the need for a functioning system: in an airplane, oxygen masks are provided for every passenger. In teaching, professionals need systemic support (like reasonable workloads, mental health resources, and adequate compensation) to be able to take care of themselves. Without such systems in place, just as in an emergency without oxygen, it becomes impossible to sustain the well-being of both educators and those they serve. In short, this analogy highlights the importance of self-care not as a selfish act but as a critical foundation for effectively caring for others.

Collective Care Empowers Us All

Just as this book calls for an interdependent classroom to equitably distribute the labor of care among networks of students, this chapter makes a similar call for teachers. We cannot treat barriers to care as individual issues. At the same time, individuals (especially care professionals) need care. When I consult with institutions and organizations who want to address burnout, disengagement, and other similar challenges, I begin by establishing interdependent professional development opportunities. Sure, we can send individuals to conferences, but we can also—more importantly—create holding environments in which everyone feels connected, supported, and valued. Mentorship models, interest groups, and structured networking can all contribute to an interdependent organization that sends the clear message that everyone belongs. Care needs to be explicitly valued and incorporated into professional development goals in order for it to take root in the professional culture.

I will always remember a conversation I had with the Associate Provost of Faculty Affairs at Quinnipiac University, Khalilah Brown-Dean. Not only was Khalilah my direct supervisor, but she was also a towering figure—known nationally because of her work as a political scientist as well as for hosting *Disrupted*, the award-winning show on National Public Radio. She had grown concerned with my efforts directing Quinnipiac's Center for Teaching and Learning, mostly because I had become overextended, managing almost 20 consultations a week as well as multiple programs and workshops. She advised me to "say no" to additional requests in order to protect my time.

While I agreed with her and appreciated her care for me, I said, "When I say no, though, it's to someone who needs help."

Khalilah responded:

Our time on this planet is very short. When you look back at life, I can promise you that you will not think, "I wish I would have spent more time working."

You will think, "I wish I would have spent more time with loved ones, in cherished places, soaking up those fleeting moments."

The reframe rattled me. One, I did not expect my supervisor to take my side over the institution's. Two, I never considered my work from a position of self-care. From that moment on, I have tried to evaluate every decision from the perspective of a future self, who hopes to be healthy and happy as he reflects on a life well lived. Pope-Ruark (2022) emphasizes the importance of self-reflection, encouraging faculty to assess their values, goals, and personal limits. By recognizing the early signs of burnout, individuals can take proactive steps to realign their work with what truly matters to them and set healthier boundaries. Pope-Ruark advises faculty to prioritize tasks that align with their core goals and values, while being selective about additional commitments that may drain their energy. She encourages faculty to cultivate a strong sense of community, building connections with colleagues who understand the demands of academic life.

Redefine Work–Life Balance

Tonkin and Whitaker (2016) highlight the importance of engaging in playful activities outside of work that bring joy, relaxation, and fulfillment. Faculty can carve out time for hobbies, exercise, mindfulness, or creative pursuits that rejuvenate them and help maintain balance. On a broader level, Jagodics and Szabó (2023) encourage both students and faculty to advocate for systemic changes within their institutions like pushing for more realistic workloads, better mental health resources, and a shift in the culture of academia to value well-being over constant productivity. We need explicit attention paid to how we define work–life balance.

I was recently invited to present to a group of caregivers working in higher education. The room of 50 or so professionals included faculty, academic staff, and administrative staff. They each balanced the difficult demands of academic life with family or loved ones who heavily relied on them for survival. Before presenting, I always make it a point to learn about those in the room, either via informal small talk as people enter the room or through some intentional thin-slicing introduction. During this engagement, a history professor shared that a tragic accident in her family resulted in her now becoming the legal guardian for her nephew and three nieces, while also raising her own two children. The administrative assistant for a university president shared that he feels terrible guilt when he cannot attend to his parents with Alzheimer's because he is too busy at work.

"I'll save up my paid time off until I can take a week off from work," the administrative assistant said.

> But that entire week goes to my parents' care—taking them to doctor appointments, cleaning up after them, handling mental breakdowns during

particularly bad episodes. From the institution's perspective, I took a "week off" like it's a vacation. But I don't get vacations. I don't get to care about me.

In one activity, I asked the audience to describe their current emotional state using a single word. They wrote the word on an index card and then we had time to walk around, introduce ourselves to others, and form groups with those whose index cards included similar words. Large groups began to form as people realized the majority of them felt "guilt," "overwhelmed," or "exhausted." From that point, I guided the groups using a variation of the Care Kit shared below, modeling a quick starting point to form a community and connect over shared concerns. The purpose of the presentation was not to magically solve deep-seated problems related to caring for everyone in an industry that rarely cares for us in return. Our purpose was far simpler: help caring people find others who will help create interconnected networks of care. At the end of the presentation, someone approached me and said, "This is just what I needed."

Cultivating an ecology of care will always be emotionally and intellectually difficult work. Even when we incorporate interdependence by taking the time to develop dynamic student relationships and peer support, we will feel exhausted. In order to nurture caring connections within our classrooms, we need to maintain our own health and well-being. Rejecting the commodification of scholarship and pedagogy can lead to the acceptance of an academic environment with roots in inclusivity, anti-racism, and social justice. Turning away from spaces of conformity and productivity turns us toward spaces where "experimentation, creativity, different epistemologies, and dissidence" are cared about (Mountz et al., 2015, p. 1254).

Care Kit: Support Communities of Practice

It is critical that teachers find and sustain their support networks, especially considering the labor inequities and burnout that college faculty face. In my experience organizing communities of practice, faculty working together to design new curriculum and implement new support programs have had encouraging results. Throughout the communities of practice I helped to organize, faculty observed each other's classes and provided feedback, designed repositories for inclusive teaching, and coordinated a university wide assembly that explored opportunities for more inclusive teaching and learning. They received institutional recognition for their activity and protected their personal well-being at the same time.

Lave and Wegner (1991) offered insight into the ways participants learn, develop, and grow as a result of sociocultural participation. They studied and encouraged the implementation of learning communities that can help promote expertise as a practitioner in a particular field. Primarily, they found that communities operate through shared identity and interdependent support that follows care-based processes. They arrived at the concept of a community of practice (CoP). There is no standard for how a CoP should look or function as the organizational context will shape what is possible. As the originators of CoPs as a concept for learning and development, Etienne Wenger-Trayner and Beverly Wenger-Trayner (2015) does provide a useful roadmap on their website, assisting teachers who want to incorporate CoPs at their institutions. They explain the foundational theory of CoPs, emphasizing the interplay between community, domain, and practice as the core elements. Their site highlights practical applications of CoPs, showcasing how they can enhance teaching by promoting collaborative learning among students and creating opportunities for faculty to share expertise and develop professionally. By applying these principles, college teachers can build interdisciplinary networks, enhance student engagement, and foster environments conducive to shared learning and growth. While there is no wrong way to go about gathering humans into collective care and interdependent support, this Care Kit illustrates how I have successfully implemented CoPs to meet these ends.

Remedy

Start with critical relationships rather than a critical mass. Maybe two teachers share a desire to address a particular problem of practice—this is a more effective start than recruiting ten teachers into a decontextualized community. If all ten teachers do not agree on the problem of practice, facilitating the CoP can be difficult, if not impossible. Within the critical relationship, clarify the problem of practice and then invite others who are impacted by the problem.

Allow all members the chance to collectively reflect on and revise the problem of practice. A CoP does not require standardization; each member might experience contextual differences in how the problem emerges in their practice, and these differences can be illuminating for others. As the CoP facilitator, leverage expertise and curiosity in ways that promote inquiry and support as opposed to immediate solutions. In other words, ensure that the CoP has ample time to sit with the problem and understand it better from diverse perspectives.

As a community, agree on the activities that will help the members learn more about resources, strategies, and opportunities to explore and address the problem of practice. Again, the goal is not a fast and easy solution. Rather, the goal is to foster care for one another as each member contributes to a body of knowledge that helps everyone involved. Possibilities include inviting speakers to address the CoP, attending events as a CoP, organizing workshops for the CoP, or hosting and presenting workshops to external individuals as a way of showcasing the CoP.

As an iterative structure, a CoP can conclude its work addressing a particular problem of practice and move to other related issues, invite different membership, or dive deeper into the initial problem. The purpose is to keep people connected, remind others of their expertise and value to an organization, and foster confidence and engagement between practitioners who otherwise work in disconnected silos.

Root

Communities of practice are inherently dynamic, evolving to address emerging challenges or embrace new members and topics. They can, sometimes, create new permanent structures that offer a more sustainable strategy for caring-with teachers. What follows is an example of a multi-year community of practice that turned into an institutional structure in the form of a fellowship. I led centers on the shared joy of learning something new. This approach demonstrates how stepping into the role of an amateur can inspire teaching practices, rejuvenate educators, and ultimately enhance professional development.

Edward Said (1994) offers an important reconsideration of the amateur, which for him means being rooted in a committed love for something. Of course, what and how we love is shaped by how we are positioned in society: "Every human being is held in by a society, no matter how free and open the society, no matter how bohemian the individual" (p. 69). One way we are positioned is as "professionals." Said (1994) identified "professionalism" as a serious threat to intellectual development. Professionalism frames intellectual activity as

> something you do for a living, between the hours of nine and five with one eye on the clock, and another cocked at what is considered to be proper, professional behavior—not rocking the boat, not straying outside the accepted paradigms or limits, making yourself marketable and above all presentable, hence uncontroversial and unpolitical and objective.
>
> (p. 74)

A professional society, therefore, limits the development of intellectual pursuits by insisting they adhere to very rigid organizational norms. In almost revolutionary contrast, amateurs are defined by

> the desire to be moved not by profit or reward but by love for and the unquenchable interest in the larger picture, in making connections across lines and barriers, in refusing to be tied down by a specialty, in caring *for* [emphasis added] ideas and values despite the restrictions of a profession.
> (p. 76)

Specialization is necessary for competence, which will always be domain specific, but when it results in the "sacrifice of one's general culture to a set of authorities and canonical ideas, then competence of that sort is not worth the price paid for it" (p. 76). Specialization can risk killing one's "sense of excitement and discovery, both of which are irreducibly present in the intellectual's makeup" (p. 77). Said (1994) also identifies expertise as an outcome of professionalization. Expertise requires certification from, and therefore allegiance to, particular institutions that assert authority or power over a field, project, or even the experts themselves. Cognitively, expertise also presents direct challenges to instruction. According to psychologist Michelene Chi (2006), who draws from a prior study conducted by Hinds (1999):

> [O]ne would expect experts to be able to extrapolate from their own task-specific knowledge how quickly or easily novices can accomplish a task. In general, the greater the expertise the worse off they were at predicting how quickly novices can perform a task, such as using a cell phone.
> (p. 26)

Considering the institutional pressures to publish in academic journals, experts tend to communicate mostly to one another, relying on insider language (e.g., jargon) that, as specialization continues, become more inaccessible to nonexperts. As Said (1994) remarks, experts favor "an esoteric and barbaric prose that is meant mainly for academic advancement and not for social change" (p. 71). Hinds (1999) referred to this phenomenon as the "curse of expertise" (p. 205), which informs Heath and Heath's (2007) "curse of knowledge" that was discussed in Chapter 3 (p. 20). Both Said and the Heath brothers offer the same strategy: to inhabit the mindset of the amateur.

The amateur is not an inferior position to the professional. The relationship between the two are not necessarily vertically arranged. Rather, the amateur is a position slightly more liberated from the institutional, political, and authoritative pressures of the professional. Said (1994) defines "amateurism," as an

> activity that is fueled by care and affection rather than by profit and selfish, narrow specialization. . . . The intellectual's spirit as an amateur can enter and transform the merely professional routine most of us go through into something much more lively and radical; instead of doing what one is supposed to do one can ask why one does it, who benefits from it, how can it reconnect with a personal project and original thoughts.
>
> (pp. 82–83)

At its core, the CoP I facilitate invites faculty to immerse themselves in a discipline or activity outside their area of expertise, challenging the tendency for specialization that, as discussed in Chapters 2 and 3, remains a holdover of industrialized models of learning. For example, a Math professor might learn to sail, a Theater instructor could delve into Chemistry, or a Biology professor might explore poetry. The goal is to create an experience that challenges participants, highlights the learning curve, and encourages reflection on how teaching practices can ease the process for students.

In the CoP, faculty *amateurs* design their own learning journeys by selecting activities that are feasible, engaging, and aligned with their interests. Institutions can support these efforts by providing small stipends, covering costs for workshops or materials, and encouraging proposals that include students as collaborators. Faculty amateurs might document their experiences through reflective narratives, identifying how their learning process informs their teaching. Regular discussions with peers or mentors can further enhance these reflections, connecting personal insights to broader educational theories.

A key component of this approach is translating personal learning experiences into actionable insights for the broader teaching community. Faculty can identify specific challenges they faced—such as managing cognitive load or sustaining motivation—and use these as starting points to rethink their own teaching practices. They can also develop strategies or tools to share with colleagues, fostering collective growth.

Possible ways to share these insights include organizing workshops, publishing articles, creating digital resources, or presenting them at conferences. These activities not only amplify the benefits of the learning journey but also contribute to a culture of professional development that values exploration and collaboration. Faculty who take this approach model the importance of lifelong learning and demonstrate how self-care through intellectual growth can enhance teaching and learning.

> Giving ourselves permission to step into the role of an amateur is a powerful way to inspire innovation in teaching practices and restore a sense of joy in learning. This process nurtures empathy and creativity, reminding educators of the challenges their students face and helping them design more supportive learning environments. It also fosters a sense of solidarity among faculty, creating opportunities to build meaningful connections and share insights.

CoPs—or community in general—remind us of the importance of integrating care into our professional lives. As Felten et al. (2023) note, care within a community requires a multidirectional network of relationships—restoring one connection restores many others. By prioritizing their growth and sharing their insights, educators not only enhance their teaching but also contribute to a vibrant culture of care and innovation. Institutions that adopt similar approaches will find that professional development becomes not just a goal but a shared journey toward excellence, enjoyment, and well-being.

References

Allegretto, S. (2022, May 10). The teacher pay penalty has hit a new high. *Economic Policy Institute.* https://www.epi.org/publication/teacher-pay-penalty-2022.

Allen, K. A., Slaten, C. D., Arslan, G., Roffey, S., Craig, H., & Vella-Brodrick, D. A. (2021). School belonging: The importance of student and teacher relationships. In *The Palgrave handbook of positive education* (pp. 525–550). Springer International Publishing.

Berg, M., & Seeber, B. K. (2016). *The slow professor: Challenging the culture of speed in the academy.* University of Toronto Press.

Brenan, M. (2022, December 6). Nurses retain top ethics rating, but below 2020 high. *Gallup.* https://news.gallup.com/poll/467804/nurses-retain-top-ethics-rating-below-2020-high.aspx.

Brewer, E. W., & Shapard, L. (2004). Employee burnout: A meta-analysis of the relationship between age or years of experience. *Human Resource Development Review, 3*(2), 102–123.

Chi, M. T. (2006). Two approaches to the study of experts' characteristics. In *The Cambridge handbook of expertise and expert performance* (pp. 21–30).

Felten, P., Lambert, L. M., Artze-Vega, I., & Tapia, O. R. M. (2023). *Connections Are Everything: A College Student's Guide to Relationship-Rich Education.* JHU Press.

Giattino, C., Ortiz-Ospina, E., & Roser, M. (2020). Working hours. *Our World in Data.* https://ourworldindata.org/working-hours.

Hartman, Y., & Darab, S. (2012). A call for slow scholarship: A case study on the intensification of academic life and its implications for pedagogy. *Review of Education, Pedagogy, and Cultural Studies, 34*(1–2), 49–60.

Heath, C., & Heath, D. (2007). *Made to stick: Why some ideas survive and others die.* Random House.

Hinds, P. J. (1999). The curse of expertise: The effects of expertise and debiasing methods on prediction of novice performance. *Journal of Experimental Psychology: Applied, 5*(2), 205–221.

Iasevoli, B. (2018, March 6). Survey shows support for an Oklahoma teacher strike. *Education Week*. https://www.edweek.org/teaching-learning/survey-shows-support-for-an-oklahoma-teacher-strike/2018/03.

Lasater, K. B., Aiken, L. H., Sloane, D. M., French, R., Martin, B., Reneau, K., . . . & McHugh, M. D. (2021). Chronic hospital nurse understaffing meets COVID-19: An observational study. *BMJ Quality & Safety*, *30*(8), 639–647.

Lave, J., & Wenger, E. (1991). *Situated learning: Legitimate peripheral participation.* Cambridge University Press.

Li, L. Z., Yang, P., Singer, S. J., Pfeffer, J., Mathur, M. B., & Shanafelt, T. (2024). Nurse burnout and patient safety, satisfaction, and quality of care: A systematic review and meta-analysis. *JAMA Network Open*, *7*(11), e2443059.

Martela, F. (2014). Sharing well-being in a work community: Exploring well-being-generating relational systems. In *Emotions and the organizational fabric (Research on emotion in organizations, vol. 10)* (pp. 79–110). Emerald Group Publishing.

Mountz, A., Bonds, A., Mansfield, B., Loyd, J., Hyndman, J., Walton-Roberts, M., ... & Curran, W. (2015). For slow scholarship: A feminist politics of resistance through collective action in the neoliberal university. *ACME: An International Journal for Critical Geographies*, *14*(4), 1235–1259.

National Education Association. (2021, June 15). Survey: Alarming number of educators may soon leave the profession. *NEA Today*. https://www.nea.org/nea-today/all-news-articles/survey-alarming-number-educators-may-soon-leave-profession.

Pope-Ruark, R. (2022). *Unraveling faculty burnout: Pathways to reckoning and renewal.* JHU Press.

Rizvi Jafree, S., Burhan, S. K., & Mahmood, Q. K. (2023). Predictors for stress in special education teachers: Policy lessons for teacher support and special needs education development during the COVID pandemic and beyond. *Journal of Human Behavior in the Social Environment*, *33*(5), 615–632.

Said, E. W. (1994). *Representations of the intellectual* (1st American ed.). Pantheon Books.

Serafin, L., Kusiak, A., & Czarkowska-Pączek, B. (2022). The COVID-19 pandemic increased burnout and bullying among newly graduated nurses but did not impact the relationship between burnout and bullying and self-labelled subjective feeling of being bullied: A cross-sectional, comparative study. *International Journal of Environmental Research and Public Health*, *19*(3), 1730.

Sinclair, S., Raffin-Bouchal, S., Venturato, L., Mijovic-Kondejewski, J., & Smith-MacDonald, L. (2017). Compassion fatigue: A meta-narrative review of the healthcare literature. *International Journal of Nursing Studies*, *69*, 9–24.

Skovholt, T. M., & Trotter-Mathison, M. (2010). *The resilient practitioner: Burnout prevention and self-care strategies for counselors, therapists, teachers, and health professionals.* Routledge.

Stimpfel, A. W., Fatehi, F., & Kovner, C. (2020). Nurses' sleep, work hours, and patient care quality, and safety. *Sleep Health*, *6*(3), 314–320.

Tessema, M. T., Tesfom, G., Faircloth, M. A., Tesfagiorgis, M., & Teckle, P. (2022). The "great resignation": Causes, consequences, and creative HR management strategies. *Journal of Human Resource and Sustainability Studies*, *10*(1), 161–178.

Tonkin, A., & Whitaker, J. (Eds.). (2016). *Play in healthcare for adults: Using play to promote health and wellbeing across the adult lifespan.* Routledge.

Wenger-Trayner, E., & Wenger-Trayner, B. (2015). Introduction to communities of practice. https://www.wenger-trayner.com/introduction-to-communities-of-practice/.

Wigert, B. (2020). *Employee burnout: The biggest myth.* Gallup. https://www.gallup.com/workplace/288539/employee-burnout-biggest-myth.aspx.

Zee, M., & Koomen, H. M. (2016). Teacher self-efficacy and its effects on classroom processes, student academic adjustment, and teacher well-being: A synthesis of 40 years of research. *Review of Educational Research*, *86*(4), 981–1015.

CONCLUSION

We Care!

Chapter Contents
Developing Expertise by Caring-With 144
A Communal Care Kit 146
References 148

One of the most hopeful books about education is Zoe Weil's (2021) *The World Becomes What We Teach: Educating a Generation of Solutionaries*. Although the book is written for educators working with children, Weil's central argument is more pertinent than ever, for those who teach learners of all ages. Considering the restrictions on curricula that target and learning that results in critical awareness, I return to Weil's book with renewed interest. Weil reminds teachers that their practice and impact directly shape the kinds of humans students become, which also means that teachers actively create the future. But Weil doesn't place added pressure onto teachers; rather, her reminder serves to empower our potential to prepare students to think critically, creatively, and hopefully about the significant challenges we collectively face. In this moment of disconnection, isolation, and disengagement, relationships matter the most. The more relational we make teaching, the closer we get to changing the systems that have constituted an unjust world.

Of course, as adrienne maree brown (2021) cautions, the immediate reaction of trying to "solve" problems without understanding them and our role in creating them in the first place can often make things worse. Unfettered capitalism created abject poverty, and the immediate response to abject poverty is to deregulate capitalism even more. Industrial technology created the current climate crisis, and the immediate response to climate change is to increase industrial technology. Defunding higher education created educational inequities, and the immediate response to these inequities is to defund higher education *and* the federal agencies that support education. Whether these solutions were ever meant to be legitimate solutions in the first place is one thing. Still, it remains critical that we teach students how to sit with problems, "stay with the trouble," in Donna Haraway's (2016) words, and understand how to disentangle injustice from the structures that insist the injustice continue to exist. Every syllabus I share with students, regardless of the class, includes the popular quote attributed to Albert Einstein: "If I had an hour to solve a problem, I'd spend 55 minutes thinking about the problem and 5 minutes thinking about solutions."

Rather than jumping straight into solutions, Weil (2021) argues that "if young people are to become solutionaries, they must be permitted to explore and grapple with controversial topics" (p. 32). Exploration suggestions permission to care about particular interests and grappling suggests the desirable difficulty of caring for particular interests. Connecting interests and students into interdependent ecologies requires careful emotional navigation. Weil (2021) writes,

> When people actively and energetically pursue information and gain knowledge, they often want to share their new perspectives with others. Sometimes they do so with critical *attitude*, not just critical *thinking*, and when this happens, learning and thinking suffer. It's important to ensure respectful dialogue in classrooms and reinforce good communication and listening skills.
>
> *(p. 34)*

Solutionaries commit to solving problems in ways that benefit as many people as possible. Like Kimmerer (2013) with her pond in Chapter 1, problems are always interconnected with other systems, requiring deep thought and compassion about what solutions mean for everyone. Weil (2021) reimagines education as a tool for transforming how we care about the world, shifting the focus from individual success to collective well-being. Through her concept of "solutionary" education, Weil encourages students to develop the critical thinking and ethical reasoning needed to solve these urgent problems. This approach shifts the purpose of learning from personal gain to the well-being of society and the planet. When researchers Syropoulos and Markowitz (2024) found that people who cared about future generations were more likely to engage in pro-environmental behavior, they concluded, "focusing greater attention on the responsibilities that people alive today hold" toward one another provides "a powerful mechanism for motivating the action necessary to confront this challenge" (p. 9). Echoing Weil, such evidence demonstrates the importance and the effectiveness of focusing our teaching efforts on solutionary care. Ultimately, Weil's model redirects education toward fostering compassion, collaboration, and problem-solving for the common good, transforming learning into an act of caring with the world as a whole.

Teaching interdependent care entails the creation of a pluriverse. Maggie Fitzgerald (2022) explores the concept of care in the context of the "pluriverse," a term often used to describe a world with diverse ways of being, knowing, and experiencing. She emphasizes the importance of recognizing and valuing multiple perspectives and practices of care that exist across different cultures and communities, as difference can often lead to tensions when divisions in discourse or social position ossify into ontological barriers. Fitzgerald argues that care should not be understood as a universal, one-size-fits-all concept. Instead, it should be seen as diverse and context-specific, shaped by cultural, social, and environmental factors. She suggests that embracing this diversity in care requires an explicit acknowledgment of our relational ontologies—how we exist in relation to one another, human and more than human. Accepting this reality exposes an important vulnerability in being, one that requires interdependent care. "If moral selves are constituted in and through relations," Fitzgerald (2022) writes:

> [T]hen our very subjectivity is vulnerable and inextricably dependent on those relations. We are the product of relations; should those relations change, our vulnerable subjectivity would also change. There is not some transcendental self that can traverse different relations and contexts. . . . The self rather emerges in and through relations and contexts, and is susceptible to changes in these relations and contexts.
>
> *(p. 148)*

Fitzgerald's (2022) theory of care in the pluriverse has empirical support in the relational self-construal research referenced in Chapters 1 and 2. We have also examined evidence indicating that a philosophy of interdependent care is supported in educational research as well as health science (Seeman, 1996; Christakis & Fowler, 2013). The benefits are also, of course, ecological, helping us not only teach students but also directly shape a world strongly influenced by increasing AI, separation of class, race, politics, gender, ability—division upon division. The more that individuals isolate into their own belief-reinforcing communities, the angrier they are likely to become at those who disagree (Filsinger, 2024). What many scholars suggest is an urgently needed outcome of education is the development of "relational expertise."

Developing Expertise by Caring-With

As we discussed earlier, one of the ways that higher education systems have disconnected students is through their conception of expertise. Traditionally, expertise has been framed as a fixed, individual attribute—skills, knowledge, and talent that one either possesses or lacks. This view positions expertise as internal and static, disconnected from the environments and relationships in which it is practiced. Yet as Emirbayer (1997) and others have argued, expertise is fundamentally relational. A physician's expertise, for instance, only materializes through interaction with a patient. That same expertise might be diminished in relation to colleagues or entirely irrelevant when engaging as a parent with a child. Expertise is thus context-bound and contingent, shaped by the dynamics of the relationships in which it is enacted.

As large language models and generative AI technologies rise in capability and influence, they expose the limitations of traditional, individualistic notions of expertise. Frey and Osborne (2013, 2017) predicted that nearly half of U.S. employment is at high risk of automation—including many roles previously considered immune due to their non-routine cognitive demands. Similarly, McKinsey Global Institute (Manyika et al., 2017; Lund et al., 2019) and the World Bank (2016) have projected significant workforce displacement due to automation. These predictions challenge the once-stable assumption that individuals can simply "skill up" to avoid job loss. In this new terrain, where disruption is constant, the most adaptive skillsets are not necessarily specialized but relational, developed through meaningful collaboration, responsiveness, and interdependence.

Despite this, we are witnessing an increase in specialization (Susskind, 2020), accompanied by greater social isolation (Putnam, 2000), political polarization (Brooks, 2020), and cultural homogeneity in elite professional spaces (Rivera, 2015). Educational technology often exacerbates these divides. Sherry Turkle (2011) warns that while we are more connected than ever, we are also more alone. Technology routinely promises to solve problems—speed up communication, expand connection, reduce inefficiency—but it often intensifies the very issues it claims to resolve. Take email, for example: originally intended to make communication faster and easier, it now consumes and exhausts us. As Turkle (2011) puts it:

> Now we know that once computers connected us to each other, once we became tethered to the network, we really didn't need to keep computers busy. They keep us busy. It is as though we have become their killer app. As a friend of mine put it in a moment of pique, "We don't do our e-mail; our e-mail does us." We talk about "spending" hours on e-mail, but we, too, are being spent.
>
> (p. 279)

We are constantly performing, multitasking, and switching contexts. While technology expands our reach, it often hollows out our relationships, illuminating a tragic irony that Turkle (2011) perfectly articulated: "We enjoy continual connection but rarely have each other's full attention" (p. 280). This erosion of presence undercuts the possibility of developing relational expertise skills that depend on co-presence, care, and shared meaning.

Educators cannot always choose their teaching modalities, but whether online or in-person, we must center the practice of caring-with our students. Stable internet connections are not enough; we need stable relationships. As Pakarinen and Huising (2024) argue, relational practices and mindsets offer the kind of future-proofing that higher education desperately needs. In the context of AI, a relational approach means integrating new tools into existing and emerging social relationships rather than replacing human roles with algorithmic substitutes. Relational expertise, in this sense, is less about what one knows and more about *how* one knows in concert with others.

From a relational standpoint, entities—including people, knowledge, and tools—derive meaning only through their interactions. A teacher becomes a teacher not in isolation, but through their engagement with students, shaped by the specific context and needs of that shared environment (Pakarinen & Huising, 2024). Expertise, too, is generated through these entanglements—among actor groups, material objects, and concepts (Eyal, 2013, 2019). It occurs at multiple levels: in interactions (DiBenigno, 2018), within organizations (Sandefur, 2015), and across professional fields (Star & Griesemer, 1989).

Barley (1996) distinguishes between *substantive expertise*—abstract and formal, often credentialed—and *relational expertise*, which is emergent, contextual, and practiced in real time. Because professional work is always embedded in institutional and interpersonal contexts, relational expertise becomes critical to its performance. It is not only a way of knowing but also a way of *being with* others. As Fitzgerald (2022) argues, we live in a pluriverse—a world of many worlds—where relational identities are essential for navigating uncertainty and complexity. Relational expertise enables us to respond more adaptively to these shifting realities.

To meet this moment of disruption, we must reimagine expertise as something grown and shared, like the mycorrhizal networks beneath forest soil, through which trees and plants exchange nutrients and support in times of stress. Just as these underground systems sustain life by connecting organisms, relational expertise depends on caring-with one another. It is through these interdependent ties that we can survive and thrive in a rapidly changing world.

A Communal Care Kit

The Care Kit entries we developed are yours for adaptation and revision. I do encourage you to share them with others for further revision. A communal garden feeds a community. Returning one last time to Maggie Fitzgerald (2022), a change that occurs at the level of a classroom activity or single assignment can result in changes for your entire class. A remedy can take root. But this can also happen across teachers. When people change together, systems transform and new worlds become possible.

In *Humans Who Teach: A Guide for Centering Love, Justice, and Liberation in Schools*, Shamari Reid (2024) reminds us that love must be a collective project, something we practice, share, and model with intention. His book challenges educators to socialize ourselves and our students toward interdependence by centering love as both an ethic and an action. Reid does not treat care as an abstract value but as a practical necessity that we must learn, teach, and live in community. He encourages educators to build spaces that sustain both self and others, so that care becomes an everyday, shared responsibility.

This is precisely what the Care Kit aims to cultivate: strategies for enacting care-with—where we don't just model compassion but actively teach students how to engage in mutual care. Reid (2024) urges us to reject the isolating myths of individualism and burnout that plague our profession, and instead invites us into a model of teaching rooted in love, justice, and human connection. By prioritizing our own well-being and creating space for others to do the same, we build classrooms that are not only more just and joyful but also more transformative. When educators practice interdependence, we show students how to do the same. And in doing so, we begin to shift the trajectories not just of individual students but also of collective futures.

When I reflect on my own educational journey, which included detentions in middle school, suspensions in high school, and even academic probation my second year in community college, I am often surprised I survived long enough to earn a PhD. I am even more surprised to realize how much I love education. I remember how often I would say, "I love learning, but I hate school." I grew up in a Spanish-speaking household in 1980s and 1990s Miami, Florida, a time that defined "a good Cuban-American" as one who assimilated by exchanging one cultural identity for the other. And so English was the only language I could formally learn, despite being surrounded by Spanish. As a result—this time to no surprise—I ended up in speech therapy. I struggled reading aloud, frequently to the laughter of other students.

For all of my struggles, my parents almost willed me through schooling. After stumbling to high school graduation, my parents offered to financially support me so long as I attended Valencia Community College (now Valencia College). If I chose against college, I would have to move out. My mother, like her parents, did not go to college. My father, like his parents, only partially completed college. He attended different schools off and on, collecting enough credits and work experience until he finally passed the Certified Public Accountant (CPA) exam. Because my parents loved me, they did not want my story to begin with "like my parents."

But mine did.

I struggled. I felt excluded. I felt "other." I believed I was not intelligent. And then, one semester at Valencia, I took an introduction to creative writing class and met the professor who saved my life. To be very clear, that professor simply did her job. She assigned prompts that allowed me choice in how I engaged. She listened to all of us share personal stories and then used those personal stories to connect to the content. She allowed us to choose our own readings based on our interests, and it was she who introduced me to Gabriel García Márquez's *One Hundred Years of*

Solitude, the book that was like a crystal ball, revealing so many possibilities for my imagination to consider. I fell in love with magical realism. I majored in creative writing. And then I pursued educational psychology to answer the ultimate question: how did I so dramatically transform my care for education?

(Hopefully, this book has offered an answer.)

How humans develop depends on their relations with themselves, other humans, their teachers, and the content they seek to master. In our fragmented, hurting world, we need models who know how to empathize with others, bring people together, and bravely address serious challenges. We need students who care. And we need teachers to show them how.

References

brown, a. m. (2021). *Holding change: The way of emergent strategy facilitation and mediation.* AK Press.

Barley, S. R. (1996). Technicians in the workplace: Ethnographic evidence for bringing work into organizational studies. *Administrative Science Quarterly, 41*(3), 404–441.

Brooks, D. (2020). *The second mountain: The quest for a moral life.* Random House.

Christakis, N. A., & Fowler, J. H. (2013). Social contagion theory: Examining dynamic social networks and human behavior. *Statistics in Medicine, 32*(4), 556–577.

DiBenigno, J. (2018). Anchored personalization in managing role conflict between professional groups: The case of U.S. Army mental health care. *Administrative Science Quarterly, 63*(2), 279–323.

Emirbayer, M. (1997). Manifesto for a relational sociology. *American Journal of Sociology, 103*(2), 281–317.

Eyal, G. (2013). For a sociology of expertise: The social origins of the autism epidemic. *American Journal of Sociology, 118*(4), 863–907.

Eyal, G. (2019). *The crisis of expertise.* Polity Press.

Filsinger, M. (2024). Bringing emotions in: How anger shapes the relationship between social isolation and populist attitudes. *American Behavioral Scientist*, https://doi.org/10.1177/00027642241241133.

Fitzgerald, M. (2022). *Care and the pluriverse: Rethinking global ethics.* Policy Press.

Frey, C. B., & Osborne, M. A. (2013). *The future of employment: How susceptible are jobs to computerisation?* Oxford Martin School.

Frey, C. B., & Osborne, M. A. (2017). The future of employment: How susceptible are jobs to computerisation? *Technological Forecasting and Social Change, 114*, 254–280.

Haraway, D. J. (2016). *Staying with the trouble: Making kin in the Chthulucene.* Duke University Press.

Kimmerer, R. W. (2013). *Braiding sweetgrass: Indigenous wisdom, scientific knowledge and the teachings of plants.* Milkweed Editions.

Lund, S., Madgavkar, A., Manyika, J., & Smit, S. (2019). *The future of work in America: People and places, today and tomorrow.* McKinsey Global Institute.

Manyika, J., Chui, M., Miremadi, M., Bughin, J., George, K., Willmott, P., & Dewhurst, M. (2017). *A future that works: Automation, employment, and productivity.* McKinsey Global Institute.

Pakarinen, P., & Huising, R. (2024). Relational work in an algorithmic world: Designing for meaningful human-AI collaboration. *Academy of management perspectives.* Advance Online Publication.

Putnam, R. D. (2000). *Bowling alone: The collapse and revival of American community.* Simon & Schuster.

Reid, S. (2024). *Humans who teach: A guide for centering love, justice, and liberation in schools.* Heinemann.

Rivera, L. A. (2015). *Pedigree: How elite students get elite jobs.* Princeton University Press.

Sandefur, R. L. (2015). Elements of professional expertise: Understanding relational and substantive expertise through lawyers' impact. *American Sociological Review, 80*(5), 909–933.

Seeman, T. E. (1996). Social ties and health: The benefits of social integration. *Annals of Epidemiology, 6*(5), 442–451.

Star, S. L., & Griesemer, J. R. (1989). Institutional ecology, "translations" and boundary objects: Amateurs and professionals in Berkeley's Museum of Vertebrate Zoology. *Social Studies of Science, 19*(3), 387–420.

Susskind, R. (2020). *The future of the professions: How technology will transform the work of human experts.* Oxford University Press.

Syropoulos, S., & Markowitz, E. (2024). Responsibility towards future generations is a strong predictor of proenvironmental engagement. *Journal of Environmental Psychology, 93*, 1–11.

Turkle, S. (2011). *Alone together: Why we expect more from technology and less from each other.* Basic Books.

Weil, Z. (2021). *The world becomes what we teach: Educating a generation of solutionaries.* Lantern Books.

World Bank. (2016). *World development report 2016: Digital dividends.* World Bank Publications.

INDEX

Abelard, P. 31–32
"Abolition of Work, The" (Black) 111
academia: agenda, change 38; colonial legacy 2; lived experiences, disconnect 34
Academic Capitalism in the Age of Globalization (Cantwell/Kauppinen) 38
academic failure 93–94
academic freedom, attacks (justification) 41
academic journal publishing, institutional pressures 138
academic life, balance 134
academic motivation, enhancement 93
academic outcomes, improvement 64
academic programs, communities (connection) 105–106
academic self-efficacy 64
accessibility justice 27
accreditation agencies, impact 52–53
acknowledgment, acts 8
actionable pedagogy 26
action/reaction, relationship 24–25
adaptability/growth, capacity (building) 115
Adopt a Concept (Care Kit) 120–122
adult learning: evidence-based practices 113; play, value 110–112
agriculture, replacement 33
Ahmed, S. 130

Air Nomads (*Avatar the Last Airbender*) 102
airplane analogy, functioning system (need) 133
Alternative Reality 4
amateur: defining 138; reconsideration 137
ambiguities, society (confrontation) 119
analytical thinking 89
ancestors, reciprocal relationships 19
antiracist justice 27
anti-social century, student socialization 91
anxiety: increase 239; social anxiety 93–94
Anxious Generation, The (Haidt) 10, 94
Aquinas, T. 31
Arará: culture, characteristics 18–19; interdependence, practice 19; people, enslavement 18
Aristotle 31
Ark: Survival Ascended (video game) 106–107; design, teacher classroom design (comparison) 108–110; feature 117; game context 118
artificial intelligence (AI): advancement, impact 126; development 6; disruption 109–110; influence, increase 12
Art of Gathering: How We Meet and Why It Matters (Parker) 80
attention: description, spotlight metaphor 15; scope, narrowing 26–27

Index

authoritarian governance structures, student protests 34
automation, impact 145
Avatar the Last Airbender (series) 101
awe: defining 63; dispositional awe scales 64; experiencing, prosocial effects 63; peer-rated curiosity, relationship 64
Ayni, Andean concept 21

backstories: impact 82; validation 65–67
"bad apple" mentality 46
Barr, R. 4
belief, believing 77–79
belonging: positive relationships, connection 75; sense 39
Ben-Avie, M. 91–92
benevolence, framing 5
Berg, M. 88, 131
Biesta, G. 121
"Big Six" college experience 7
"Bill Gates Should Stop Telling Africans What Kind of Agriculture Africans Need" (Belay/Mugambe) 14
Black, B. 120
Black/Latino students, SAT cultural bias 39
Blom, P. 32
bonding facilitation, dopamine (impact) 90
Boulding, K. 22
boundaries, importance 132–133
Bowling Alone: The Collapse and Revival of American Community (Putnam) 2
Braiding Sweetgrass (Wall Kimmerer) 12
brain: curiosity reliance 60–61; hardwiring 90; long-term brain health, resilience support 62; pattern learning, enjoyment 118; reward system (activation), curiosity (impact) 60; uncertainty minimization/energy conservation 41–42
Brazil: literacy issues 73; military dictatorship 73
Brock, M. 109–110
Brooks, D. 82
Brown, A.M. 46, 142
Brown-Dean, K. 87, 133–134
Brown, S. 111
Brown, W. 38
Burbano de Lara, L. 74
burnout 125–126; avoidance 132–133; confrontation 126–129; early signs 134; experience 125; faculty burnout 35; perpetuation 131; profession exits 127; reports 126–127
"business as usual" (impossibility) 125
Butler, J. 17

caciques (chiefs), leadership 20
campus activism, impact 34
Cantwell, B. 38
care: center, teacher role (reduction) 8; coddling, contrast 3; collective care, benefit 133–134; committed action 24–25; "crisis of care" (creation), capitalism (impact) 5; culture wars 38–43; defining 3–7; economic gain, equivalence 5; feminist ethics 130; gendered term 5; higher education history 31–38; holistic care 5; incorporation, complexities 13; interdependent care, teaching 144; interdependent frameworks 6; learning 2–3; neoliberal care 34–38; networks (cultivation), embedded learning communities (impact) 89; ownership, equivalence 5; pedagogy, equivalence 56–59; postmodern care 33–34; post-war care 33; prevention 129; productivity, equivalence 5; redefining 5; redirection 33; teaching 7–9, 27–28; Tronto definition 13; *see also* self-care
"cared for" experience 15–16
career: outcomes, focus 37; preparation, enhancement 93
Care Kit: Adopt a Concept 120–122; aim 147; backstories, validation 65–67; communal Care Kit 146–148; communities of practice, support 135–140; contribution 54, 88–89; cultivation aims 147; curiosity sharing 73–74; development 8–9; learning community cultivation 99–103; sharing 8; thin-slicing 81–84; usage 54; variation, usage 135
"care work is work" assertion 130–131
caring: connections, nurturing 135; content, usage 55–56; forms, co-creation 15–16; imagining, higher education (combination) 45–48; relationships, networks (incorporation) 132
caring-about: assistance 15, 113; attention, alignment 15; capacity, expansion 114;

152 Index

caring-for, distinction 14; clarification 16; connection 116; consideration 15–16; focus 15, 114; importance 114; reduction 14
caring, cost 15
caring-for 114; assistance 113; caring-about, distinction 15–16; connecting 116; considerations 15–16; ethical practice 16; labor, sharing 92; relational support, involvement 114; students, caring-for 115; support 92
caring-with 16, 115–118; amplification 78; assistance 113; attention 17; cultivation 99; experiences/interests, sharing 92; humans, development 91–92; initiation 84; intellectual/emotional caring-with 82; minoritization/underrepresentation 39; strategy 137; system, cultivation 44; teachers, strategy 137; thinking-with 17
caring world, building 45–46
Carlson, T. 35
Casey, P.J. 45
Catholic Church teachings, contradiction (avoidance) 37
Cavanagh, S.R. 6
celerity, demonstration 6
censorship, issues 3
ChatGPT, usage 109–110
cheating 36
Chevron, climate science reduction 37
Chi, M. 138
classes, relationships 22
classmates, treatment 2–3
classroom: boundaries (dissolution), quarantine (impact) 3; creation 111; culture, CST promotion 75–76; environment, care (incorporation) 7; familiar model 72; focal point 54; play space, creation 111; reframing 78; teacher design, *Ark* design (comparison) 108–110
coddling, issues 3
Coddling of the American Mind: How Good Intentions and Bad Ideas Are Setting Up a Generation for Failure (Lukianoff/Haidt) 3
cognitive load, impact 26–27
cognitive outcomes, diversity (benefits) 76–77
cognitive resilience 62
cognitive resources, requirement 116–117
Cold War, crisis 41

collaboration 36, 115; emphasis 76–77; focus 27
collaborative grading method, comparison 98
collaborative problem-solving, studies 63
collaborative work, engagement 99
collective care, benefit 133–134
collective effort, requirement 97
collective responsibility, understanding 90
collectivist orientations, psychological adjustment (correlation) 39
college education, Carlson perspective 35
college experiences: idea, innovation 31; identification (Gallup-Purdue Index study) 7
college-to-job narrative 47
collegial governance, attacks (justification) 41
communal care, impact 5
communal Care Kit 146–148
communal garden 146
communal spaces, fostering 131
communication skills: problems 45; reinforcement 143
community: creation, challenge 53; shared community, learning/caring 76; themes 105–106
community building 129; games, influence 106
community of practice (CoP): Care Kit 135–140; concept 136; multi-year community of practice, example 137
compassion fatigue 14–15
competition, stress 39
complex reasoning, promotion 76
conflict, experiences 23
Confucianism 21
Connections Are Everything (Felten et al.) 93
connection, teaching 96–99
consciousness, defining 60–61
consumerism, masquerade 44
consumption/self-care, manufactured cycle 44
content: living with 121–122; student care 103; student learning, issues 53
context: interests, stability 113–114; performing/multitasking/switching 145; student immersion 108
continuous feedback, providing 103
contradictions, society (confrontation) 119
Conuco techniques 20

cooperation, fostering 90
cooperative learning 18, 96–97; benefits 77
co-presence, dependence 145
corporate-groomed individuals, university leaders (connection) 38
cost of caring 15
Council of Soissons 32
course assessment, activity/assignment (iterative process) 83
course content, personal goals (connection) 77
COVID-19 pandemic: disruption 1–2; in-person interactions 106; interaction, learning 95–96; protective measure, nurse advocacy (bullying) 128; spread 125; stressors 39
Coyote (trickster) 119–120
creative problem-solving 100
creative thinking 89
creativity 36; defining process 118–119; fostering 110; impeding 42; nurturing 140; promotion 76
"crisis of care" (creation), capitalism (impact) 5
critical attitude 143
critical consciousness (*conscientização*), fostering 73
critical race theory, understanding 34
critical thinking 37, 143; defining process 118–119; promotion 76
cultural blending 18
cultural expectation, pervasiveness 128
cultural identities, affirmation 78
culturally sensitive teaching (CST), impact 75–76
Culturally Sustaining Pedagogies (Paris/Alim) 76
culture change, demand 78–79
culture, hegemony (preference) 76
culture wars 38–43
curiosity 55–56; cultivation 54, 64–65; decline 61; etymology 58; flourishing 89; interdependence, relationship 62–65; peer-rated curiosity 64; satisfaction 60; science 59–62; sharing 73–74; survival rate, correlation 61–62
Curiosity and Exploration Inventory (CEI-II) 64
curiosity-driven innovation, emergence 90
curriculum (curricula): design 76; designers 52–53; focus 36; space, creation 71–74
"curse of knowledge" 55, 138

DALL-E, usage 102
Dao (natural flow of the universe) 21
Daoism 21
Davidson, C. 32
de-centered pedagogical approaches, impact 4
decision-making: limited information, impact 100; processes, control 22–23
deconstruction (Derrida) 56
decontextualizaed community, usage 136
de-industrialization 46
deities, reciprocal relationships 19
democratic rights, postmodern care 33–34
Denial, C. 7, 80
Derrida, J. 56–58
"desirable difficulties" 118
Dewey, J. 25, 75, 112, 120
dialogue, adaptation/engagement ability (absence) 57
DiCarlo, S. 54, 56
disciplines, framing (games perspective) 109
disconnection 142, 144–145; normalcy, problem 94–96
disengaged students, problems/issues 9–10
disengagement 93–94, 142
dispositional awe scales 64
diversity, equity, and inclusion (DEI) 34; attack 2, 38; DEI-aligned teaching practices, impact 78; eliminations 38–39
dopamine: age-related declines 61; bonding facilitation 90; hit 60
dreamtime, usage 21
Drive: the Surprising Truth About What Motivates Us (Pink) 111
Durkheim, E. 22

Earth Kingdom (*Avatar the Last Airbender*) 102
ecology: change 47; complexity 27–28; definition 4; dependence 9; differences 13; Freire, existence 73; higher education ecology 8, 28; relationships, expansion 84; varieties, existence 12–13
ecology of care 8; creation 8; cultivation 8, 9, 135
ecology of stress: higher education, existence 126; life, unsustainability 41; navigation 39–42
education: banking concept 72; profession, exit plan levels (elevation) 127; solutionary education, concept 143

educational inequities (creation), higher education defunding (impact) 142–143
educational technology, impact 145
educational trajectories, COVID-19 disruption 1–2
efficiency: institutional focus, problems 128–129; Marxist critique 36; obsession 35
Einstein, a. 143
embedded learning communities, impact 89
emotional connection, ability (decrease) 15
emotional contagion, presence 6
emotional labor: sidelining 130–131; teacher/nurse performance 127
emotional navigation 143
emotional numbness, feelings 15
emotional symptoms, challenge 124–125
emotional well-being, prioritization 61
empathy: acts 8; nurturing 140; practicing 126–127
employment disappearance, automation (impact) 145
end-of-term evaluation 72
end-of-term surveys 83
engagement, fostering 110
enlightenment, feeling 60
entanglements, impact 146
environments, disconnection 144–145
equity-focused interventions, impact 77
equity gaps 76–77
ethnic studies curriculum, assessment 76
Eureka moment 59
Every Man in His Humour (Jonson) 58
evidence-based practices 113
exam performance, improvement 76
exclusion, perpetuation 131
experience, knowledge (contrast) 119
expertise: context-bound/contingent aspect 145; development 144–146; types 146
exploration, prioritization 48
external guidance 115
external signs, reliance 56–57
extractive practices, disentanglement 28
extraneous load, elimination 117

Facebook users, derogatory posts (sharing) 96
face-to-face promotive interaction, student requirements 97
factory workers, appearance/increase 32–33
factual information, memorization 72

faculty: burnout 35, 129; performance, quantification 36; positions/departments/programs, elimination 41; transparency, increase 35; workload, justification 2
failure: academic failure 93–94; fear 108; normalization 113; perception 25; punishment, absence 107; rates, reduction 76–77
familial/communal bonds, interconnections 19
familiar model, analysis 72
fear of missing out (FOMO) 59
fear, relief 127
Federal Aviation Administration (FAA), advice/message 132–133
feedback 115; continuous feedback, providing 103; need 79; peer feedback, student training 99; peer feedback, training (providing) 99; positive feedback 82; providing 135; student provision 96
"feelings of learning" measurement 53
female martens, care 28
feminism 16–17
fight-or-flight response 41
Fire Nation (*Avatar the Last Airbender*) 102
Fitzgerald, M. 144, 146
Flip, usage 120
Floyd, George (murder) 3
formative assessments 47
"For Slow Scholarship: A Feminist Politics of Resistance through Collective Action in the Neoliberal University" (Mountz et al.) 129–130
Frankenstein (Shelley) 6
Free Speech Movement (UCB) 33–34
Freire, P. 72–74; exile 73
Friedman, M. 41, 42
functional MRI (fMRI), usage 60
functioning system, need 133
Future of Jobs 2023 report (WEF) 89, 90
future-proofing 146

Gaither, T. 8
Galileo, G. 32
game: context 118; defining 108; loyalty 117–118; play, rules regulation 108; success conditions, teaching 109; video games, frustration 117
García Márquez, G. 147

Garza, A. 46
Gates, B. 13–14; ideology 13; philanthropy 37
gateway courses 42–43; individualistic environment 43; weeding-out process 43
Generation Z: problems 94; research 95; social experiences, absence (impact) 94
"generous authority" (embodiment) 81
geographical distances, trees (spread) 24
germane load 117
GI Bill, impact 33
Gilligan, C. 6
Giridharadas, A. 13
global economic systems, interdependence 22
globalized consumer economy, impact 33
goals, approach/work 25–26
grading systems, student perceptions 98
grammatical leniency 98
grants: loss 37; result 88
Great Lakes Feminist Geography Collective, authorship (emergence) 130
great resignation 126
Great Upheaval: Higher education's past, present, and uncertain future (Levine/Van Pelt) 32
group-based evaluations, usage 98
groups: dynamics, studies 63; functioning, student discussion 99; learning community function 103; projects, assigning/grading process 93
group work: complaints, counterintuitiveness 90; success 89–94
growth, driving (team reliance) 90
"guide on the side" 4
Gulf of Mexico, British Petroleum (impact) 14

Haidt, J. 3, 10, 94
Haraway, D. 143
Harry Potter 101
harvest, honor 28
health concerns, management 127
Heath, C. 55, 138
Heath, D. 55, 138
hegemony: impact 42; preference 76
helplessness, feelings 15
Hermes (trickster) 119
hierarchical family metaphor, challenge 57
higher education: burnout, confrontation 126–129; care, history 31–38; confidence levels 35; defunding, impact 142–143; ecological stress, impact 45; ecology of stress 40; neoliberal corporate-driven models 31; neoliberalism, coupling 47; neoliberal model 131; students, disengagement 9–10; transformation 31
higher education ecology 8, 28; care, need 30; imagining 47–48; roots 47–48; stress 45
historical materialism, theory (Marx) 22
holistic care 5
homeostatic regulation 60–61
Homo Ludens (Huizinga) 110
honorable harvests, disentanglement 28
Honorable Harvest, teaching 27–28
How People Learn: Brain, Mind, Experience, and School (NRC) 109
Huizinga, J. 110
human activity, institutionalization 111
Humans Who Teach: A Guide for Centering Love, Justice, and Liberation in Schools (Reid) 146
Hyde, L. 120
hyper-specialized majors, curricula focus 36

identity-based support spaces, usage 78
identity, instability 2–3
illegitimate (writing), distinction (issue) 57–58
impact plans 46
"in-against-and-beyond the university" attempt 130
inclusive classrooms, active learning approaches (usage) 76–77
inclusive relationships, fostering 78
inclusive research opportunities, function 77–78
inclusive teachers, impact 77
inclusive teaching 74–77; relational affirmation 75
inclusivity 42
Indigenous cultures: survey/theme 21; web of life viewpoint 20–21
Indigenous epistemologies, contributions 18
Indigenous people, survey/theme 21
individual accountability 26; promotion 97
individual goals, accomplishment 27
individual impact plans 6
individualism 5

individualist orientation 22
individualist orientations, anxiety-induced competition 39
individualist/universalist ethics, questioning 46
individuals, reciprocal relationships 19
industrialization, impact 32–33
industrial order, assemblage 72
inflation-adjusted teacher salaries, decline 128
information, clarity/predictability 23
injustice, vastness (consideration) 15
innovation, team reliance 90
in-person interaction 94; prioritization 106
in-person students, online students (separation) 3
inquiry-based learning (IBL) 67
inquiry/exploration, culture (promotion) 65
intellectual curiosity: prioritization 48; subsidization, absence (Reagan) 35
intellectual/emotional caring-with 82
intentionally equitable hospitality (IEH) 7; theory (Denial) 80
interaction dynamics 23
interconnected learning 18
interdependence 5; belonging, relationship 75; concept 17, 22; curiosity, relationship 62–65; discussion 46; disruption 25; holistic understanding 19; roots 103; simulation, games (usage) 109; theory, defining 22; understanding, dreamtime (usage) 21; understandings 7; wisdom 28
interdependent care: philosophy 144; teaching 144
interdependent classrooms 24–27, 74; creation 75; cultural shift 88; failure, normalization 113
interdependent process 62
interdisciplinary topics, communities (connection) 105–106
interest groups, contributions 133
internal state, maintenance 60–61
intersectional programs, retention promotion success 78
isolation 142

job loss 237
Johnson, D. 7, 17, 25–26
Johnson, R. 7, 17, 25–26
Jones, A. 79–80

Jonson, B. 58
journaling 66

Kauppinen, I. 38
Kelley, H. 22
Kern, C. 87–88, 92
Keynes, J.M. 22
kindergarten games 112
Klein, N. 40–41
knowing: comfort 93; issue 17
knowledge: co-construction 26; co-construction, emphasis 76–77; "curse of knowledge" 55, 138; experience, contrast 119; interdependent system 62; notions (democratization), campus activism (impact) 34; production, ethical questions 33; specialization/credentialism, increase 44; task-specific knowledge, extrapolation 138
Koch family, higher education criticism 37
Koch Foundation, education controls/restrictions 37–38
Kondos Field, Valorie (culture change demand) 78–79

labor: diverse forms, valuing 131; sustainable system, creation 131
labor-based grading method, comparison 98
Lang, J. 93
Last Week Tonight with John Oliver (TV show) 53
Latour, B. 6
learner-centeredness 4
learners, experiences (value) 75
learning: adult learning, play (value) 110–112; challenges, increase 110; cognitive resources requirement 116–117; communities, function 77–78; community, cultivation 99–103; cooperative learning 18, 77, 96–97; develop/design/deliver vision, expansion 4; embedded learning communities, impact 89; enhancement 56; goals 67; impeding 42; interconnected learning 18; outcomes, enhancement 97; perceptions 53; personal learning experience, translation 139; relational learning 42; scholarship, translation 78; science 74–77; self-regulated

learning 113–116; task 26, 118; theory 52; transformation 143
Learning Paradigm 4
legitimate (speech), distinction (issue) 57–58
Lembke, A. 59
Levine, A. 32
Lin, M. 62
listening skills, reinforcement 143
literacy, opportunity 73
Living Learning Community (LLC) program 105–106
Loki (trickster) 119
long-term brain health, resilience support 62
Lukianoff, G. 3

Made to Stick (Heath/Heath) 55
magical realism, enjoyment 148
make-believe, experience 110
managerial interests, protection 41
Manifest Destiny 5
Māori (New Zealand), interdependence (sense) 21
market-oriented principles, application 34
market value, neoliberal care 34–38
Martela, F. 131
Marx, K. 22
Matanzas Province, research 19
"matter of fact," "matter of concern" (differentiation) 16
Matters of Care (Puig de la Bellacasa) 16
McKee, R. 24
meditation 66
mental breakdowns, handling 134–135
mental health: crises 88; decrease 43
mental representations, accommodation 63
mentorship: function 77–78; models 133
mentors, justice involvements 27
meritocracy, impact 42
metacognitive awareness, fostering 115
metaphors, connection 59
middle class, growth 33
"might is right" mentality, reinforcement 42
mild cognitive impairment (MCI) 61–62
military-industrial-academic complex, formation 33
military/university collaboration, student protests 34
minds, "rewiring" 10
mind-wandering, encouragement 48
Mitákuye Oyás'iŋ ("All My Relations") 21

modalities: distributions 88–89; multiplicity 30
monsters, "love" 6–7
motivation, sustaining 115
mutual dependence 22–23
MySpace, debut 2

national security, post-war care 33
Native peoples, "civilizing" 5
natural world, reciprocal relationships 19
Nazir, C. 62
necropolitics 46
neoliberalism 34; acceleration 41; growth, social institution response 44; higher education, coupling 47; promise, failure 43–44; questions 43
neoliberal meritocratic ideologies 43
neoliberal university ("governing rationality") 38
New Deal, welfare issues 41
New Education: How to revolutionize the university to prepare students for a world in flux (Davidson) 32
Newton, E. 55
Newton, I. 32
Noddings, N. 6, 14–16, 113, 114
nomophobia, feature 60
non-routine cognitive demands 145
nonviolence, force 17
Nonviolent Response: Strategies for Responding to Writing (Rysdam/Torres) 78
norepinephrine, age-related declines 61
nurses: burnout, institutional culture/organizational structure (impact) 128–129; burnout rates, patient safety decrease (correlation) 127; earnings, problems 128

One Hundred Years of Solitude (García Márquez) 147–148
one-on-one professor-student meeting 95
one-size-fits-all concept 144
one-size-fits-all strategies, limitations 77–78
on-the-job questions 37
ontological barriers, ossification 144
Openness to Experience factor 64
oppression, mechanism 130
others: care 24; caring-with 115–118
overprotection, issues 3
overwork, problem 88
oxytocin ("bonding hormone"), release 90

Padlet: gallery 120–121; usage 102
Papacy, spiritual authority 31
paradoxes, embodiment 119
Parker, P. 80–81
Pasquarella, L. 6, 35, 45
patterns, brain learning (enjoyment) 118
pedagogical prerogative 36
pedagogical structures 112–113
peer: collaboration, academic advantages 75; discussions 139; interactions 91; pressure, power 71; ratings, usage 64; review, engagement 98
peer feedback: student training 99; training, providing 99
peer-rated curiosity 64
personal development, enhancement 93
personal learning experience, translation 139
personal motivations, focus 64–65
personal relationships, building 95
perspective-taking skills 76
Peterson, Justin 105–106, 118
Phaedrus (Plato) 56–57
physical education instructors, rules (teaching) 109
physical health, outcomes (prediction) 61–62
physical symptoms, emergence 124–125
Pink, D. 111, 120
pity, problematic experience 14
Plato 56–57; hierarchy 57
"Plato's Pharmacy" (Derrida) 56
play: content, usage 112–118; examination 111; free activity, equivalence 110; relationships, involvement 118–120; value 110–112; work, contrast 112
playful activities, engagement (importance) 134
pluriverse 144
polarization 47
political speeches, analysis 114
political tensions, increase 2
Pope-Ruark, R. 126, 129, 134
positive interdependence: occurrence 25–26; sustaining 26
positive relationships, belonging (connection) 75
Post-It notes, usage 120–121
power: extension 14; influence, distribution 22–23
"PowerPoint Improv" activity 100–101
prioritization, process 15
privacy, violation (student debate) 95

privilege, impact 21–22
problem-based learning (PBL) 67
problem-posing education model (Freire) 72–73
production: efficiency 44; modes, relationships 22
productivity: care, equivalence 5; measures, limitations 131; obsession 2, 35
pro-environmental behavior 143
professionalism 137–138
professionalization, outcome 138
program administrators, impact 52–53
project management, team reliance 90
promotive interaction 26
protest policies, administrator enforcement 37
PTSD symptoms, severity/duration (exacerbation) 3
public life, corporate values (entrenchment) 45
public opinion, pressure 127–128
publishing, institutional pressures 138
Puig de la Bellacasa, M. 6, 7, 16–17
Putnam, R. 2

quarantine, impact 3, 125
questions: meditation 66; sets, creation 67

racial segregation, student protests 34
Reacting to the Past (RTTP) 109–110
ready-made categories, conformance 17
Reagan, Ronald (state university funding cuts) 34–35
real-life social interactions, struggle 94
reason, Enlightenment care 32–33
reflection, defining process 118–119
reflective practices, encouragement 48
Reid, S. 146–147
relational expertise 146
relational hosts, teacher role 79–80
relational-interdependent self-construal (RISC) 23–24
relationality, attention 46–47
relational labor, sidelining 130–131
relational learning 42
relational realities, co-creation 17
relational self-construal 24
Relationship-Rich Education (Felten/Lambert) 91, 93
relationships: authenticity 24; curricula, space (creation) 71–74; disconnection 144–145; importance 142–143

religious doctrine, medieval care 31–32
remote learning, pivot 127
research university model 32
resilience 3–4
resources, control 22–23
risk-avoidance behaviors, focus 95
risk, sense 82
risk-taking, encouragement 65
root-level change 92
Rosenau, J. 22
Rysdam, S. 78

safe spaces, issues 3
safety, focus 95
safetyism 3
"sage on the stage" 4
Said, E. 137–139
San Lázaro ceremonies 19
scholarship: engagement 36; reduction, problems 130; relationship-rich education, scholarship 93; teaching/learning translation 78
science, technology, engineering, and math (STEM) 36–37; classes 42; courses, student performance 76–77; fields, women graduates (participation) 39; LLC focus 105; women of color, involvement 78
Scott, Rick 38
screen time, dangers 59
Seeber, B. 88, 131
self-awareness, shaping 61
self-care: consumption/self-care, manufactured cycle 44; devaluation 127; importance 8, 132–133; increase 44; permission 129–132; reframing 132; self-compassion/self-indulgence, comparison 129
self-concept: maintenance 24; stability, maintenance 24
self-consistency, assessment 23–24
self-efficacy 117; elevation, demonstration 109; increase 77
self-evaluation strategy 98
self-indulgence 129
self-reflection, usage 129
self-regulated learning: promotion 113; reference 114–115; usage 115–116
self-specific benefits, favoring 6
selves, boundaries 17
sex identity justice 27
shared community, learning/caring 76
shared environment, needs 146

"shared experience" groups, formation 74
shared home, term (usage) 4
shared interests, learning 62–63
shared labor, fostering 90
shared trust, establishment 27
Shelley, M. 6
shock doctrine 40–41
Sic et Non (Yes and No) (Abelard) 31–32
sickcare system, derision 129
Silko, L.M. 5
situational interest: defining 114; sustaining 115–116
Slow Professor: Challenging the Culture of Speed in the Academy (Berg/Seeber) 88, 131
slow scholarship: call 130; framing, alternative 131
social anxiety 93–94
social connection, instructional outcome 93–94
social constructions 118–119
social contexts, behavior 23–24
social development 95–96
social engagement, curiosity (link) 62–63
social interaction: contextualization 96; issues 8–9
social interdependence: idea, exploration 22; theory, application 25
social interdependent learning theory (SILT) 17, 89–90; emphasis 7; existence 25; pedagogical concept 88–89; practice, translation 96–97; studies, review 26; usage 98
social isolation, increase 145
socialization, games (impact) 106
social justice, attacks 38
social learning theories, usage 89–90
social media: belief reinforcement, company incentive 80; rise/impact 95–96; usage 79–80
social skills, building 95
societal narratives, impact 128
sociocultural participation 135–136
socioemotional selectivity theory 61
soft skills 93–94
solidarity, prevention 36
solutionaries, becoming 143
solutionary education, concept 143
somatic markers, stress (impact) 42
spaces, creation 47, 71–74
specs-based grading method, comparison 98
speech, metaphor 57

spirits, communication 20
spotlight, metaphor 15
status-seeking actions, issues 88
stories, sharing 66
stress: cognitive responses, desensitization 42; ecology, navigation 39–42; impact 42; normalization 88; profession exits 127; relief, desire 127; structure, equivalence 42–43
structural change, necessity 128–129
structural equation modeling, usage 64
structural transformation 46
structured networking 133
"student among students" role 74
students: achievement, improvement 76; Black/Latino students, SAT cultural bias 39; care 87, 105; caring-for 115; collaborator role 139; complementary roles/tasks, collective effort (requirement) 97; context, student immersion 108; course content, personal goals (connection) 77; curricula protests 34; disengaged students, problems/issues 9–10; diversity, increase 30; engagement, improvement 76; full personhood 77; grading systems, student perceptions 98; groups, silencing 41; in-person students, online students (separation) 3; job readiness 45; low-stakes risk, creation/opportunity 82; mentoring 36; needs, increase 127; non-academic activities, list (creation) 122; nontraditional labeling 39; relationship-rich education, scholarship 93; student-centered pedagogy 42; student-driven pathways 48; teacher care 70; teacher encounters 81; teacher management 25; timelessness, experience (rarity) 40; weeding-out process 42
Studio Wildcard 106
subjective experience, interference 16
substantive expertise 146
success, systemic characteristic 25
suffering, exposure 15
suppression, modes 37
"survival of the fittest" mentality 42
syllabus coverage, issues 81
syncretic practices 18
systemic problems 47
system racism/sexism/ableism, political tensions (increase) 2

Tagg, J. 4
Taíno: people, environment (symbiotic relationship) 20; worldview 20
"tappers and listeners" experiment (Stanford University) 55
task-specific knowledge, extrapolation 138
tasks, prioritization 134
teachers: care 70, 124; care center role, reduction 8; classroom design, *Ark* design (comparison) 108–110; communiques, issuance 72; content, care relationship 52; exhaustion 31; relational host role 79–81; student encounters 81; teacher-student relationship 73–74
teacher-student relationship model 73–74
teaching: fulfillment, disappearance 1; modalities, educator selection (problems) 145–146; scholarship, translation 78
Teaching Games for Understanding (Griffin/Butler) 108
teams, reliance 90
teamwork skills, importance 89
technology, solutions/problems 145
"test of learning" measurement 53
Thibaut, J. 22
thinking: analytical thinking 89; creative thinking 89; issue 17
thinking-with 17
thin-slicing 81–84
Thompson, Derek 91
Thorndike, E. 25
timelessness, student experience (rarity) 40
top-down epistemology, power structure (student functioning) 111
transactional care, power extension 14
transformation, encouragement 119
Trickster Makes the World (Hyde) 119
trigger warnings 3
Tronto, J. 6, 13, 46, 103, 130
Trump, Donald (social justice/DEI attacks) 38
trust, building 62–63
Twenge, J. 95

"Umuntu ngumuntu ngabantu" ("I am because we are") (Zulu proverb) 21
unanswerable questions, cognitive complexity 48
understaffing, problems 128–129
Undoing the Demos: Neoliberalism's Stealth Revolution (Brown) 38

ungrading method, comparison 98
unionization, prevention 36
universe, natural flow 21
universities, neoliberal transformation 130
University of Berlin (research university model) 32
Unraveling Faculty Burnout: Pathways to Reckoning and Renewal (Pope-Ruark) 126, 129

Valencia Community College (Valencia College), attendance 147–148
Van Pelt, S. 32
video games, frustration 117
Vietnam War 33
violence, absence 17
Virtual Reality (VR), usage 4
Voodoo, evil forces (perception) 18

Wall Kimmerer, R. 4, 12, 27–28, 143
Water Tribe (*Avatar the Last Airbender*) 102
Weil, Z. 142–143
well-being: impact 21; maintenance 23–24
Wenger-Trayner, B. 136
Wenger-Trayner, E. 136
Western lifestyles, questioning 126
Western world, perpetual crisis 40–41

whakapapa (Maori connection) 21
What We Value: Public Health, Social Justice, and Educating for Democracy (Pasquarella) 35
Winner Takes All: The Elite Charade of Changing the World (Giridharadas) 13
women, caregiver role (expectation) 46
work: conditions, isolating effects 130; ethic 64; examination 111; play, contrast 112
workers, task specialization 36
working memory: exhaustion 26–27; limitations 117
work-life balance, redefining 134–135
World Becomes What We Teach: Educating a Generation of Solutionaries (Weil) 142
World Economic Forum (WEF), *Future of Jobs 2023* report 89, 90
World War II 33
writing, generative power 57–58

young people: epidemics 10; solutionaries, becoming 143
yucayeques (villages), organization 20
Yuja, usage 120

zemí (protection/fertility/balance) 20

For Product Safety Concerns and Information please contact our EU
representative GPSR@taylorandfrancis.com
Taylor & Francis Verlag GmbH, Kaufingerstraße 24, 80331 München, Germany

www.ingramcontent.com/pod-product-compliance
Lightning Source LLC
Chambersburg PA
CBHW071411300426

44114CB00016B/2264